BEING A JUDGE IN TI

Being a Judge in the Modern World

Edited by

JEREMY COOPER

OXFORD
UNIVERSITY PRESS

Great Clarendon Street, Oxford, OX2 6DP,
United Kingdom

Oxford University Press is a department of the University of Oxford.
It furthers the University's objective of excellence in research, scholarship,
and education by publishing worldwide. Oxford is a registered trade mark of
Oxford University Press in the UK and in certain other countries

Published in the United States of America by Oxford University Press
198 Madison Avenue, New York, NY 10016, United States of America

British Library Cataloguing in Publication Data

Library of Congress Control Number: 2016960621

ISBN 978-0-19-879660-2

Printed and bound by
CPI Group (UK) Ltd, Croydon, CR0 4YY

Acknowledgements

A number of people helped in the gestation of this publication. I would like in particular to express my gratitude to the Heads of the Law Faculties at the Universities of Birmingham, Bristol, Cardiff, Leeds, Manchester, and the University of Law in London, together with the Warden of Keble College Oxford, Sir Jonathan Phillips for hosting several of the lectures that made up this series; to Sheridan Greenland and His Honour John Phillips of the Judicial College for their generous engagement with and support for this project since its inception; to Brian Evans and David Thomas of the Judicial College for managing the administrative complexities of the programme with impeccable efficiency; to Clare Picking for her timely assistance in proof reading the manuscript; and to Howard Davis, whose professional encouragement ensured the project would come to fruition.

Jeremy Cooper
January 2017

Contents

List of Contributors

Desirée Bernard Mrs Justice Desirée Bernard retired from the Caribbean Court of Justice in 2014, after being appointed its first female judge in 2005. She has sat in the High Court of the Supreme Court of Guyana and in the Court of Appeal of the Supreme Court of Guyana, and in 2001 became the first female Chancellor and Head of Judiciary of Guyana, in charge of the administration of justice and President of the Court of Appeal. She has been awarded the Cacique Crown of Honour, and the Order of Roraima, Guyana's third- and second-highest national awards respectively.

Robert Carnwath Lord Carnwath of Notting Hill is currently a United Kingdom Supreme Court judge. He was Senior President of Tribunals from 2007 to 2012, leading the tribunal system reform following the Leggatt report. He has sat as a High Court Judge in the Chancery Division and later the Court of Appeal, as well as being Chairman of the Law Commission and serving as Attorney General to the Prince of Wales.

Shami Chakrabarti Baroness Chakrabarti worked as a lawyer for the Home Office before joining Liberty as in-house counsel in 2001. Two years later she became director of Liberty and spent twelve years in this position, being appointed a CBE in 2007. She released her first book, *On Liberty* in October 2014 and is now Chancellor of the University of Essex, and a Life Peer.

Jeremy Cooper Professor Jeremy Cooper was until July 2016 Joint Director of Training in the Judicial College, London. He sat as a Tribunal Judge in both the First Tier Tribunal and the Upper Tribunal, also serving as Southern Regional Chairman of the Mental Health Review Tribunal. He is an Honorary Visiting Professor at the Universities of Kent and Middlesex. Prior to becoming a Tribunal Judge he was Dean of the Law Faculty and Professor of Law at Southampton Institute.

Brenda Hale Lady Hale of Richmond is currently a United Kingdom Supreme Court judge and was appointed Deputy President of the Supreme Court in June 2013. She was the first woman to be appointed to the Law Commission in 1984, following which she became a High Court judge, then the first female Lord of Appeal in Ordinary and the first woman Justice of the Supreme Court in 2009. Prior to her judicial appointment she was a senior law academic at the University of Manchester. She is Chancellor of the University of Bristol and Visitor of Girton College, Cambridge.

Lord Judge was the Lord Chief Justice of England and Wales from 2008 to 2013. Prior to this, he sat as a High Court Judge, later becoming a Lord Justice of Appeal before being appointed Deputy Chief Justice, then President of the Queen's Bench Division. He was created Baron Judge of Draycote in 2008 and is an Honorary Fellow of Magdalene College, Cambridge.

John Laws Lord Justice Laws was appointed a Lord Justice of Appeal in 1999. Prior to this, he was First Junior Treasury Counsel (Common Law) and a Recorder, holding both positions until his appointment to the High Court in the Queen's Bench Division. He retired from the Bench in October 2016.

Joshua Rozenberg Joshua Rozenberg qualified as a solicitor in 1976 and became the BBC's first legal correspondent, holding the position for fifteen years. He has since become a freelance writer, commentator, and broadcaster, having published a number of books and presenting a BBC Radio 4 series. In 2016 he was appointed an honorary QC for his work as the 'pre-eminent legal analyst of modern time'.

Alan Rusbridger Alan Rusbridger trained as a reporter, moving from writing to editing in 1988. He spent ten years as editor-in-chief of Guardian News and Media from 1995, during which time the paper was nominated 'newspaper of the year' on five occasions. He was named 'editor of the year' three times. Rusbridger was also awarded the Spanish Ortega y Gasset award for journalism and the 2014 European Press Prize. He was elected Principal of Lady Margaret Hall, Oxford in 2015.

Ernest Ryder Lord Justice Ernest Ryder has been the Senior President of Tribunals since September 2015. He currently chairs the Lord Chief Justice's steering group on judicial performance and deployment strategy. Prior to this he was appointed a Judge of the High Court of Justice, Family Division, during which time he spent a year as Judge in Charge of the Modernisation of Family Justice, as well as being Family Division Liaison Judge and Presiding Judge of the Northern

Circuit and then a Judge of the Court of Appeal. He is also a Deputy Lieutenant of Greater Manchester and Chancellor of the University of Bolton.

John Thomas Lord Thomas of Cwmgiedd has been the Lord Chief Justice since October 2013. After being appointed Judge of the High Court of England and Wales in 1996, he later became one of the Presiding Judges of the Wales and Chester Circuit, Judge in Charge of the Commercial Court in London, and then a Lord Justice of Appeal. He has also been President of the European Network of Councils for the Judiciary. He is an Honorary Fellow of Trinity Hall, Cambridge; a Fellow of the Universities of Cardiff, Aberystwyth, Swansea, and Bangor; and an Honorary Doctor of Law of the Universities of South Wales, the West of England, Cardiff Metropolitan, and Wales.

1

Introduction

Professor Jeremy Cooper

The provenance of this book is rooted firmly in the Judicial College. The College is the body with responsibility for training judicial office holders across many parts of the United Kingdom.[1] It was my privilege, together with my colleague John Phillips,[2] to have been one of the two Directors of Training for the College, from its inception in April 2011 to July 2016 when our fixed-term secondment came to an end.[3] It was a stimulating and at times white-knuckle journey overseeing the College's creation, in effect leading the development of the body responsible for training a large number of the nation's judiciary,[4] and nurturing the College vision to be 'a world leader in judicial training'.[5] Throughout this journey one factor was of overriding importance, namely getting it right when it came to providing our

---

[1] The Judicial College is responsible for induction and continuation training for approximately 30,000 judicial office holders, most of whom are located in England and Wales but some of whom sit in reserved tribunals in Scotland and Northern Ireland. Training is provided 'nationally', where judicial office holders from all over the country come to an event, and also 'regionally', where judicial office holders from a particular area come together.

[2] HHJ Phillips was Joint Training Director for the Judicial College from 2011 to 2016, with special responsibility for courts. Prior to that, he was Director of Studies of the Judicial Studies Board.

[3] Note that from July 2016, the Directors of Training are HHJ Andrew Hatton (Courts) and Employment Judge Christa Christensen (Tribunals).

[4] The term 'judiciary' is used in this chapter to include all judicial office holders for whom the Lord Chief Justice and the Senior President of Tribunals have responsibility, plus the coroners. The term 'judicial office holder' includes judges (both salaried and fee-paid), specialist tribunal members (of whom there are several thousand), magistrates, and coroners.

[5] Judicial College Strategy 2011–14, and 2014–17.

judiciary with the support and the training tools they require to carry out this most demanding of roles. But we wanted this to be located within a much broader environment, one that encourages debate, reflection, and an understanding of the challenges faced by the community in which judges sit and serve.

The judiciary in this country carry out a number of very important roles. They try criminal cases in the Crown and magistrates' courts; they try civil cases in the High Court and county courts; they adjudicate a wide range of inter-party disputes and disputes between the state and individuals in tribunals; they determine cases involving children and family matters; they sit as coroners; and in the highest courts they hear appeals and ultimately they make law. Salaried judiciary are well paid, but they work immensely hard, often for long hours under extreme time pressures. The integrity and commitment to justice rightly demanded of judges is unstinting. The job is hard, at times relentless, but deeply rewarding. It is public service of the highest order. Judges are the custodians of the rule of law and must carry out this role without fear, favour, affection, or ill will.[6] A strong, independent, highly trained judiciary is a *sine qua non* of a functioning democracy.

The judiciary operate in a wide range of jurisdictions, some thirty-four in total,[7] which require them to develop a range of sophisticated and at times highly specialised skills. The entry criteria to apply for a judicial post are high level and rigorous. The procedures that are followed in the appointment of judges, now under the supervision of the Judicial Appointments Commission (JAC),[8] are complex and, above all, thorough. All this tends to ensure that the body of men and women who carry out the judging function are carefully honed and appropriately trained to carry out their tasks.

---

[6] It is normal practice today for all judicial office holders to take the judicial oath 'to well and truly serve our Sovereign Lady Queen Elizabeth the Second in the office of judge; and to do right to all manner of people after the laws and usages of this realm, without fear or favour, affection or ill will'. The magistrates' (Justice of the Peace) oath is a variation of the same pledge.

[7] These include the High Court; the Upper Tribunal; the criminal, family, and civil courts; the magistrates' and the coroners' courts; and the following tribunal jurisdictions: employment, social security, and child support; immigration and asylum; mental health; care standards; special educational needs; family health lists; tax; information rights; charity; property; war pensions; and asylum support.

[8] Created by the Constitutional Reform Act 2005, section 61.

Until the latter part of the twentieth century there was, in many parts of the establishment (including the judicial establishment), a sense that because judges by the time of their appointment were already skilled professionals with an intimate knowledge and deep understanding of law and procedure grafted (in most cases) upon a long and successful career at the Bar,[9] they needed no further training. Indeed in some quarters, training was seen as a direct challenge to the concept of judicial independence. By 1979, however, the winds of change were gently blowing in a more structured direction and the rudiments of judicial training (still voluntary) were slowly pieced together. This process was managed for the courts judiciary through the Judicial Studies Board (JSB) and, in the tribunals' and magistrates' courts' sector, through a number of bespoke arrangements tailored to their specialist requirements.[10]

The JSB was, in its short lifetime from 1979 to 2011, in the words of Lord Judge, 'a great success story—the jewel in the judicial crown', with a series of 'remarkable chairmen, and ... energetic, dedicated directors of studies'.[11] In parallel, many of the tribunal jurisdictions were developing their own innovative approaches to training their judges and members, often doing exceptionally good things on a perilous budget.[12]

By 2005 two judicial training juggernauts, the Judicial Studies Board and the Tribunal Service,[13] were found to be overlapping in their training initiatives and values to the extent that a merger of the two wings of the training judiciary seemed sensible, indeed inevitable. In the summer of 2009, the then Lord Chief Justice, Lord Judge, and the Senior President of Tribunals, Lord Justice Carnwath, jointly invited Lord Justice Sullivan to chair a working group charged with the investigation of the pros and cons of creating a single training

---

[9] In most cases, at least ten years practising as a lawyer was an essential prerequisite for application.

[10] See *Judicial Studies and Information: Report of the Working Party, chaired by the Right Honourable Lord Justice Bridge* (HMSO, 1978) for a detailed background to the evolution of judicial training.

[11] Lord Judge, 'Judicial Studies: Reflections on the Past and Thoughts for the Future', in his *The Safest Shield: Lectures, Speeches and Essays* (Hart, 2015), at 297.

[12] See Jeremy Cooper, *Judicial Training in the Tribunals Services: A Report to Sir Robert Carnwath CVO, Senior President of Tribunals* (Ministry of Justice, 2010).

[13] The training for tribunals was by now co-ordinated through a body know as the Tribunals Judicial Training Group (TJTG), set up by and reporting to the Senior President of Tribunals, and chaired by Jeremy Cooper.

body for the whole of the judiciary and, if in favour, suggesting a framework to give life to the concept. The working group was established in 2009. It reported back in quick time that the arguments in favour of such a development were strong,[14] and an announcement of the creation of the Judicial College followed in 2010. A year of interim development took place and the College came formally into being in April 2011.

The Judicial College currently delivers well over 400 training programmes a year to around 30,000 judicial office holders in the United Kingdom. In 2014–15, for example, 446 courses were delivered for judiciary in the courts, coroners' courts, and tribunals, attended by a total of 18,643 participants. For 'lay' magistrates (Justices of the Peace), while some courses such as Bench Chairmanship are delivered directly by the Judicial College, in most cases the College prepares training materials for local delivery by magistrates and accredited legal advisers.

In addition to providing bespoke training in the areas of law and procedure required by each specialist jurisdiction, and in the social context of judging,[15] the College offers cross-jurisdictional training for all judicial office holders in such areas as judicial skills and judgecraft, case management, reason writing, the delivery of oral judgments, training trainers, leadership and management training, and diversity issues. Since July 2016, this cross-jurisdictional aspect of the College's overall training programme has become of such significance that it is now co-ordinated and further developed within a College Faculty, created for this purpose. As a direct consequence of this intense concentration of training activity, the quality, range, and vision of the Judicial College has become a global brand in a short space of time. The College's assistance is regularly sought by judicial training institutions the world over. This status was further consolidated in 2014, when the European Commission published a major

---

[14] Judicial Office, *Towards a Joint Judicial Training College: The Case Explored. A Report to the Lord Chief Justice and the Senior President of Tribunals by the Unified Judicial Training Advisory Board* (2010).

[15] See Judicial College Strategy 2011–17. It is the firmly held view of the Judicial College Board, that as judging does not occur in isolation from the wider society in which courts and tribunals operate, every judge and judicial office holder should understand the social context in which the disputes which they are required to adjudicate take place. This approach therefore forms a central plank of all the training that the Judicial College provides.

study of the state of training for judges and prosecutors across the European Union which identified England and Wales as having more examples of best training practices for the judiciary than any other European member state.[16]

One important consideration that influenced the College Board when agreeing its core strategy was the belief that judges need and welcome the opportunity to reflect upon their lives and their work in a secure and comfortable setting, free from the specific constraints of a training programme. We decided that it was the responsibility of the College to create a parallel programme designed to achieve this goal: thus was born the Judicial College Academic Programme, of which this volume is one of the first fruits.

The series that formed the first programme was based around the concept that forms the title of this volume, *Being a Judge in the Modern World*. There are a number of pressures upon, and challenges to, judges at every level of the judiciary today that have not always been there in the past. To date, judges have managed to face these new challenges with vigour and with fortitude, to the extent that opinion polls consistently suggest that over 80 per cent of the general public continues to hold judges in high esteem (with only vets, GPs, and schoolteachers achieving similarly positive ratings!). But the pressures remain and they escalate: cuts in legal aid; the intrusive impact of social media; the operation of more intensive performance indicators, including hearing-time pressures; increases in workload; the move towards digitalisation of court proceedings; court closures; seismic shifts in application rates in certain tribunals in response to external pressures;[17] tensions between domestic and international human rights' norms; unbridled intrusion of the Internet into the workings and priorities of everyday life—the list seems limitless.

It was against this background that our theme emerged, and it seemed irresistible in its simple appeal. Our idea was to invite a series of senior judges, together with figures with an established critical public eye for matters judicial (in the capacity of 'critical friends'), each to deliver a lecture with the same title, but with absolute freedom to address the issue in any way they saw fit with neither guidance nor censorship from the Judicial College. The

---

[16] See *European Commission Final Report Tender JUST/2012/JUTR/PR/0064/A4-Implementation of the Pilot Project—European Judicial Training*.
[17] For further discussion of this issue, see Chapter 8 below, at footnotes 10–11.

lectures were publicised internally to all members of the judiciary and were held in locations across the country (mostly university law schools) to maximise the chance for judicial office
holders from all parts of the country to attend at least one lecture. Typically, each lecture would last fifty minutes, followed
by close questioning, and would be attended by a mix of judges,
tribunal members, magistrates, law faculty, and students. The
invited speakers were, in date order: Carnwath (then Lord Justice,
now Lord), Lord Judge, Mrs Justice Desirée Bernard, Ms (now
Baroness) Shami Chakrabarti, Mr Joshua Rozenberg, Mr Alan
Rusbridger, and Lord Thomas. Two further senior judges were
subsequently invited to deliver lectures on related themes—Lady
Hale on judicial diversity, and Lord Justice Laws on judicial law
making. This volume is completed by the addition of four lectures delivered in the very recent past by Lord Thomas and Lord
Justice Ryder, both of whom are acknowledged reform-oriented
judges with major leadership roles in the various judicial reform
programmes that are taking place. I provide an overview on the
growth of tribunals over the past ten years and the place they now
hold in the overall delivery of justice.

The lectures have been arranged thematically to provide the reader
with greater coherence and context. So far as possible, the text of each
lecture has been left unedited, in order to retain the integrity of the
event at which it was delivered and also to ensure that the reader can
absorb the thinking of the speaker within the real time frame of the
series. This means, for example, that we resisted the temptation to
invite each speaker to update their speech in the light of subsequent
developments. Thus the text of each speech retains the range of con-
temporaneous reflections and at times surprises offered to their audience by each speaker. By agreement each speaker was not briefed on
possible content—this was left deliberately to them alone—and the
text of each speech was never circulated to us in advance. As a consequence, the reading of these speeches should provide the reader
with a sense of intellectual freewheeling excitement in the knowledge
that each speaker will take the reader where he or she wishes to go
with the rigorously independent mind one would expect from such a
distinguished group.

The volume begins with the reflections of the immediate past
and the current Lord Chief Justices, the Right Honourable Lord
Judge, and the Right Honourable Lord Thomas of Cwmgiedd.

Lord Judge offers a fascinating reflection on the many changes that have occurred in his lifetime in the law. He is keen to separate, in this respect, the wheat from the chaff:[18]

> Being a judge in the modern world has at its heart the notion that judges should understand the modern world, not embracing the latest fad or fashion because these are ephemeral and short-lived ... but because where real change is apparent, the judicial system must understand, represent, and respond to it.

And Lord Judge is quite clear about the moral duty of the contemporary judge to put this understanding into practice:[19] judges 'must be alert to the practical realities of the world in which they live ... and understand the realities with which those who appear in court have to grapple'. The practical realities upon which he subsequently expounds are both insightful and trenchant.

The clarity of vision shown by Lord Judge is equally present in the contribution of his successor, Lord Thomas. The theme that Lord Thomas selects as his priority is: how judges must harness and implement reform. Taking as his text the constitutional commitment to the rule of law contained in the Constitutional Reform Act 2005,[20] Lord Thomas reiterates the principle that the separation of powers nevertheless requires the judiciary to take on a role as part of the apparatus of the state:

> If the judiciary is to play its proper role in ensuring that the administration of justice is efficient and effective and thus helping to secure equality before the law, it cannot but play an active role in the reform process. It has ... a duty to do so.[21]

And the key enabling process, through which all these roles are fulfilled and maintained, he believes to be the principled reform of the delivery of justice. The examples that he gives of required reform are wide-ranging.

In Chapter 13, in a parallel lecture directed at an international audience, Lord Thomas stresses the universality of these norms, reiterating that 'the centrality of justice through an independent judiciary is the basis on which democracy, prosperity, fairness, and the rule of law depend in our increasingly diverse societies'.[22]

---

[18] Chapter 2 below, at 17.   [19] Ibid., at 17.   [20] Section 1.
[21] Chapter 3 below, at 27.   [22] Chapter 13 below, at 169.

The next group of lectures in this volume were delivered by distin-guished individuals who, while close observers of the judicial system, are not part of it: Ms (now Baroness) Shami Chakrabarti, Mr Joshua Rozenberg, and Mr Alan Rusbridger—speakers whom we might best describe as 'critical friends'. Their contributions to our analysis of the question Being a Judge in the Modern World provide fascinating and illuminating insights.

Shami Chakrabarti is one of the United Kingdom's best-known civil liberties lawyers, and described the prospect of providing judges with her views on the question Being a Judge in the Modern World as 'daunting'. The context against which she shares her thinking on the topic is the series of recent issues that have served to erode people's trust in the establishment in general and the Government in particu-lar in the course of the past two decades. Against this sorry list of issues, Ms Chakrabarti is quick to point out that 'when we [Liberty] poll people on their kind of trust index for different institutions and different professionals in Britain … the judiciary polls incredibly well'.[23] The problem she identifies as the most challenging for the judi-ciary in contemporary Britain is one she describes as 'constitutional illiteracy'.[24]

Joshua Rozenberg is at the top of his game as a legal analyst and draws upon many years observing the judiciary at close quarters. His theme—to paraphrase—is that of the 'embattled judge'. Noting, as do others, that a judge has to make unpopular, principled decisions and cannot defend them outside the courtroom, he cites 'quiet fortitude' as the first requisite for the judge in the modern world. He also readily concedes that being a judge in the modern world is not easy, recognis-ing that 'those who do the job deserve our admiration and respect'.[25] The challenges faced by the intrusive presence of electronic and social media in every aspect of judging are, inter alia, dealt with in some picturesque detail in the course of this lecture.

At the time he delivered his lecture on judges and the media,[26] Alan Rusbridger was the highly experienced editor of *The Guardian* news-paper, and the insights he brought to the table conveyed a real edge of contemporary tension. His lecture revisited the theme that seemed

---

[23] Chapter 4, at 42.   [24] Ibid., at 42.   [25] Chapter 5, at 66.
[26] Shortly afterwards Alan Rusbridger left *The Guardian*, after thirty-five years on the paper (twenty as editor), to take up the post of Principal of Lady Margaret Hall, Oxford.

to become a leitmotif of the series—the real, if currently unfathomable, impact of the electronic media (or as Mr Rusbridger would have it, 'the digital revolution') upon modern communication and other forms of discourse. He offers a number of ideas for the judiciary to consider as a way of shoring up the toxic interface between a rampant and at times unprincipled press and a benign 'no comment' judiciary.

Mrs Justice Desirée Bernard delivered her lecture to a packed audience in the Lord Chief Justice's magnificent Court at the Royal Courts of Justice in London. She was visiting London at the invitation of the Institute of Advanced Legal Studies and graciously accepted our invitation to share her thoughts on our general theme from the perspective of a judge whose work is centred in the Caribbean. The reader will be interested to note the examples of new and emerging areas of law that the Caribbean Court is being asked to adjudicate—computer crime, collateral issues related to surrogacy, same-sex marriages, human trafficking, cloning—and her trenchant observation that 'the lack of advanced technology reduces the capacity of courts to deliver justice in a timely manner'.[27] She notes that many more women are now entering the legal profession in the Caribbean region and anticipates that this will in due course change the complexion of the Caribbean judiciary, and she also notes that there is a far greater requirement for judicial transparency, both procedural and in the context of personal conduct and ethics than in the past, with the Caribbean media taking a closer interest on both these issues.

The next two lectures in the series focus upon the rise of the tribunal judge as a counterweight to the traditional hierarchical notion that 'real' judges are limited to those who sit in the courts, affectionately known in some quarters as 'the uniformed branch'. The phenomenon of the Judicial College in which judges and judicial office holders of all ranks and specialisms share knowledge, and train and learn together, does appear to have done a great deal finally to put that hierarchical notion to bed. The statutory requirement that tribunal judges now take on the formal title of 'judge' has completed the circle.

In Chapter 8, I provide an account of the key changes that have occurred in the tribunal world in a very short space of time (essentially 2000–15) to ensure their place as an essential component in the

---

[27] Chapter 7 below, at 87.

rich patchwork of judicial arbitration in this country. The chapter labels this process a 'quiet revolution' and identifies the key factors at work driving this revolution forward.

The lecture by Lord Carnwath, the first person to be appointed Senior President of Tribunals, has a special place in this volume. It was the very first lecture to be delivered in the programme. Furthermore, it presents a unique piece of real-time history, through Lord Carnwath's personal reflections on the days prior to, during, and immediately after the creation of the new world of tribunals; he is the man who, with the exception of Lord Justice Leggatt himself, did more than any other to bring the new tribunal system to fruition.

The volume includes two lectures that did not form part of the Being a Judge in the Modern World academic series, but were delivered in the time frame of this series. Their content is so closely allied to the themes of the volume that to include them seems more than appropriate. Both lectures were delivered by Lord Justice Ryder, one of the leading reformist judges of his generation.[28] Lord Justice Ryder adheres closely to the philosophy of Lord Thomas, i.e. embrace change or face the consequences. In his case he uses this maxim to analyse how we can best reform the adjudication processes to provide individuals with access to a first-class system of readily accessible courts and tribunals. In an attempt to redress the imbalance between the citizen and the state in a court setting ('going to court can be a daunting prospect for many of our citizens'[29]) Lord Justice Ryder's vision is bold, if not without risks.

The final two chapters of this volume address two discrete topics that are central to an analysis of the role of the modern judge: the question of diversity and the extent to which judges do, or should, make law. The contributors of these two chapters are both pre-eminent experts in the subject matter of their topics. Lady Hale provides a scholarly and penetrating analysis of the importance of diversity among the judiciary ('difference' is her favoured term), which she demonstrates through detailed objective evidence in the course of this lecture to be, at the present time, wanting.

---

[28] Lord Justice Ryder was the judge in charge of the family justice modernisation project and thereafter he chaired the Lord Chief Justice's steering group on performance and deployment strategy.

[29] Chapter 11.

In the final lecture of this volume, Lord Justice Laws provides an erudite analysis of whether judges do and should make law. His conclusion, based upon constitutional principles combined with scholarly textual analysis of a series of cases, is a resounding yes, to both questions. Lord Justice Laws opines that:

> In the common law world the interpretation and application of the law are interwoven with its creation, because the judges mediate Parliament's legislation to the people so that, so far as possible, it conforms to civilised constitutional principles, whose guardians are the courts.[30]

Drawing upon a number of examples from leading cases across a range of topics, Lord Justice Laws succeeds in building a formidable case in support of his proposition.

Thus the volume ends with scholarship and analysis of the highest order. We hope that reading these lectures as a single collection will prove both stimulating and insightful in equal measure.

---

[30] Ibid., at Chapter 15 at 199.

2

Reflections of a Retired Lord Chief Justice

*Lord Judge**

This lecture was delivered at the Cardiff University Law School on 21 February 2013.

Perhaps the starting point is to underline how many changes there have been in my lifetime in the law. Let me give you a few examples.

My client was seeking a divorce on the grounds of his wife's adultery with the co-respondent. He claimed £300 damages for her loss. If I had valued my wife at £300, I think she would have gone off with the co-respondent. But it is laughable to think of it now.

Another example: if you wanted a divorce and you yourself had committed adultery, you had in your humble petition for divorce to seek the exercise of the court's discretion in your favour notwithstanding your own adultery. And you had to provide a full, frank, total admission of all the occasions when you had committed adultery yourself. And after you had given evidence, even if the case was undefended, an envelope was solemnly handed to the judge, who carefully opened it and read the contents. One of my clients was a sailor. He had committed adultery in eighty-four different ports throughout the world with eighty-four different completely unknown women. Nevertheless, the list had to be written. By contrast, another petitioner, not my client, about whom I was told, came from rather a grand family in England, and his discretion statement included list upon list of the assembled nobility, beginning with duchesses, then listing countesses, the wives of barons, and the wives of mere knights, with only

* © Previously published in Lord Judge, *The Safest Shield: Lectures, Speeches and Essays*, Hart Publishing, an imprint of Bloomsbury Publishing Plc, 2015.

the odd commoner thrown in. My point is that this was all solemnly part of the ritual which was required before you could get a divorce.

None of that avoided the rather difficult evidential point that what was said in the statement proved that the person making the statement had been having sexual intercourse with someone else, but that did not prove that someone had been having sexual intercourse with him.

Looking back on it, those examples are all funny. But I also had a client who, as an adult, committed buggery with another adult, in private. This was private consensual sex between adult men. He was sentenced to three years' imprisonment. I thought then and I still think that was a shocking sentence, but it reflected the times. And, still in my time in practice, in *R v Merthyr Tydfil Justices, ex parte Jenkins*, a future Lord Chief Justice expounded his view of the content of his experience of having spent the summer on circuit in Wales:

> It is quite clear that the proper language for the court proceedings in Wales is the English language. Indeed the use of Welsh impeded 'the efficient administration of justice in Wales'. As to language difficulties which might arise in Wales, they could be dealt with by discretionary arrangements for an interpreter, precisely in the same way as language difficulties at the Central Criminal Court are dealt with when the accused is a Pole.

So perhaps the most obvious example of changes is that here today in Cardiff the Lord Chief Justice is not the Lord Chief Justice of England, but, since just before 2000, the Lord Chief Justice of England and Wales, and I would add, in Wales, Lord Chief Justice of Wales and England. The examples I have given, and this last example in particular, symbolise that being a judge in the modern world has at its heart the notion that judges should understand the modern world, not embracing the latest fad or fashion because these are ephemeral and short-lived and today's fashion inevitably gives way to tomorrow's fashion, but because where real change is apparent, the judicial system must understand, represent, and respond to it. Here in Wales the modern judge must be alert to the developments of the legal life of Wales, not because he or she has a personal belief one way or another, but simply because the legal life of Wales is in flux and rapid development. Judges must not seek to push or to hold back, but they must be alert to what is happening.

This lecture is being given under the auspices of the Judicial College. It is now the Judicial College, not least because of yet another area of new understanding and arrangement. The men and women who sit in the tribunal system are exercising a judicial function, no less than those who sit in what I may describe as the ordinary courts of the land, the High Court, the Crown Court, and the county court, as well as others. The new Judicial College simply brings together what were formerly the separate arrangements for judicial training of judges and tribunal judges. HMCTS is just that: Her Majesty's Service for Courts and Tribunals, a single service. So when I speak of judges, I am including judges who sit in tribunals. That, too, is a significant change. The modern judge may be sitting in a suit in a tribunal rather than in what we recognise as a court. And the modern judge may also be sitting as a magistrate, also in a suit, in something that does look like a court. In other words, the modern judge comes in all kinds of judicial shapes and sizes, with differing responsibilities, but ultimately committed to the administration of justice.

But I want to go back to those first days of the Judicial Studies Board. We are back in the late 1970s and early 1980s. I was appointed a Recorder of the Crown Court in 1976. I sat for two years as a Recorder before I received any training at all. I was simply a barrister practising on the Midland Circuit who was thought to be up to the responsibility. The omission of training was no reflection on my remarkable talents, it was simply that there was no training at all. At the end of two years I was summoned to a brief seminar, held in the Court of the Lord Chief Justice, and a desultory exchange of views between a Lord Justice of Appeal and the judges and recorders then took place. I can still remember that the main message of the day was that provided you said, and re-emphasised, that the decision on the facts was for the jury, it was open to the judge to make any comment, however damaging to the defendant, that the judge thought fit. In other words, the judge could run the trial on the basis that provided he repeated and emphasised that the jury was entitled to reject any comment made by him, he could make virtually any comment he liked. That is not how we do it these days.

What is more, in the first years after the Judicial Studies Board was formed, there was significant judicial antipathy to the process. Many of us welcomed the training, but many did not. Many thought that this newfangled idea constituted an interference with judicial independence. And notice the importance of the title of the organisation—it was Judicial 'Studies'—not what in truth it was, Judicial 'Training', and if you ask what's in a name, the answer was a great deal. You do not reconcile those who are hostile to the idea if you demean them by implying that they might need training in the performance of their responsibilities.

I speak of these matters from personal knowledge, because I was part of a tiny team which ran the Judicial Studies Board in those far-off days.

Let us briefly go back to those days. For some of you it will be inconceivable, but we are talking in the years before the Police and Criminal Evidence Act 1984 had come into force. The judges' rules were applied, their objective being to ensure that any evidence which might amount to a confession of guilt was properly obtained and accurately recorded. Police officers were believed to have the kind of memory that holds sway in the elephant kingdom. They were able, hours later, to remember verbatim the precise questions and answers of a conversation with the defendant. And my clients all seemed to be vested with the kind of intellectual quality of a professor of modern languages when it came to their offering a free account, always in their own words, of their criminal activities. Logical, coherent, with a beginning, a middle, and an end, none of it prompted.

I never detected very many such qualities in many of my clients. Often they were confused, and many inarticulate. But here I can bring two threads together, making the same point. I can remember a very senior police officer who told me how much he would welcome the use of tape recordings during police interviews, and, indeed—and these are days long ago—filming of the interview process. He was in a tiny minority. In the face of much opposition it was introduced. We can now be certain that we know exactly what the defendant said, and the context in which he said it, and the question he was answering, as well as the answer itself, which, taken out of context, could be immensely damaging. No one would wish to go back to the old days. What a welcome use of what was then at the forefront of modern technology. Most welcome to us all.

And the same applies to the Judicial College. Continuing education is integral to the working life of a judge. We all are sure of its value. Every judge knows that training has no bearing whatever on his or her independence. The process enables them to be better informed and therefore better able to discharge their responsibilities. Judges now book into the seminars which are appropriate for their needs.

They value continuing training and education. Being a judge in the modern world does not merely require such education and training; it requires a frame of mind in which these positive advantages are welcomed. And they are.

Before you rush to condemn the older generation of the judges, perhaps you would bear in mind that they were simply reflective of what to them was the modern world. Their world was 'modern' to them, just as it was to all their contemporaries in all the professions. In their modern world football players in the First Division, now the Premier League, were paid £10 per week with a £2 bonus for a win and £1 for draw. Men who had the honour of turning out to represent Wales at Cardiff Arms Park were amateurs. Woe betide you if anyone discovered that you were accepting money or benefits in kind—you were expelled, and in those days no one in the legal profession, or, as far as I am aware, in any other profession, had continuing education. What we now treat as common and obvious was not common and obvious then. And before we get too carried away with our own rectitude, bear this clearly in mind, that in twenty-five to fifty years' time, the then Lord Chief Justice of Wales will be addressing just such a meeting as this in Cardiff, and there will be gasps of surprise at how extraordinary our processes and the way we do things now were. Yet, of course, subject to improvement, because we are always trying to reflect our best view of the best way things should be done. And if you examine this process more deeply, you end up, do you not, with this reflection. Just as judges must not follow fads and fashion, they must be alert to the practical realities of the world in which they live and understand it, and understand the realities with which those who appear in court have to grapple.

Put in this broad way, perhaps what I have just said is rather nebulous. There are a number of direct, concrete matters which fall within my broad proposition. We need to address the impact of modern technology on our justice system, and in particular our criminal justice system. You may very well appreciate that we use modern technology in the Crown Court. But our system is different from the various police forces, and the Prison Service, and the Probation Service. So the different bodies cannot simply all send the relevant documents to each other by pressing a single button. We can ask ourselves, how could that possibly be? But where do you stop with modern technology? Twitter and Facebook are less than ten years old. In other words, if I had been giving this lecture in, say, 2003, they would have been unheard of, and if heard of, then of no moment, not least because our eyes were focused on the extraordinary constitutional changes which were going on. Do you remember? The Lord Chancellor to be abolished: that did not get through the House of Lords. But he ceased to be head of the judiciary. That responsibility passed to the Lord Chief Justice. No one bothered to ask the Lord Chief Justice what he thought about this proposal, let alone whether he agreed with it. Well, that is modern political life. And we have had a remarkable change in our constitutional arrangements, not just in the context of devolution in Wales and greater independence in Scotland, but in the context of the judiciary as the third arm of our constitution. The judiciary is no longer represented around the Cabinet table by a minister whose function exclusively is to ensure that Cabinet decisions do not impinge on the independence of the judiciary, and the judiciary is no longer able to speak for itself in Parliament, because the right of the Lord Chief Justice to stand up and speak in Parliament has been abrogated. The impact of these constitutional changes has not yet been fully appreciated, and we must watch very closely how it develops.

Let us return to technology. So which piece of modern technology, as yet uncreated, of which we are all ignorant, will arrive to change the face of the administration of justice? I do not know, and, by definition, you do not know either. But we can be certain, can we not, that there will be dramatic changes, and that they will have, and should have, a dramatic impact on processes. We can be sure that the most modern technology today will be utterly out of date by 2025, if not significantly earlier. Should we, can we, go on with our time-honoured practices? The fact that they are time-honoured and tested gives them some merit, but they have not been tested against the possibilities which modern technology can open up. So how do the modern judge and the judicial system accommodate this extraordinary phenomenon— extraordinary, but unfixed and unknown?

We have to manage it. We cannot be insulated from it, any more than any other aspect of society. It is like the tide, coming in, eventually to fill every nook and cranny of society. Health, education, government, businesses large and small, football clubs, anything you care to think of does not merely need current IT, but needs vision about the uses to which IT can be deployed, enhancing, in our case, the administration of justice. Again, we have to be careful not to be after the latest fad or fashion: but we do have to examine, we certainly shall have to examine, whether the processes with which we have been familiar for generations can reflect the valuable assistance of modern technology without diminishing the quality of justice.

Let me just ramble. Do we need vast files of paper? Do we need so much focus on the oral tradition? In civil appeals, can all the material not be put onto a screen? In criminal appeals, unless there is fresh evidence, can the defendant not always be linked to the court by video, so as to avoid him a most uncomfortable journey, and the cost of fetching him to and from prison? Can we, perhaps most of all, recognise the dire danger of burying our system, our common law system, under mounds and mounds of so-called authorities, decided cases which are supposed to assist the judge by directing him or her to the relevant principle? If we could use modern technology to distil the essential principle to be applied by the court into two or three paragraphs, rather than two or three folders of so-called authorities, that would be a triumph.

Let us remember that when the Incorporated Council of Law Reporting was set up in the mid-1860s, its purpose was to ensure proper reporting of cases which decided legal principle. Well, modern technology has produced the unreported, neutral citation, judgment which decides no legal principle, under which to bury the judge, so perhaps it may one day expiate its guilt and produce a new system for reporting cases which actually matter. And if I may say so, finally on this topic, let us not be beguiled by the latest sales talk into buying equipment which will be redundant in three or four years, after a massive capital expenditure: if we are investing vast sums of capital, can the word 'flexibility' be built into it?

Let me give a particular example of the impact of modern technology in the context of criminal trials. We already have too many cases where jurors ignore the directions of the trial judge that they should decide the case on the evidence presented to them and not seek information from whichever species of modern technology they choose to use. This is not an attempt by the judiciary to preserve a piece of flummery. You can all see, when you think about it, that it is elementary that if you are charged with a criminal offence, not only must your trial be held in public, but also you should have an opportunity to deal with any evidence which is said to prove your guilt. You would be absolutely horrified if, in today's processes, you, as the defendant, were asked to leave court while some material, apparently damaging to you, was presented to the judge and jury. You would want to know what it was, and you want to try and deal with it. The juror who seeks information outside the court process is doing just that: he or she is using material which is secret from you, and which you have no chance to address, to decide whether you are guilty or not. The same complaint could be made by someone who is the victim of crime. If you wish to preserve the jury system as it is, we need all the best technology that we can find to enable masses of evidence to be presented and all of the processes to be clearer, simpler, and speedier. But just because technology is 'modern', its impact is not always to the public advantage. So we have to be careful to welcome the technology, and to learn how to handle it, but to handle it cautiously so as to ensure that the administration of true justice is undiminished. If the jury system has to change because of modern technology, and over the centuries it has been susceptible to change, then this must not be done behind the scenes by a nod and wink, but must be addressed directly and explicitly in our legislative assemblies. It is those who work in these places, those we elect to represent us, who have the responsibility for making these decisions about the sort of society in which we and our children and grandchildren will live, and the rules which will be agreeable to them in their modern society. That, of course, is for the future.

And for the future, however it is addressed, the qualities we seek in a judge will be identical to those that we seek in a judge today. The eternal verities do not change. We make great demands of our judges. They must have wisdom, patience, a sense of practical realities, an understanding of people and the way of the world, fairness and balance, independence of mind and knowledge of the law, and a total commitment that justice should be administered according to the law. These are qualities which are needed by judges at whatever level they sit, and wherever they sit, giving judgment without fear or favour, affection or ill will. But there are a number of particular further features which are sometimes overlooked.

First, a judge must have the ability to make up his or her mind and give a decision. Anyone can see a number of different possible solutions to a problem and different ways to address it. In many cases that is precisely why they have come to the judge, because they cannot agree it. The judge cannot take refuge in the answer being one thing or another: the judge must decide.

Second, judges have to make decisions that are profoundly unpleasant and have very serious consequences. But they have to make them. To send someone to prison when his spouse believes that he is innocent; to take children away from one or other, or even both, parents because it is no longer safe for them to be living with that parent; to tell the government of the day or all the many authorities that have power over us that they are acting unlawfully is a difficult responsibility. This is not a fun job. And you have to do it. The parties and the public are entitled to a decision from you. And you must give reasons for it. And you must give it to the best of your abilities. And you must give it even if you know that another court may take a different view.

Third, the modern judge is increasingly involved in what can be described as administration. The days are over when the judicial function was performed by the judge turning up at court at 9.00, reading the papers for the day's work, going into court at 10.00 or 10.30, sitting the court hours, adjourning at 4.30 or thereabouts, working on the day's work in preparation for the summing up or the judgment, and then going home. Many judges have out-of-court responsibilities. They are members of different boards or councils; they have pastoral responsibilities as resident judges, designated family judges or designated civil judges. They help with diversity issues; some of them work with schools and places of education. Ultimately, the administrative responsibilities devolve downwards from the Lord Chief Justice. Properly to perform his function, he has to deal with the Lord Chancellor, the Permanent Secretary of the Department and senior officials, other ministers in the department, and then all the boards and bodies which work to make the system more efficient and more accountable, such as, for example, the Judicial Appointments Commission and HMCTS. All of us help to ensure the efficient and effective system which the Lord Chancellor must provide to carry on the business of the courts. Judges have to devote time to these and many similar responsibilities. The modern judge is likely to be involved directly or indirectly with many responsibilities out of court, which have nothing whatever to do with his or her judicial judgments. All this is new, but the burdens are likely to increase rather than to diminish. Do not get me wrong: they add greatly to the interest of the job, but the time in which to do it does not increase. I am very grateful to the many judges up and down the country who are prepared to offer themselves to help ensure that the administration of justice runs efficiently, not merely when they are conducting their cases in court, but overall, in each of its many aspects.

So this leads to the final feature I wish to highlight. Judges must have moral courage or fortitude, in particular to make decisions that will not be popular with the politicians or the media or indeed the vast majority of the public. And judges have to defend the right to equality and fair treatment before the law of any individual citizen, even and perhaps most of all a citizen who is unpopular, currently demonised, currently beyond the pale. That is the rule of law, and in its practical application it is not always very popular. And, what is more, the judge cannot respond to personal criticism. This makes fortitude, an old-fashioned virtue, much underrated in our present society. Quiet fortitude: a requisite for the judge in the modern world.

But you will notice that none of these qualities have anything whatever to do with the gender of a human being, or the colour of the skin of the human being, or the sexual orientation, or the physical abilities, or the religion they follow, or their social origins. None of these matters have the slightest relevance to the identity of those we are seeking to persuade to take on judicial office, or indeed to the judiciary as a whole. We are still far from a diverse judiciary. I do not underestimate the value of diversity as an essential ingredient for its own sake. My view is, however, more intensely focused: that diversity is a necessary requirement of the judiciary, because the individuals best suited to judicial office include women just as much as men, include human beings whose skin is brown or black as well as white, includes those whose social origins are the most humble, and includes those who would not win a gold medal in the 100 metres at the Olympics. None of these things matter. What matters is that the judiciary should be made up of individuals who are qualified for appointment and are of the highest calibre, vested with the qualities that make a good judge. We do, after all, vest in our judges considerable responsibilities, and power. Only the best will do.

Somehow or other the pool of candidates for appointment to judicial office is not as large or as wide as I would like it to be. Putting it bluntly, the larger the pool of those with an interest in judicial office, the greater potential for increasing quality in our judges. When I was studying to become a barrister the vast majority of those around me were white men. There were very few brave women breaking into what was then an overwhelmingly male profession. There were tiny numbers from ethnic minorities. None of this was special to the Bar. It was true of solicitors and consultants and major companies and indeed politicians, and so far as men were concerned, white men form the international cricket, soccer, and rugby teams. That has changed and is changing and I earnestly hope will continue to change. But you have to start thinking about a judicial career very early. I want the young students at the University of Cardiff who are thinking of entering the legal profession, whether as solicitors or barristers or indeed as members of the Chartered Institute of Legal Executives (CILEX), to think now, in the years when they are students, and while they are qualifying for their professions, to ask themselves whether after twenty to twenty-five years in their chosen profession, the judicial bench might also represent an interesting new challenge. The old barriers have gone. The old doors are open. All that we need is for some of those under the under-represented parts of our community on the Bench, if they are good enough, to join it. I am not looking for quotas. That is insulting.

We have far from resolved the diversity issue, but it is at least fair to say that in society today no one is surprised to come before a judge who is a woman, or whose skin colour is not white, or who needs a stick, or a wheelchair. That is progress—slow, slow, but progress towards the time when our diverse community is served by a diverse judiciary.

Ultimately being a judge in the modern world requires us to have and keep open minds about every single current and new facet affecting the lives of those who live in the same community which we as judges are privileged and proud to serve. We are serving the community. We have to understand that world. They are living in it today, and so are we.

3

Reflections of a Serving Lord Chief Justice

Lord Thomas of Cwmgiedd

This lecture was first delivered at Birmingham University Law School on 12 March 2014.

It is a pleasure to have been asked to take part in the Judicial College's lecture series on Judging in the Modern World.[1] Some might say that the very idea that judges are in any way part of the modern world is fanciful at best. We all know the stereotype. The crusty old buffer who has difficulty knowing who The Beatles are, never mind anything more up to date than that, what text-speak or blogging might be or that a tweet is not simply a sound a young bird makes. Too much port at lunch and a round of golf in the afternoon rounds off the stereotype. In fact newspapers sometimes think this is reality; let me explain. When sitting in the Court of Appeal Criminal Division about twelve years ago, counsel forgot to ask for bail over the lunch adjournment. The press report contained a complaint by the appellant that he had been left in the cells whilst the senior judge had been at his Inn consuming port and stilton—the stereotype. The actuality was that he had been working on the judgment he was about to give and eating a sandwich in his room.

As fun as they can sometimes be, such stereotypes—like all stereotypes—are, however, a shortcut away from thought. The reality is, of course, very different. Judges are very much part of the modern world. In their various ways the lectures that form part of this series have illustrated this. In this lecture I want to look at another

[1] I am grateful to Dr John Sorabji, Principal Legal Adviser to the Lord Chief Justice, for his assistance in preparing this lecture.

aspect of the modern judge's role: the work they have to do that goes beyond the courtroom, but which is inextricably linked with the delivery of justice. I want to focus on how judges harness and implement reform. This has a number of facets and will, I believe, become increasingly important.

I want to take as my starting point what in court would be presented as a preliminary issue: should judges engage in reform in the first place? Should they rather adopt the position, variously attributed to Lord Melbourne, the Duke of Wellington, Mr Justice Astbury (an early twentieth-century chancery judge) and no doubt many others. When faced with the prospect of reform, they are supposed to have reacted with the lines 'Reform? Reform? Aren't things bad enough already?' Should modern judges take a similar line, and argue for the status quo or give reform a wide berth?

The answer to this has to be a firm no. Judges not only should engage. They must do so. They are in fact under a duty to do so. Why do I say this? There are at least two reasons. The first, and most obvious, is that the Astbury approach is as fatuous as it is ridiculously pessimistic. It suggests no good can come of reform; that we should endure a far less than ideal situation because we cannot be sure, or rather because we must anticipate that, any attempt to improve things is doomed to make them worse. It may play to the gallery, but it stands no scrutiny. If, as a piece of advice, it had ever been followed we would no doubt all be strangers to civilization.

The second reason lies in our constitutional framework. As we all know, we are a country committed to the rule of law. That we are is an established constitutional principle, now acknowledged by section 1 of the Constitutional Reform Act 2005. While our courts have not yet opined on the exact nature of this section, a number of its aspects are well established. One of those is the constitutional right of access to the courts; the idea that we must secure equal justice before the law.[2] This constitutional principle is, it seems to me, one that imposes a duty on all branches of the state: Parliament to provide the legislative framework for the justice system; the Government to see that Parliament provides the necessary funds for the system; and the judiciary to ensure that within the framework and finance provided the courts are properly accessible to all.

---

[2] *Bremer Vulkan v South India Shipping Corporation Ltd* [1981] AC 909 at 917.

If the judiciary is to play its proper role in ensuring that the administration of justice is as efficient and effective as possible and thus helping to secure equality before the law, it cannot but play an active role in the reform process. It has, as I said, a duty to do so. The rationale behind this, however, goes beyond the fundamental commitment to the rule of law. A number of relatively recent statutory changes are also relevant. I intend to return to these later, when I discuss the judiciary's role concerning procedural change. However, for the moment let me say this about them. They flesh out the wider duty. They make specific provision for a number of members of the senior judiciary, the Lord Chief Justice, Master of the Rolls, and President of the Family Division, and others, to take a leading role in scrutinizing the administration of justice. That oversight role cannot but be an active one. It is one that requires them to consider reform, and where necessary promote it. What cannot be done is for the Astbury line to be adopted.

I should say, however, that accepting that there is a positive duty on the senior judiciary to take an active part in the reform process is not also to accept that reform is either inevitable or beneficial. That conclusion clearly does not follow from the initial premise. Some reforms may be ill-conceived, some may be impractical, some may be premature or ahead of their time. Certainly not all reform is good reform. In playing an active part in the reform process it is the role of the judiciary to ensure, as far as it can, that the reform process is widely informed, by informal and formal consultation; that problems are brought to light; and that those reforms which are pursued will bring benefits. With this in mind I want to focus now on the role judges have in the development of policy changes.

Policy, except for policy concerning the proper administration of justice, is the responsibility of the Government and Parliament. Questions on whether to bring forward legislation, what should go into that legislation, and the aims which it intends to further are very much the province of the democratically elected branches of the state. Judges do not, as a consequence, offer advice to either of the other branches of the state on questions concerning, for instance, the constitutionality of legislation, whether proposed legislation is likely to comply with Convention rights, or, simply, whether it is a good or a bad idea to bring forward some proposed statutory reform.

If legal advice, or advice on the constitution, is desired, the proper source of such advice is the Attorney General. If advice is required on the merits of any legislation there are plenty of organizations, think tanks, policy fora and, of course, law schools that can offer it. Judges cannot. As Lord Merrivale put it in 1928 (and it remains as accurate a statement today as it was then):

> It is no part of the business of His Majesty's judges, and never has been part of their business, at any rate since the Act of Settlement, to have any advisory concern in the acts of the Administration; or to take any part in advising the Administration.[3]

There is, however, one form of advice that the judiciary have given and continue to provide and do so quite properly: technical advice. What do I mean by this?

Judges have a wealth of experience regarding both the operation of substantive and procedural law. Let me take an example. It is sometimes the case that the Government determines that it is appropriate to reform court procedure. It did so, for instance, in the Justice and Security Act 2013 in order to introduce closed material proceedings into the civil process. The nature of this reform was, as all know, highly controversial. It gave rise to serious policy questions. Such matters were not matters in which the judiciary could become involved. How the proposed reform would or could operate was, however, a technical, a practical, matter. That was an issue entirely divorced from the primary policy question. It was something that could be commented on. It could because it went to the heart of the proper administration of justice, upon which the judiciary was well placed to comment. That is not to say that the Government was in any way required to act on that advice.

How far, then, can technical advice go? It can properly encompass the practical consequences of proposals. It can outline how they would interact with existing procedure. Such interaction may produce otherwise unforeseen consequences in seemingly unrelated areas. Imagine, for instance, to choose a neutral example, it was suggested that we alter the disclosure process in order to reduce its attendant cost. The suggested reform is that the default rule becomes that parties only have to disclose that which they intend to rely on. That would certainly reduce both the scope of disclosure and its cost. No longer, for instance, would parties have to carry out any search of their own documents to ensure that they had disclosed those adverse to their case or which might assist their opponent's case.

---

[3] Cited in Tom Bingham, *The Rule of Law* (Allen Lane, 2010), at 94.

Such a reform might appear attractive from a cost perspective. But let us assume the proposal on disclosure was to be the default position. The reform would permit parties to continue to make applications for specific disclosure of documents that they believed their opponent had or controlled and which assisted their own case or harmed their opponent's. Might the reform simply result in a massive increase in contested specific disclosure applications? Equally it might lead to more appeals from such decisions than the disclosure process currently creates. Might it thus increase costs, and use more court time and resources in dealing with them, than the present approach? It would be incumbent on the judiciary to point out these practical consequences to those who were developing such a reform. The aim is not to pass judgement on the merit of the proposal. It is to ensure that if it goes ahead it will work as well as it possibly can.

I now turn to the role judges have in relation to procedural change. There is nothing novel in this role. Judges have always been intimately involved in both formulating procedural reform and implementing it. For example, Lord Mansfield, although far better known as the judge who founded modern commercial law, instituted major reforms to the procedure of the King's Bench. Judges sat on and often chaired, in the nineteenth century, the various reform commissions that looked at what procedural improvements could be made. Proposals made by the judiciary in 1892 were probably the most far-reaching—they included the establishment of the Commercial Court and the Court of Appeal, Criminal Division, the grouping of courts for the trial of cases out of London in place of the Assizes, strict control over disclosure, and a right on the part of the Attorney General to appeal where the sentence was inadequate. A legal paper, the *Law Times*, commented in welcoming it as the most important reform of modern times ('excellent though they are in many ways, they are not complete'[4]). The author was, however, sceptical as to whether the proposed reforms would be carried through on the lines drawn by the judges, or in a more emasculated form. You can guess the answer. Some are still to be completed.

In the twentieth century and in this century prior to 2005 the standard approach would be for the Government to appoint a judge, or committee variously made up of judges and other individuals drawn

---

[4] 93 *Law Times* 371 1892 at 384.

from academia, Government, Parliament and the legal profession, to investigate and make reform recommendations. The judge would, in such circumstances, be carrying out what could properly be described as an executive function.

The picture has changed since the Constitutional Reform Act 2005. It remains possible that the Government may, in future, appoint a judge or judges to chair a reform process of the historic kind, just as in 1994 Lord Mackay LC appointed Lord Woolf to carry out the Access to Justice review. The post-2005 settlement, which made the Lord Chief Justice head of the judiciary, provided a power for the Chief Justice to make representations to Parliament on the administration of justice and gave a number of other leadership roles to the senior judiciary. Following the pattern of the Civil Procedure Act 1997, which created the office of Head of Civil Justice, the 2005 Act created the offices of Head of Criminal Justice and Head of Family Justice. The rationale behind these offices was, amongst other things, to provide an over-sight and leadership role in the development of these aspects of the justice system, to secure effective resource use, and keep them under review. As Lord Woolf, whilst setting out the rationale for creating the office of Head of Civil Justice in his Interim Report, put it: 'The holder of this office, in consultation with others, would include among his responsibilities:– the proper monitoring of the operation and admin-istration of the civil courts and the smooth introduction of any neces-sary reforms.'[5] Taken together, these various reforms have, it seems to me, altered the landscape in the way I indicated earlier: they provide the specific statutory basis that now underpins the duty imposed on the judiciary by the constitutional right of access to the courts. In par-ticular they require the judiciary to undertake, of its own initiative, the types of reform effort that had previously been initiated by the Government. We no longer now have to wait for the Lord Chancellor to appoint a latter-day Lord Woolf to review civil litigation. The Heads of Justice can now act, as Lord Clarke, Master of the Rolls, did when he appointed Sir Rupert Jackson to review civil litigation costs. In a similar vein, Lord Phillips appointed Sir Henry Brooke to consider the case for a single civil court; the Chancellor of the High Court, Sir Terence Etherton, appointed Sir Michael Briggs to review the

---

[5] H. Woolf, *Access to Justice: Interim Report to the Lord Chancellor on the Civil Justice System in England and Wales* (HMSO, 1995), Chapter 10, para. 8.

operation of the Chancery Division; and, to bring things completely up to date, I appointed Sir Brian Leveson, President of the Queen's Bench Division, to review the work of the Crown and Magistrates' Courts in order to ensure that they operate as efficiently as possible.

In each of these instances, individual judges have been—and will no doubt periodically continue to be—appointed to bring their expertise to bear on a question relating to the administration of the justice system. They, of course, do not do so alone. They canvas the views of others; they, as Sir Rupert Jackson did, gather research and evidence from a wide range of sources. They formulate ideas and test them. They look to the universities for ideas and help and invariably receive it, for a university law school is a place where issues are analysed and scrutinized. For example, Professor I. R. Scott of this university provided many ideas on the ways in which the courts should be administered and resourced.

One objection to this new approach, and it is one that does not bear much scrutiny, is that in carrying out such reviews the judiciary has in some sense overstepped the mark; that it has strayed onto the territory that a proper respect for separation of powers would leave to Parliament and the Government. The flaw in this objection is straightforward. It misunderstands the role the judiciary plays. First, it fails to properly appreciate the duty imposed on the judiciary by both constitutional principle and the statutes to which I referred earlier. Second, it misunderstands the nature of the reform proposals. Such proposals are invariably discussed with the officials of the relevant Department of State. Moreover, some proposals will require action by the Executive and Parliament. The Jackson Reforms, for instance, required both primary and secondary legislation. Once made, they were subject to Government and then Parliamentary scrutiny. Some were also subject to scrutiny by the Civil Procedure Rule Committee before implementation. Judicial proposals were subject to scrutiny by the other branches of the state before they were implemented, or, as in the case of the proposal to abolish the indemnity rule, not implemented. Separation of powers was, and is, clearly respected.

What the duty has increased, though, is a clear sense that the judiciary is no longer the passive recipient of procedural reform as it was in much of the twentieth century. The days when it was necessary to suggest to the Lord Chancellor that it might be an idea to consider reviewing the system and then waiting for someone to be appointed have gone. It is no longer someone else's responsibility. It is clear that the judiciary has a responsibility. As a consequence the judiciary cannot but play a more active part than it has in the recent past.

So far I have considered the role the judiciary can and should play in the development of reform. It does not end there. It is all very well devising a seemingly perfect set of rules or laws, but effective implementation is as important as properly formulated reform. Given this it can hardly be acceptable for the judiciary to engage actively in the development of reform and then to sit back and do nothing to ensure proper implementation. Whether or not judges agree with reforms, the law remains the law and is there to be upheld by the judiciary. 'Be you ever so high, the law is above you'[6] applies to the judiciary just as it does to the other branches of the state, the police, local authorities, the armed forces and every private citizen and business. There is no picking and choosing.

There are a number of ways in which the judiciary implements reform; most obviously given what I have just said by applying it in court. As closed material proceedings are now utilizable in civil proceedings, the courts must apply the procedure relating to them. Perhaps less obviously, successful implementation can also require the judiciary to ascertain how it is to take place. Take, for instance, the reform that flowed from the Constitutional Reform Act 2005. It transferred the role of head of the judiciary of England and Wales from the Lord Chancellor to the Lord Chief Justice. It was not immediately clear what that would entail for the judiciary. It was fairly clear that it would require the senior judiciary to have a dedicated civil service, what is now well known as the Judicial Office, of which the Judicial College is a fundamental part. How it would work was not, however, so clear. Working out structures, ways of working, took time. Equally, working out how the judiciary and Executive were to relate to each other took time. In many ways this was to be expected. Any reform takes time to bed in.

Reforms also require training, something at which the Judicial College excels. New laws and new procedures need to be understood. Procedural reforms need to be implemented consistently across the entire judiciary. Where culture needs to change to make it work, that has to be changed too. A good example is the treatment of

---

[6] Thomas Fuller (1733) cited by Lord Denning MR, *Gouriet v Union of Post Office Workers* [1977] QB 729 at 762.

victims/alleged victims of crime in court. Traditionally in much of the Western world (and elsewhere in systems influenced by the Western world) a criminal trial was seen as a contest between the state and the defendant; the alleged victim or victim was seen very much as occupying a minor role. That has changed. The Judicial College's courses have been profoundly influential in bringing about the change of culture to make that change a reality.

It is no good introducing reform if it is to be subject to piecemeal implementation and affords litigants the choice of forum shopping between courts. Piecemeal implementation leads to arbitrary justice. It undermines the rule of law. The development of effective training courses is, as a consequence, essential. They, of course, take time and resources to properly develop and deliver. They require work by judges devising the courses and delivering them, work that takes them out of the courtroom. They require detailed work by you at the College. None of this work is an optional extra. It is not a luxury. It is a necessity. Effective implementation requires time and effort. It requires active engagement by us all.

The duty to engage actively in reform goes further than the provision of advice and implementation. It also requires judges to anticipate further reform. As Lord Clarke, then Master of the Rolls, summarised a discussion of the Woolf and Jackson reforms, reform is a process, not an event.[7] The managerially minded might say that this means we have to engage in something called 'horizon scanning'. That only suggests to me eye-strain, however. Put in a more mundane, and more accurate, way, the need to anticipate further reform requires two things. First, it means we have to consider the consequences of present reforms. What might they be? Secondly, it means we have to consider what reforms may become necessary in the light of possible changes in future circumstances? Let me elaborate.

The recent Crime and Courts Act 2013 elaborates the first issue. It effected a number of reforms. Can I refer to three? First, it merged the county courts into a single county court, as had previously been recommended by Sir Henry Brooke in his report on the feasibility of a single civil court. An instance of where the judiciary led, Government policy and legislation followed. Second, it created the single Family Court,

---

[7] A. Clarke, 'The Woolf Reforms: A Singular Event or an Ongoing Process', in D. Dwyer, *The Civil Procedure Rules Ten Years On* (Oxford University Press, 2009).

to draw together jurisdictions that had previously been exercised by a welter of different courts—an example of the judiciary helping to devise a reform (which originated in a recommendation in David Norgrove's Family Justice Review) as developed and implemented by the President of the Family Division and Lord Justice Ryder.[8] Third, it amended a large number of statutory provisions that establish which judges can sit in which courts and tribunals. The aim here was to provide the Lord Chief Justice with a wider range of options when exercising her or his statutory duty to deploy the judiciary. It also had a number of other aims. Through creating a wider range of deployment options it was also to be a means to promote judicial diversity, as well as facilitate the development of experience.

These various reforms are in the process of coming into effect. The Family Court, for instance, opened its doors on 22 April 2014 and is starting to develop as a jurisdiction in its own right. The provisions regarding deployment are, in the main, already in force. In respect of both, work is being carried out by the judiciary and by the Judicial Office, and in some respects by the Executive, to ensure these provisions work well in practice. If I can take flexible deployment, implementing it effectively requires some considerable work. What, for instance, are the proper criteria to apply in considering where and how to deploy judges? It may look a straightforward question whether a tribunal judge or High Court Master can sit in the county court, but this raises resource implications. It requires a consideration of what training, if any, needs to be undergone before a judge can be deployed into a court other than the one to which they were appointed. That, in turn, gives rise to further resource considerations. How much time and money will training incur? How many other judges will need to come out of court to conduct such training, and what is the knock-on effect of that? The essential point is that present reforms, and for that matter other reforms since the turn of the century, require us to think carefully about their consequences from, at least, an organizational, administrative, and procedural perspective.

What of the second point, the need to consider what reforms may become necessary in the light of possible changes in future circumstances? Such considerations are much more open-textured than

---

[8] Lord Justice McFarlane was a member of the Review Panel. See www.gov.uk/government/uploads/system/uploads/attachment_data/file/217343/family-justice-review- final-report.pdf.

those arising under the first point.[9] They require us to consider not only what may happen, but what that might mean for the courts and judiciary. They may arise from questions of cost and investment, from any further change to litigation funding, whether that refers to legal aid, third-party funding, or legal insurance. They may arise from recommendations such as those in the recently published Silk Commission Report, concerning the development of the justice system in Wales.

Looking wider than this, they may also arise from the continuing evolution of legal services regulation, which cannot by any means be said to have reached its end point. If the judiciary is to discharge its duty, it cannot be the passive recipient of such possible future changes. It needs to consider what they might be, what effect they may have, and what that might mean more broadly for the justice system. In this respect there is a need for the judiciary both to do its own thinking, but also to engage constructively with external think tanks, the universities and, where appropriate, the Executive. In order to do so as beneficially as possible it will no doubt have to adopt a structured approach to such engagement; a scattergun approach would be as ineffective here as it is anywhere else.

The classic picture of the judge is of a magisterial figure, decked out in red robes, sitting calmly impassive in court while counsel presents the evidence and legal argument. It is the image of the umpire, as Pollock and Maitland described the English and Welsh judge.[10] The picture is far from the truth. Historically, it undersold the active nature of the judges', and Masters', roles in the Court of Chancery. It undersold the picture of criminal trials, at least until the development of the modern adversarial criminal trial from the late eighteenth century, as keen viewers of *Garrow's Law* well know. Since the development of case management to deal with multiparty disputes from the 1980s and then the introduction of formal, active case management in civil, family, and criminal proceedings from 1999, it certainly does not capture the true nature of the judge's role in court.

---

[9] *Silk Commission on Devolution in Wales* (Second Report 2014, The Welsh Assembly).

[10] Pollock and Maitland, *The History of English Law* (Cambridge University Press, 1968, 2nd edn reissue), Vol. 2 at 670 (667 in the original page referencing), 'We are often reminded of the cricket match. The judges sit in court, not in order that they may discover the truth, but in order that they may answer the question, How's that?'

The picture was also far from the truth in another way. It was because it was, as I imagine any representation cannot but be, only ever partial. It only told the story from the perspective of the court-room. Historically, however, our judges were always active outside court. Lord Mansfield was, even though Chief Justice, a member of the Cabinet from 1757 to 1765. Lord Ellenborough, Mansfield's successor but one, was a member of Lord Grenville's so-called ministry of all the talents, sitting in the Cabinet from 1806. He was the last to do so. It has been unlikely that a judge could do so for some time.

In addition to the former practice of engaging in overtly political activity, judges have always engaged in non-political matters, specifically those concerned with reform, as I mentioned earlier. But engagement in reform of the administration of justice is entirely different. It is an essential part of the duty of the senior judiciary, as I have explained. The sheer number of reforming efforts we have made over the past 200 years regarding our justice system is legend. Judges have been involved with all of them.

Modern judges are not only required to be active in the courtroom, but have to take on a wide range of administrative duties. In addition to those, the senior judiciary and many other judges have to take on a wide range of activities concerned with reforming the justice system. They have to do so because we are under a duty to do so; a duty born of our commitment to the rule of law and the need to, amongst other things, secure the constitutional right of access to the court. The intensity of the activity required will vary with the times. Today we are in an intensively active period of reform driven largely by the necessity to introduce modern technology, to reduce cost, and to deliver justice more speedily. In that last, we need all the help we can obtain, particularly scrutiny and constructive criticism, for it is in everyone's interest that reform is what I have described as 'good reform'. I therefore look forward to hearing from as many of you as feel able to contribute.

4

Walking the Tightrope of Independence in a Constitutionally Illiterate World

Baroness Chakrabarti CBE

This lecture was delivered at Manchester University on 25 April 2013.

It is, of course, a daunting privilege indeed to be before so many judges at once; daunting enough for most people to be before one, but to be before so many! They used to say that it was when the policemen and the teachers looked younger that you knew you were heading for old age yourself, and we can add to that when the judges look younger you know you really are quite old, or perhaps I should say middle aged.

I feel it is not really my place to even begin to lecture judges on what it is to be a judge in the modern world, or the ancient world, or any world. I am not a judge, so mine is an external perspective on the challenges that you all face, but hopefully an interested, interesting, and friendly perspective, based on the experience of primarily having been a Government lawyer, and then a thorn in the side of Government, having been a human rights campaigner for the last twelve years now, since I left the Home Office.

You will know that Liberty is the National Council for Civil Liberties (NCCL). It was formed nearly eighty years ago and we will celebrate our eightieth anniversary next year. Of course a lot has changed since the Council was formed. In 1934 certain newspapers that are still in circulation—I will leave you to guess which ones they are—would regularly run headlines about how appalling it was that there were so many migrants flooding into this country from Eastern Europe, and of course we know that would never happen today! In 1934, between the wars, the far right was in the ascendancy all over Europe and we even had the Blackshirts here in England. So you can see my concern about the dangers of history repeating itself. But the particular catalyst for the formation of Liberty was that hunger marchers came from the north of England, eventually to assemble in Hyde Park in central London, and they were promptly crushed by the Metropolitan Police. Of course we know that that would never happen today.

Interestingly, to be a bit more specific about what happened, we think, in 1934 undercover police officers dressed as hunger marchers went amongst them and acted as agents provocateurs, which ignited the troubles. I was reminded of that situation recently over the case of Mark Kennedy and others who joined protest movements, living for years and years in those movements, and formed relationships with women who now feel, understandably, quite wronged by that. Arguably I would call it potentially an abuse of power. There are many senior police officers with whom I have debated this issue who say, 'No, I mean, how can you be genuinely undercover if you're not able to be seen to be in relationships?' So that was why we were formed.

A group of people, far smaller than the group here today, sat in the Crypt of St Martin-in-the-Fields in Trafalgar Square and wrote a letter (I suppose today it would be a tweet or a blog) to the *Manchester Guardian* newspaper; today, of course, *The Guardian* newspaper. Considering that some of the names that signed that letter were great men and women of letters, for instance H. G. Wells, E. M. Forster, and Edith Summerskill, the letter itself is quite verbose and not particularly well written, but the sentiment is highly important. They had been horrified by the police response to the peaceful demonstrators and had decided, just as audaciously as I feel addressing a group of judges, that on that day, in February 1934, they would form a National Council for Civil Liberties to 'keep watch over the entire spirit', they said, 'of British liberty'.[1]

I think one of the most interesting moments on the journey from 1934 to the present day comes after World War II, because that is when we stopped thinking about British liberty in that 'leave-me-alone-overweening-state-please-protect-me-from-the-policeman's-boot' way. It is good to be protected from the policeman's boot, but

---

[1] See www.liberty-human-rights.org.uk/tags/national-council-civil-liberties.

actually we moved to a broader human rights' agenda that is not just libertarian, but is as much about protecting and promoting the rule of law and race equality. It is an international human rights' agenda with NCCL/Liberty as a sort of domestic organization promoting that agenda, rather than just a reactive one. I think that was a very important moment for the international rule of law and for human rights around the world, where individual freedom struggles come together and settle behind this very precious framework of fundamental rights and freedoms, agreed on by people slightly to the left of politics, slightly to the right of politics, representatives of all the great world faith communities and people of no religious conviction at all. That is to be found initially in the universal declaration, but then in regional legal instruments like the much-maligned European Convention of Human Rights (ECHR). The ECHR is almost as important to us at Liberty as our formation in 1934, the settling on that framework by, amongst others, Winston Churchill and Eleanor Roosevelt. And now we see ourselves very much at the heart of an international human rights movement, but remembering, of course, that human rights begin at home, or, as Eleanor Roosevelt said, 'Small places close to home, so small that you will never find them on any map of the world'.[2]

Of course, some of you will know us at Liberty, because we do litigate. We are completely unashamed of the fact that you do need a legal, enforceable backstop for human rights. They do have to live in the courtroom, but clearly you will understand they have to also live in the classroom, in the living room, in the newsroom, and in the Parliament chamber if human rights are to be protected and promoted for the future. That is what we do. If you are not familiar with our work, we are multidisciplinary human rights campaigners; we litigate; we intervene, with the permission of courts, in other people's cases because, unlike Christabel Pankhurst, I have never promised to behave myself. *The Sun* newspaper once called me the most dangerous woman in Britain, but if this is as dangerous as it gets, I think you can probably relax. So we litigate; we intervene in important cases that are likely to affect the public discourse or the law substantively in an important way; and we lobby Parliamentarians. So we have a lot

---

[2] Speech by Eleanor Roosevelt at the presentation of 'In Your Hands: A Guide for Community Action for the Tenth Anniversary of the Universal Declaration of Human Rights', Thursday, 27 March 1958, United Nations, New York.

of dealings with Whitehall and Westminster, with the Legislature and the Executive, including policymakers, and we take on a lot of media work, but all connected with the same issues: promoting fundamental rights and freedoms and the rule of law.

So, from that perspective, what do I think are the challenges in being a judge in the modern world? What a daunting title.

I think that I would obviously highlight some external challenges which I am sure you think about all the time and are well aware of. First, I would remind you, I think, that in recent years in this country especially, but elsewhere in the world too, it has been a particular grand drama or opera, even. There have been crises, really quite huge crises, in trust in very, very important institutions in this country in recent years, certainly in my time as director of Liberty. You could take it back to the Executive crisis in faith and in the Executive, possibly over the Iraq war. Whatever your view of the Iraq war it did lead to a crisis of trust in Government. We saw this affect our work and our campaigns, and it became easier to arouse people's interest in the limitations, for example, of secret intelligence and the limitations of the security state as a result of people's shock at what they heard—'45 minutes', 'dodgy dossiers', and so on. That was a crisis in trust.

Then, of course, you have a crisis in trust in Parliament, which was about MPs' expenses. The last decade was a very authoritarian period in British politics. The law-and-order debate ratcheted up in my adult lifetime, if I think about coming out of college and then being called to the Bar in 1994, and around that time the great authoritarian arms race that began with Mr Michael Howard and Mr Tony Blair as they faced each other across the despatch box, as Home Secretary and Shadow Home Secretary. I really trace it back to that time, with things like the Criminal Justice and Public Order Bill, as was, then Act, of 1994 and the idea that law and order are not just for the home affairs pages; they are for the front page. Of course, in time, these two men went on to lead their parties, and this had previously been their big brief, and you see that ratchet continue as Mr Blair becomes Prime Minister and Mr Howard becomes leader of the Conservative Party. Lots of judge bashing (and we will come back to the judge bashing in a moment: I'm sure you're looking forward to that bit!).

We had this very authoritarian period, in my view, in British politics. But think of all the criminal justice bills that some of you had to grapple with, had to implement, had to read and understand and make work—not always easy to make work—not all of it brought into force, of course, which is another issue of which you will be aware, when the machine churns out all of these criminal justice and police powers bills. So the public was lectured for years and years about law and order and about not being dishonest and not being workshy and then the same people who had been wagging this authoritarian fore-finger on law and order appear to be rifling through the expenses till with the left hand. You saw the crisis of trust that that issue led to in Parliament, just before the last general election. So that is another huge seismic crisis in trust that we experienced in recent years.

Then, of course, you cannot even trust the bank managers any more, it seems. You are better off putting your savings under the mattress because of the whole 'casino' metaphor, and just when we thought that was all done, these crises of trust in these powerful insti-tutions in this great democracy of ours, the final act: the media, the journalists who are supposed to help us as citizens to look at other powerful institutions and hold them to account. They were misbehav-ing as well, hence the Leveson inquiry.

Now I can tell this as a sort of colourful anecdote, but I do not glory in it and I do not think of it as good news, because the thing about democracies is they do need these institutions, do they not? Yes, it may be good that the modern world is a bit less reverent than it was previously. Yes, it is not a bad thing if people have their wits about them and do not take everything on trust: I would say this as Director of Liberty! It is also good, perhaps, that people are a little more scepti-cal of 'securocrats' than they were pre-Iraq, but, nonetheless, you do have to have a government and you do have to have a security state that goes with it. And you do have to have parliamentarians and poli-tics and legislators and you do have to have banks and you do have to have news media, including, I would argue, professionally trained journalists, and it is very worrying that there is a crisis in funding in that area.

I know we are probably not all the best friends of the media, and people have probably got a few stories of their own, but everyone can be a citizen journalist now, just as everyone can learn to do first aid. But sometimes a little surgery is better done by someone who has a few ethics and has trained and so on, and that is not always going to happen just via the Internet. So I think one of the issues that we are grappling with, with being any kind of important institution in the modern world, in modern Britain, is the fact that there have been these really quite significant crises in trust in institutions.

I think the good news, though, for you, is that the judiciary has come out of this quite well. When we do polling at Liberty and have focus groups, we do all that political stuff because the bad guys do and we need to know what people are thinking. When we run focus groups, the difference between our polling and our focus groups is that we do not necessarily change our values on the basis of what we find out. We sometimes alter the communication tools and try and hone the arguments but we do not actually say 'torture's okay now because people are supporting torture'—which they are not, by the way—but when we poll people on their kind of trust index for different institutions and different professionals in Britain you will be happy, but I hope unsurprised, to hear that the judiciary polls incredibly well.

You might think, and I would agree with you, that one of the challenges that you face is our general legal and constitutional illiteracy in this country. I really do think that is a problem and you may have your own thoughts about that. So whilst there is, I think, a very low level of basic legal and constitutional literacy in this country, including, sadly, amongst the political classes and in Parliament, there is nonetheless instinctive and cultural trust in the judiciary amongst ordinary people. That is what the polling suggests, that when people are worried about something that is very important to them, they would trust a judge over a politician. They would actually trust a chief constable over one of the elected police and crime commissioners as well.

I think constitutional illiteracy is a challenge for all of you, as it is for us at Liberty. It is a common idea in parts of the political establishment—really clever people, by the way, really highly educated people who have been to university and should know better—the idea that the only source of legitimate authority in a democracy is elected power; the only people who have a proper place making decisions that affect people's lives are elected politicians. Have you not heard senior politicians rail against 'unelected judges'? Now what is the answer to that, to elect the judges? Is that what is being seriously posited? Well, it is never quite put that way, but you have heard senior—the most senior—Cabinet ministers you could imagine railing at the interfering decisions of 'unelected judges' who make them feel physically sick, when it is about criminals and prisoners.

It is not just Strasbourg judges. That is another area of concern, because that is then national sovereignty. It is also domestic judges. Yes, it is the Supreme Court and, yes, the High Court, but it can be any unfortunate judge who finds him/herself reported or misreported in the local or national press—because there is no such thing, by the way, as local and national and international media any more. There is practically no real distinction between old and new media any more and that, of course, is another challenge in itself. So we have this constitutional illiteracy, but the good news is that we, nonetheless, have a high trust index in the institution of the independent judiciary. So ordinary people understand it, although they might not be able to articulate the rule of law. Among the political classes there is a narrative that says that judges are unelected and therefore lack legitimacy, I, of course, say they are independent and that is what gives them their legitimacy. You start electing the judges and Barabbas will always walk free, I think, for those of you who like those kind of biblical allusions.

So I think that is an interesting tension. The other interesting tension about politicians and judges that I have observed is another slightly mischievous irony, if you will forgive me, that we have had politicians—of all colours, by the way, this is not a party-political point—for a number of years railing at interfering judges; railing at due process, you know, as 'old fashioned', 'nineteenth century', 'Byzantine', 'too slow'; it does not always get you the results that you want; railing at lawyers, at the 'gravy train' of legal aid and all the 'fat cats'. Well, there is not much 'fat' left now. There is not much of a 'train' left now, actually, which is going to be another enormous challenge. And yet, and yet, it is back to Lord Justice Leveson, when there is a genuine political scandal amongst the political classes and they are really in a corner and they do not know how to lance this boil and deal with the public clamour of the political scandal, who do we call? Who are you going to call? Not Ghostbusters, no. You're going to call Lord Justice Leveson or some other poor judge that gets stuck with the task, which is interesting, is it not? You can almost imagine a kind of dystopian future where there is no traditional litigation any more because, as you know, there is no money for it and there is no legal process … you know, there are no more civil disputes or criminal trials. It is all going to be sorted out by computer or perhaps by voting, like *The X Factor* or *The Voice*. We will just turn on our TVs and take a look at the contestant/defendant and decide whether he is guilty or not guilty; we can vote on our iPhones. We can get rid of criminal trials; we can get rid of civil trials; but there will still be work to be done by judges and lawyers and it will be called public inquiries, sorting out political, polycentric, complex problems like what self-regulation of the press should look like and war and peace and economics and all the things that were traditionally in the sphere of the elected politicians rather than the rule of law, that worked so well in a courtroom.

Now, of course I am being deliberately mischievous, but there is a point there nonetheless, that the constitutional illiteracy is forgetting that a democratic constitution needs fixed points as well as moving parts. Of course the moving parts, the elected, the elections, and all the raucous party politics and the heat and light of that are all incredibly important, but we also need no torture, free speech, fair trials, personal privacy, equal treatment under the law, this small bundle of non-negotiable rights and freedoms, and it does have to be protected by the judiciary because, otherwise, today's democracy descends into something very different, very quickly.

Markets will eat themselves when they are unregulated and democracy can eat itself as well when the press is censored or opponents are arrested and the police are corrupted. We have seen this, have we not, in our lifetimes all over the world. Of course we are complacent about all that stuff in Britain but I think the complacency in Parliament is because there are not enough lawyers in Parliament any more. We would never have said that twenty years ago. We would have made self-deprecating jokes about being a lawyer and how many lawyers does it take to change a light bulb and all of that kind of stuff. The time for that is over. I do not do it any more. I used to make jokes, when I was first in this job, about being a lawyer in recovery, or perhaps in remission. I do not do it any more because it is not funny, because of this challenge that I think you all face, as much as I do, of the illiteracy, this lack of understanding, of real political understanding, of why the law is important and why it is not anti-democratic, but is actually essential in a democracy.

Of course, there is not enough basic legal literacy provided in schools either. So this is feeding right down. It is particularly troubling in the highly educated legislators. We are churning out legislation they can barely read, let alone understand. Of course, it feeds then into attacks on human rights. I spoke to someone who was a very senior minister in the Blair and Brown years recently who did not realize that the Human Rights Act contains no strike-down powers for judges in relation to primary legislation. I think that is pretty troubling, don't you? So, you have got people pontificating about unelected judges and interfering, using these wicked human rights to get in the way of Parliament, and they do not even realize that the exquisite constitutional compromise provided by section 4 of the Declaration of Incompatibility in the Human Rights Act means that judges, even in the Supreme Court, cannot overrule the will of Parliament in the end—strike down executive actions for the Home Secretary, or whatever, but that is not Parliamentary sovereignty, that is Executive sovereignty and I did not ever understand that to be, at least, the theoretical, governing principle of our constitution. But I think that is the level of illiteracy I am talking about. How many Fleet Street editors, Cabinet ministers, members of the Shadow Cabinet understand just the basic mechanics of something like the Human Rights Act and its limitations, let alone principles of judicial review, let alone the reality of legal aid as opposed to the spin about fat cats and so on? That is a challenge for a judge, I would argue, in the modern world.

On the one hand you have the attacks on the judiciary and on human rights and so on, but then on the other hand this potential danger of co-option. There are different kinds of potential co-option that can be challenging for the judiciary as well. Now, one type of co-option is controversial; some of you may not agree with me, but I think all of these secret courts and secret commissions and legal quasi-judicial processes, where judges are asked to sit in a room with one side of a case and basically look at lots of secret intelligence that cannot properly be called evidence because it cannot be challenged, I think that that is a dangerous potential form of co-option which may, in time, when scandals emerge, not be good for the reputation of the judiciary. The Justice and Security Act that has just passed, sadly, is an absolute scandal and hopefully we will get a new policy one day and it will be overturned, but I do not see how it is good for anybody, for the Executive, for the *spooks*, for the judges, for any of these vital institutions in a democracy to be part of a little stitch up that goes on in a room that cannot any longer be called a court, but they are not dealing with a fair civil trial where two sides get to have an argument with a judge as a referee. We are co-opting the judge who is off with one team in the locker room looking at secret material that can never be tested. How can the judge really test it? That is one, I think, very obvious dangerous potential route to co-option, and we saw it, and of course that's a trend that began post-9/11 with internment and Belmarsh.

You could argue that all public enquiries can be a form of co-option in themselves. I'm not talking about the Leveson Inquiry, in particular, because the judge there was, at least, given quite a free hand about his remit and whom he could call as witnesses and so on, but the Gibson Inquiry,[3] that my colleagues and I boycotted, which was not an appropriate inquiry because the powers of the judge were so limited and because the whole thing was subject, essentially, to Cabinet Office veto in terms of what documents would be seen and what would be published, even by the judge in the final analysis. I am glad to say that that inquiry was brought to an end because when is a judicial inquiry not a judicial inquiry? When the puppeteer is the Cabinet Secretary or, effectively, the director general of MI5, or whatever, it is not going to work. Remember, these inquiries are created to rebuild trust because trust has been broken. You are not going to rebuild trust with a process that does not look independent; you are just going to undermine trust in the judiciary that have been co-opted into that process. So that is something to think about as a judge in this weird, potentially slightly dystopian, modern world.

Of course, there are obvious challenges in relation to the media that I have alluded to, and I do not want to scare anybody, but it is worth remembering that, so even sitting in your local court thinking, 'This is a completely innocuous little case and there is nobody here from the press', but of course there is no such thing! Everybody is a citizen–journalist, everybody is tweeting and blogging, and everything can be distorted, and have we not all heard the little joke that the magistrate or the immigration judge made, which was perfectly fine and jolly in its setting and ends up with 'catgate', and Theresa May saying, 'scrap the Human Rights Act, because somebody got to stay because of their cat'. I am not trying to turn you all into sort of guarded politicians, but it is worth bearing in mind that the media are everywhere. Big Brother is everywhere in terms of the potential traps in relation to pronouncements or musings that you make in court. Of course, the obvious challenge, partly technological, is that every mobile phone is a camera. The police find that to their cost now. It is very interesting on demonstrations. The police have their cameras on their helmets to watch the demonstrators and the demonstrators are walking round with their mobile phones.

---

[3] On 6 July 2010, Prime Minister David Cameron appointed Sir Peter Gibson to head the Detainee Inquiry, which would look into allegations that the UK intelligence services were complicit in the torture of detainees, including those from the Guantánamo Bay detention camp or subject to rendition flights. The interim report of the inquiry was finally published on 19 December 2013. It concluded that the British intelligence services had been complicit in extraordinary rendition.

Of course there is so much new technology with implications, not just for different areas of life and policy, but probably for your work as well. We could probably have a whole-day seminar on developing technologies in relation to surveillance that would be relevant to evidence in the future or in relation to health and medical evidence and so on. That, of course, is another aspect of what it is to adjudicate cases in the modern world. I think that this is a shrinking, interconnected modern world and everybody should remember that. What happens here is immediately reported on the other side of the world. People have loyalties and family connections all over the world. That is why I will always support human rights rather than citizens' privileges, because they are not going to help a Gary McKinnon or a Christopher Tappin who has not even left his own country, but is sitting on a computer and is charged with crimes by another government elsewhere. They have not even got a passport, let alone left the country, but they are sitting there and it is a shrinking, interconnected world.

What is the nationality of the Internet? This idea that the Human Rights Act might, for example, be replaced by a British Bill of Rights, that we should go back to citizens' rights, that is the road to Guantánamo Bay, if you think about it, because some clever White House lawyer can argue that the United States Bill of Rights is just for citizens and say, 'Well, Mr President, I've got a wizard wheeze, as long as they are not American, and as long as the detention without trial is in Guantánamo and not in New Jersey, we can do it.' If every government around the world adopted that approach and we had citizens' rights documents and not human rights documents, people are not going to be protected. It seems to me, therefore, we decide whether to be human beings everywhere or foreigners pretty much everywhere, or in everywhere except one place.

Of course, there are challenges, huge challenges, to all of you caused by austerity Britain and austerity Europe, probably for some time. Some of it is inevitably associated with anger and disharmony and you may already see the effects of that in your courtrooms. Legal aid has to be mentioned because if we are not careful, your work could change hugely and you may stop being dispassionate, highly educated referees and find yourselves social workers, mediators with very distressed, vulnerable, inarticulate people from whom a lawyer struggles to take instruction, so then a judge attempts to help in real time in court. I am very, very bleak about that at the moment. At Liberty, the only thing that we can really do is to try and get different policy commitments from various political parties in time for the manifestos of the next election, but at the moment the law has changed. I believe that legal aid is being decimated in this country, which brings profound challenges for most of you, I suspect.

Then, finally, there are some challenges that come from inside and are not external threats. So just a couple of words about the composition of the Bench. I am never going to be the person who says that you cannot get a fair hearing from someone of another race or gender or age bracket or class demographic or anything like that. Of course not. It is just not true. Equally, given what I have said about crises in trust and political attacks on the independent judiciary, I do think that diversity matters, that a more diverse Bench is happening. But it needs to happen more quickly, and particularly at the top end. Then it will be more robust from that kind of attack, not at all because you cannot get a fair trial from someone, or I cannot get a fair trial from someone who is an Etonian, not a bit of it. The judiciary is not just a group of individuals; it is a great institution of state in our country and appeals and precedent and all sorts of things mean that having a more diverse judicial body is a good thing, and I do not agree at all with the idea that diversity is 'intention with meritocracy', because although I am sure that you are all the best judges that there could possibly be, the status quo is not meritocracy and I do think that it would be a competent, wise and ambitious judiciary that looked outward towards bringing in people from a wider pool. We need to look at what the qualifications for that kind of service are, just as qualifications were changed so that women could do men's jobs when men were off at war, and they did the jobs and they were fine and then the qualifications were changed back after the war again. There are ways in which one alters qualifications for different kinds of service at different times. I think that it will be a more empathetic, more in touch, more legitimate, more robust, and more competent judiciary that is less vulnerable, frankly, to attack from the *Daily Mail* every time those appointments are made, with those photographs, always with the full-bottom wigs, that they print in the *Daily Mail* when people are appointed as judges. It will only be a good thing for the senior judiciary, in particular, to be a little bit less timid about opening up to a broader pool.

5

The Embattled Judge

Joshua Rozenberg QC

This lecture was delivered at Keble College, Oxford, on 13 June 2014.

It is quite a challenge to be asked to give a talk on Being a Judge in the Modern World. I like to think I live in the modern world—whatever that may be—but I have no experience of being a judge.

So you would have been much better off listening to the lecture by Lord Judge.[1] Lord Judge was, of course, the Lord Chief Justice—and he has been a 'Judge' from the moment he was born. So was his father, Raymond Judge. But I am not going to talk about nominative determinism tonight—although you might like to consult the *British Journal of Urology* for those famous papers on incontinence that were written in the late 1970s by A. J. Splatt and D. Weedon.

Lord Judge did not make jokes about anybody's name in his lecture, though he did tell some rather interesting stories. From these, he was able to conclude that 'being a judge in the modern world has at its heart the notion that judges should understand the modern world … because where real change is apparent, the judicial system must understand, represent, and respond to it'.

There is one passage from his lecture that I particularly want to read you because it sums up his own approach so well. He said:

Judges must have moral courage or fortitude, in particular to make decisions that will not be popular with the politicians or the media or indeed the vast majority of the public. And judges have to defend the

---

[1] Chapter 2 above.

right to equality and fair treatment before the law of any individual citizen, even and perhaps most of all a citizen who is unpopular, currently demonised, currently beyond the pale. That is the rule of law, and in its practical application it is not always very popular. And, what is more, the judge cannot respond to personal criticism. This makes fortitude, an old-fashioned virtue, much underrated in our present society. Quiet fortitude: a requisite for the judge in the modern world.[2]

Despite saying that judges must not attempt to be popular, I think the defining characteristic of Lord Judge is his sensitivity to the public mood. On more than one occasion, I think, people who have been treated unnecessarily harshly by the system have announced that they would be seeking to appeal—only to find that permission has already been granted and the case has been listed before Lord Judge with a hearing next Tuesday.

It was typical of Lord Judge to grasp the importance of social media before many people even knew what the phrase referred to. In December 2012, two and a half years ago, the Lord Chief Justice acknowledged that tweeting, blogging, or even formal reporting from inside the courtroom was unlikely to interfere with the proper administration of justice. Individuals, he announced, could apply to use a 'mobile phone, small laptop or similar piece of equipment, solely to make live text-based communications of the proceedings'.[3] It was a few weeks later that I decided to join Twitter myself. That was shortly after I had the chastening experience of rushing out of a courtroom and into a television studio to report on a hearing that had just begun—only to find that tweets from inside the courtroom were on the television screen before I was. The accused, incidentally, was Julian Assange—one of the few defendants I can think of to sentence himself to detention and then commence a lengthy period of confinement without waiting to be convicted or sentenced.

In December 2011, a year after Lord Judge had issued his interim guidance, the Lord Chief Justice announced that members of the media, and legal commentators, could tweet without asking formal permission—unless, of course, the trial judge had decided otherwise. 'Twitter as much as you wish', he said, rather endearingly. And we did.

---

[2] Ibid., p. 21.
[3] See www.theguardian.com/technology/2010/dec/20/twitter-court-lord-chief-justice links to the original guidance.

Shortly after the Lord Chief Justice allowed reporters to tweet without asking first, I was interviewed on BBC Radio 2 about a sentencing decision at the Old Bailey. I happened to be out of the country, though the programme didn't know that; they were speaking to me on the phone. The hearing had been delayed because the victims' family had been caught in traffic and sentencing was taking place while the programme was on the air. Because a newspaper reporter whom I know and trust was tweeting from court, I was able to sit in front of my computer and read out the reporter's tweets while the judge was speaking. Listeners to the broadcast knew the outcome at virtually the same time as those in court.

Twitter works the other way too. I had a huge and flattering response to my interview with Lord McNally, the legal aid minister, on this week's *Law in Action*. Gone are the days when broadcasting was a one-way process, at a time to suit the broadcaster. Because the programme went out on BBC Radio 4 at four o'clock on Tuesday afternoon, many of my listeners downloaded it and listened to it later. Those of you who prefer to tune in to the wireless can hear it at eight o'clock tonight.

Of course, even the judges are on Twitter now, in the sense that their excellent communications office will alert followers to important new judgments. But any judge here who wants to start blogging should begin by reading the guidance issued last August by Lord Justice Goldring, who was Senior Presiding Judge at the time. That advised judges to be careful: 'Judicial office holders should be acutely aware of the need to conduct themselves, both in and out of court, in such a way as to maintain public confidence in the impartiality of the judiciary.'[4] Blogging by members of the judiciary is not prohibited. However, judicial office holders who blog (or who post comments on other people's blogs) must not identify themselves as members of the judiciary. They must also avoid expressing opinions which, were it to become known that they hold judicial office, could damage public confidence in their own impartiality or in the judiciary in general.

This guidance was apparently aimed at a Justice of the Peace (JP), who had been publishing an excellent and highly opinionated website since 2005. He called it *The Magistrate's Blog*. After thinking

---

[4] See www.familylaw.co.uk/system/redactor_assets/documents/491/Blogging_by_Judicial_Office_Holders.pdf.

about the guidance for a few days he relaunched his website as *The Magistrates' Blog*—moving the apostrophe from before the 's' to after it—while adding a note to the effect that the blog was now written by a team, 'who may or may not be JPs'. His blog is still going strong.

Full-time judges in the higher courts probably don't blog or tweet. But they certainly understand the importance of communicating their decisions to the public. Judges routinely provide copies of their sentencing remarks to the media in high-profile cases, both in court and online. No longer do I have to ring judges at home to find out whether a local news agency report is accurate, only to be told—as I once was—'My husband never speaks to the press'. It was because Lord Judge realised how important it was for the public to receive fast accurate information—ideally without the need even for reporters to leave court—that he embraced modern methods of communication with such enthusiasm.

And the future? Section 32 of the Crime and Courts Act 2013 allows for video recordings to be made in the courts of England and Wales. The provision is not yet in force but preparations are being made to start broadcasting proceedings from the Court of Appeal in October. Both civil and criminal appeals will be covered, though we shall have to wait for the secondary legislation and, no doubt, practice directions to find out exactly how it is going to work. The Lord Chief Justice made it clear earlier this year that the modern appeal judge is one who has been trained to deal with the demands of television.

I can also commend to you the lecture in this series by Lord Carnwath. As you would expect, he has a great deal to say about tribunals and how they were welcomed into the judiciary by what I think is sometimes referred to as the 'uniformed branch'. The reforms introduced by the Tribunals, Courts and Enforcement Act 2007 do seem to have been one of those quiet revolutions that we do so well in this country, unlike the rather noisier revolution that happened ten years ago this week.

I will come on to that in a moment, but I want to begin with a horror story. It is a case that I have been reluctant to write about because I know and like the judge concerned—one of the downsides of specialist journalism. It is a case that will undoubtedly feature in the training given by the Judicial College to all judges at every level. Indeed the only reason that some of you may not know about it already is that judgment in *IG Markets Ltd v Crinion* [2013] EWCA Civ 587 was delivered by the Court of Appeal civil division only three weeks ago, on 23 May 2014.

The original claim was brought by a company that promotes online trading in derivatives. I have never really understood what a derivative is but, as far as I can see from the company's website, all you have to do is to bet on whether particular markets are going to go up or down. It looks very seductive and I imagine you can make a lot of money if you know what you are doing. You can also lose a great deal: more than €2 million in the case of Declan Crinion and his father Tommy, it seems. So IG Markets sued Crinion *père et fils* in the Birmingham Mercantile Court for recovery of the money they were owed.

The case came before a specialist mercantile judge who, as you might expect, was very computer-savvy. The judge heard evidence and adjourned for closing submissions. These were made orally but counsel supported them with written submissions that were emailed to the judge as an MS Word file. In a written judgment, handed down at the beginning of last year, the judge upheld the company's claims in full. There was really no defence.

Unexpectedly, though, the two defendants were granted permission to appeal and the case was heard by Lord Justices Longmore and Underhill sitting with Sir Stephen Sedley, a former Lord Justice of Appeal.

The appeal had nothing to do with the underlying claims. Instead, the defendants appealed on the basis that almost all of the judge's written ruling had been cut and pasted from the closing submissions of junior counsel for the claimants. What the judge had done was to take the Word file he had been sent by counsel and revise it to include some, though not much, material of his own.

He did, of course, change the title from 'written closing submissions' to 'judgment'. He deleted counsel's name at the end. Whenever he came across the phrase 'it is submitted that …' he struck it out. And he added a standard section—one he had used before—on the judicial evaluation of witnesses, derived from an article written by Lord Bingham and two leading authorities. Well, he intended to add it to the version he circulated to counsel in advance but, in fact, he forgot to paste it in until later.

The two appellants calculated that—ignoring the standard section on witness evaluation which was not specific to this case in any event—some 94 per cent of the words of the judgment represented junior counsel's drafting—and there was no alteration whatever to counsel's structure. The appellants also pointed out that if you opened the 'properties' file in the Word version of the judgment you would see the author's name shown. As Lord Justice Underhill said, 'that may be something of a debating point, but the appellants say that it reflects the reality.' The appellants' counsel told the court that the impression given was that the judge had abdicated his core judicial responsibility to think through for himself the issues that it was his job to decide. He had also failed to address the appellants' case. There had been a serious procedural irregularity.

The judge, of course, was not represented in the appeal. A judge never is: the judgment speaks for itself. But counsel for the original claimants IG Markets—the respondents to the appeal—sought to justify what the judge had done. If the judge had accepted the entirety of junior counsel's submissions, as he evidently had, and if he believed they were well expressed, then—counsel argued—there could be nothing objectionable in his adopting them as the basis of his judgment.

The Court of Appeal disagreed. Lord Justice Underhill again:

> Appearances matter. For the judge to rely as heavily as he did on Mr Chirnside's [junior counsel's] written submissions did indeed risk giving the impression that he had not performed his task of considering both parties' cases independently and even-handedly. I accept of course that a judge will often derive great assistance from counsel's written submissions, and there is nothing inherently wrong in his making extensive use of them, with proper acknowledgement, whether in setting out the facts or in analysing the issues or the applicable legal principles or indeed in the actual dispositive reasoning. But where that occurs the judge should take care to make it clear that he or she has fully considered such contrary submissions as have been made and has brought their own independent judgment to bear. The more extensive the reliance on material supplied by only one party, the greater the risk that the judge will in fact fail to do justice to the other party's case—and in any event that that will appear to have been the case.

What, then, was the Court of Appeal to do? Allow the appeal and order a retrial—at huge expense to the parties and, no doubt, embarrassment to the judge? No, said Lord Justice Underhill:

> In the end, and not without some hesitation, I have come to the conclusion that the judgment in this case does show, when examined carefully in the context known to the parties, that the judge performed his essential judicial role and that his reasons for deciding the dispositive issues in the way that he did are sufficiently apparent.

Lord Justice Sedley added a few withering comments of his own:

> Unequivocal acceptance of one party's case has always posed a problem for judges. To simply adopt that party's submissions, however cogent they are, is to overlook what is arguably the principal function of a reasoned judgment, which is to explain to the unsuccessful party why they have lost. Such an omission is not generally redressed by a perfunctory acknowledgment of the latter's arguments. Even a party without merit is entitled to the measure of respect which a properly reasoned judgment conveys.

Information technology has made it seductively easy to do what the judge did in this case. It has also made it embarrassingly easy to demonstrate what he has done. In principle, no doubt, it differs little from the modus operandi of the occasional judge, familiar to an earlier generation of counsel, who would pick up his pen (sometimes for the first time) and require the favoured advocate to address him at dictation speed. But in practice, for reasons which Lord Justice Underhill has described, the possibility of something approaching electronic plagiarism is new, and it needs to be said and understood that it is unacceptable. Even if it reflects no more than the judge's true thinking, it reflects poorly on the administration of justice. For, as Lord Justice Underhill says, appearances matter.

Although I agree, even so, that enough can be teased out of the judgment to satisfy the legitimate demand of the appellants for reasoning which deals with their respective cases otherwise than through the prism of the respondent's argument, I hope that a judgment like the one now before us will not be encountered again.

And Lord Justice Longmore concluded thus:

> We trust that no judge in any future case will lift so much of a claimant's submissions into his own judgment as this judge has done and that, if substantial portions are to be lifted, it will be with proper acknowledgment and with a recitation of the defendant's case together with a reasoned rejection of it. It is only in that way that unnecessary appeals can be avoided and the litigant be satisfied that he has received the justice that is his due.

So there is a cautionary tale for judges in the modern world of word processing. Let me move on to some of the broader challenges.

My starting point is a book I wrote almost twenty years ago, called *The Search for Justice*. Despite a rather portentous title, the book was little more than a snapshot of current legal issues. Inevitably, there was a section on the Lord Chancellor, and I took the opportunity to lay into Lord Mackay of Clashfern, the Conservative incumbent, who had refused to countenance any change to his tripartite role as a Government minister, speaker of the House of Lords and the country's most senior serving judge.

'However anomalous they may seem when taken together in one job', Lord Mackay had said in 1991, these three features

> do represent a practical and, I would say, a sensible answer to the difficult question how best to manage the relationship between a sovereign legislature, a powerful executive government springing from it, and an independent judiciary.[5]

In *The Search for Justice*, I disagreed. 'Nobody should be expected to do the three main jobs of the Lord Chancellor; because they are in conflict, nobody can do all three of them properly', I thundered:

> It is time for the Lord Chancellor to hang up at least one and preferably two of his three wigs. We would then have an independent speaker in the House of Lords, an independent judiciary without a government minister presiding over it, and a minister of justice sitting in the House of Commons.[6]

Be careful what you wish for. As a journalist, it's pretty rare to get everything you demand. By rights, I should be delighted. Why, then, am I not? I suppose because I can now see that not all change is for the good. Modernisation may sometimes make things worse.

Yesterday marked the tenth anniversary of Tony Blair's decision to sack his Lord Chancellor, Lord Irvine of Lairg, and introduce the political changes that I had called for—together with the Supreme Court that came as part of the package. It was on a Thursday and the most senior judges in England and Wales first heard about this constitutional revolution in the late afternoon when they arrived at a pub in the Cotswolds, just a few miles away from here. That was a decade ago, almost to the minute. The judges had been planning to have a weekend meeting with senior officials from what, until that afternoon, had been the Lord Chancellor's Department. Once they heard what had happened to their department, the officials decided that they needed to be back at their desks by Friday morning. This

---

[5] Lord Mackay, Mishcon Lecture, 1991, paras 5 and 65.
[6] Joshua Rozenberg, *The Search for Justice* (Hodder & Stoughton, 1994), p. 14.

was a wise move: the judges, led by Lord Woolf, were furious that a deal had been struck behind their back. Tony Blair's officials were bemused, thinking the senior judges would welcome a supreme court of their own.

It was a deeply traumatic event for those most closely involved and Lord Irvine has never spoken about it. He did write about it once, in 2009, and I went back to his comments to the House of Lords Constitution Committee recently for an article in the *Law Society Gazette*.

The constitutional revolution of 2003 began earlier in June with press rumours that Lord Irvine's post was to be abolished. Was it, he asked Tony Blair? The Prime Minister told him that no decision had been taken. Lord Irvine asked Tony Blair how a decision of this magnitude could be taken without consulting those affected. 'The Prime Minister appeared mystified', Lord Irvine recalled, 'and said that the machinery of government changes always had to be carried into effect in a way that precluded such discussion because of the risk of leaks'.[7] Lord Irvine left Downing Street surprised that Tony Blair thought abolishing the office of Lord Chancellor was similar to a routine transfer of departmental responsibilities. He was also surprised that 'the Prime Minister had no appreciation that the abolition of this office of state, with a critical role in our unwritten constitution ... required extensive consultation, most careful preparation and primary legislation'.[8]

When the two men met again the following Monday, Lord Irvine concluded that Tony Blair had not received proper advice from officials. At that stage, the Prime Minister had simply been planning to transfer Lord Irvine's responsibilities to Peter Hain, who was to sit in the Commons as Secretary of State for Constitutional Affairs. In that case, said Lord Irvine, the Prime Minister would have lost an opportunity to restructure the system, transferring responsibility for criminal law and procedure to a new Ministry of Justice. The next day, Lord Irvine told Tony Blair, in writing, that the whole process had been botched. 'The Lord Chancellor as head of the judiciary is presently the central organising principle of the administration

---

[7] See www.publications.parliament.uk/pa/ld200910/ldselect/ldconst/30/09070105.htm.
[8] See www.publications.parliament.uk/pa/ld200910/ldselect/ldconst/30/09070105.htm.

of justice in the country, and that is being swept aside without any assessment of its value.'[9]

Lord Irvine told Tony Blair it was not too late to set up a proper Ministry of Justice headed by a Commons' minister. He offered to see the reforms through 'and bow out on its completion', elaborating on his offer in a written note to the Prime Minister a day later. 'This alternative proposition was, I understand, rejected after Cabinet on Thursday 12 June 2003',[10] Lord Irvine recalled in 2009. 'That afternoon I returned the great seal to Her Majesty and ceased to be a member of the government.' The Prime Minister then set up a Department for Constitutional Affairs, headed by Lord Falconer.

Tony Blair himself told the committee that giving the Lord Chancellor's political functions to a politician was an 'obvious modernisation'.[11] In a letter sent at the end of 2009, the former Prime Minister acknowledged that Lord Irvine would have implemented the reforms if asked.

'However, I felt, as his memorandum implies, he was unsympathetic to my desire to change the Lord Chancellor position', Tony Blair wrote.

> So I thought it right to make a change of person as well as a change to the office. It is correct that I could have retained him in government to see through the change and then leave; but I thought it better to have the process of change led by someone [who] was then going to be part of it.

Turning the Lord Chancellor into just another politician was indeed an obvious modernisation. But its disadvantages are all too apparent now. The Lord Chancellor had evolved over the centuries into a uniquely valuable constitutional pivot. Nobody would apply that description to the present holder of that office, Chris Grayling. It is not so much that he is not a lawyer. It is of much more concern that he is a party politician, with ambitions higher than being Lord Chancellor.

And, since the Constitutional Reform Act 2005, he has no longer been head of the judiciary; that office is now occupied by the Lord Chief Justice. So the judges can no longer rely on the Lord Chancellor to speak up for them in Cabinet.

---

[9] See www.publications.parliament.uk/pa/ld200910/ldselect/ldconst/30/09070105.htm.
[10] See www.publications.parliament.uk/pa/ld200910/ldselect/ldconst/30/09070105.htm.
[11] See www.publications.parliament.uk/pa/ld200910/ldselect/ldconst/30/09070108.htm.

Those who have served in Government until recently have told me that the Lord Chancellor never was the judges' cheerleader in Cabinet. Even the much admired Lord Mackay had his run-ins with the judiciary. I wonder. Certainly, Lord Judge thinks the changes introduced by the Constitutional Reform Act may be eroding something rather important. Giving evidence to the Lords' Constitution Committee in January, the Lord Chief Justice said: 'There's nobody in the Cabinet who is responsible for representing—to those members of the Cabinet who may need advice on an issue—how a particular proposal may impact on the judiciary.' And the 2005 Act had removed the Lord Chief Justice's right to speak directly to legislators during debates in the House of Lords. He was not even allowed to vote in parliamentary elections.

'I'm not being portentous', Lord Judge continued, 'but the process of evolution has some way to go yet'. The judiciary was regarded as the 'third arm of the constitution' with a duty to represent the interests of the citizen and uphold the rule of law. It was there to ensure that those with power exercised it lawfully—a 'crucial part of the constitution', he suggested.

In the modern world, then, the job of speaking up for the judges falls on the judges themselves. It is a role that calls for considerable judgement. Should you speak out? Or should you remain silent?

Some of you may have read about the Kilmuir Rules. They were not rules at all, in fact; merely a letter written in 1955 by the then Lord Chancellor to the chairman of the BBC, in which Viscount Kilmuir said it was undesirable, as a general rule, for judges 'to broadcast on the wireless or appear on television'. As Lord Kilmuir explained, 'so long as a judge keeps silent his reputation for wisdom and impartiality remains unassailable: but every utterance which he makes in public, except in the course of the actual performance of his judicial duties, must necessarily bring him within the focus of criticism'. The Kilmuir Rules were abolished by Lord Mackay at his first press conference in 1987. I remember it well.

So it is now up to the judges themselves to decide whether to speak out on issues of the day. There are two examples I want to explore. On one, the judges have kept quiet. On the other, they have spoken out.

First, pensions. Last September, Lord Judge appeared relaxed about the prospect of reaching agreement with the Lord Chancellor on the plans that Chris Grayling had published a couple of months earlier. 'The proposals from the Lord Chancellor about judicial pensions came to us in July and there has to be a long conversation about it', Lord Judge said at his annual news conference. But negotiating with the Lord Chancellor in public would be 'totally inappropriate and indeed somehow rather disrespectful'.

By March of this year, it was clear that the Lord Chief Justice's respectful tactics had failed. There were press reports that a circuit judge's annual pension would be reduced from £64,000 plus a lump sum of £144,000 to £55,000 with no lump sum. Even that assumes twenty years' service—although there will be tapering provisions.

I wanted to check these figures as I was drafting this lecture last weekend and it occurred to me that there might be something on the subject in the annual report of the Review Body on Senior Salaries, which published its most recent annual report in April. Sure enough, I discovered, your accrual rate will go down from one-fortieth of your final salary to one-forty-third of your average earnings. That means your pension will be lower. And if you want to take a lump sum when you retire, it will be lower still.

Lord Judge had told the Review Body that the judges' concerns over pensions overshadowed pay. The report said:

> Strength of feeling was such that over 1,200 judges had responded to the Government's consultation. The Lord Chief Justice said that some had indicated that they would resign before the changes became effective on 1 April 2015 if they did not qualify for relief, as they considered that the conduct of the Government in unilaterally reducing the remuneration of judges would discharge them from any obligation given at the time of their appointment not to return to legal practice.

What? Judges have said they will resign and return to private practice? There's a story. Has anyone ever reported that? Not as far as I could see. So I immediately drafted a column for the *Law Society Gazette*.

As I am sure the judges here are well aware, members of the full-time judiciary are barred from legal practice while in post. Their terms of service add: 'The Lord Chancellor ... regards a judgeship as a lifetime appointment. Any offer of appointment is therefore made on the understanding that appointees will not return to practice.'

I am not a lawyer but I do not see how this 'understanding' can be legally binding. We can infer from the passage that some judges are accusing Chris Grayling of changing the rules of the road after they have set off down a one-way street.

Although the Lord President of the Court of Session and the Lord Chief Justice of Northern Ireland were not aware of any judges in their respective jurisdictions who were threatening to resign, the senior Scottish judge told the Review body that it would be 'unprecedented and in his view highly undesirable' for a senior judge to return to practice.

Those views are likely to be shared in England and Wales. In my view, resignations would damage morale among the remaining judges and discourage lawyers from joining the Bench.

Although practising lawyers sit as part-time judges and many former judges sit as arbitrators or mediators, there have always been concerns at the idea of judges stepping down from a full-time appointment and going back to where they left off. A former judge might appear before a court whose members the former judge had previously overruled. Having a former judge around the partnership table might be seen as giving a solicitors' practice an unfair advantage.

Even if these fears are not justified in practice, there would be a public perception that things were not as they should be. Eyebrows were raised when Lord Sumption appeared in the High Court a couple of years ago, after his appointment to the Supreme Court had been announced.

In 1970, there was consternation when Sir Henry Fisher resigned from the High Court after less than three years because he found himself temperamentally unsuited to the job. However, there was no such reaction when it was announced last month that Sir Nicholas Stadlen, aged sixty-two, was retiring after five years in the High Court because of his wife's ill health. He has not returned to practice.

In his evidence to the Senior Salaries Review Body, Lord Judge expressed his concern that

> by making it harder to recruit the best judges, the changes could affect the quality of the justice system, including its ability to attract international business which contributed to the national balance of payments.

He believed it was wrong to offer only those judges closest to retirement the opportunity to stay in the existing scheme while changing the pension arrangements of those who had joined the judiciary more recently. Actuarial evidence obtained by the judiciary showed that judges would see a reduction in pension benefits of between 34 per cent and 46 per cent for service after April 2015.

Recommending a modest rise of 1 per cent in judicial salaries from April 2013, the Review body said it was more concerned about the impact of the Government's pay policies on the judiciary than on senior civil servants and the armed forces.

It noted that successful applicants to the High Court bench typically suffered a cut in earnings of 59 per cent. The current pension scheme could not bridge the financial gap between private practice and public service, but it had 'a psychological impact well beyond its financial value, signalling acknowledgment of what had been given up for ever and marking public respect for the judiciary as an institution'.

While the Review Body thought there would still be senior practitioners willing to join the judiciary, it said that

> the combination of the reduction in the value of the pension and prolonged pay restraint will result in a tipping point when there will be too few of the right quality willing to make the transition.

The Review concluded:

> We believe we may be at that tipping point now.

This is a pretty powerful story. But why had it not come out sooner? The Review Body's report was published two months ago.

First of all, legal journalists—myself included—would not think to read the annual reports of the Review Body on Senior Salaries. Secondly, Lord Judge has chosen not to speak publicly about judicial pensions—or even to alert us to authoritative and alarming reports such as this. He takes the view that whinging about their pay and pensions will not do the judges any good at all. The public regard all judges as both immensely powerful and staggeringly wealthy. They would have no sympathy for judges who complained that their pensions were being cut by more than a third.

That is probably true. I suspect Lord Judge would prefer it if I did not write about judicial pensions. I know that he regards my freedom to write about anything I lawfully can as much more important than any embarrassment my story might cause him. But to avoid posing this dilemma to him, I decided not to tell his office I would be reporting the evidence he gave to the Review Body. That way, nobody can say my story came from him.

Pensions was the issue on which the judges kept quiet. What about the story on which the judges spoke out?

It was, of course, the Government's consultation paper on Transforming Legal Aid. The Council of Her Majesty's Circuit Judges sent in a response, along with some 16,000 other individuals and associations—although the Ministry of Justice says that some of the responses were duplicates. Among the responses was one from the Judicial Executive Board, which comprises the Lord Chief Justice, the Master of the Rolls, the President of the Queen's Bench Division, the President of the Family Division, the Chancellor of the High Court, the Chairman of the Judicial College, the Senior President of Tribunals, and the Senior Presiding Judge.

Judicial responses to public consultations normally appear on the judiciary's website. One was published this week, dealing with the code of practice for victims of crime. But although that response was published on 10 June 2014, it was dated 14 May 2014. There is a convention that publication of these responses is delayed by thirty days. Maybe somebody once thought it would be courteous to give the Government a month to read the judges' comments. Or maybe someone thought it would be best to sit on the response until it was no longer newsworthy. Nobody seems quite sure.

In any event, you won't find anything on the judicial website about the Lord Chancellor's consultation on Legal Aid. But you will find the story in last week's newspapers, or at least their online versions. 'Judges Attack Grayling's Legal Aid Shake-Up' was the *Times* headline. 'Crown Court Judges Criticise Grayling's Legal Aid Plans' was the more restrained *Guardian*.

Let me read you some extracts from the circuit judges' response:

> We are dismayed that in a consultation of this importance there has not been allowed the normal period for reflection and response.
>
> We are saddened that the measures proposed seem to be based upon bald assertions concerning the cost of provision of legal aid in the United Kingdom but without analysis of the factors involved.
>
> It appears ... from the consultation paper that justification for the proposals is based on assertions that legal aid has lost much of its credibility with the public, that it has been used to fund frivolous claims, to foot the bills of wealthy criminals and to enrich lawyers; yet no evidence is cited to support those assertions.
>
> Little or no consideration has been given to the impact upon the courts of limited and, when available, poor-quality representation and the potential for injustice to victims and to those accused.

And finally a comment on the proposal to introduce price-competitive tendering for criminal legal aid contracts:

> We regard this as a dangerously inappropriate model.

Strong stuff, but how did it find its way into the newspapers? Well, of course, it was leaked—by which I mean circulated unofficially. I'm not saying that the Council of Circuit Judges did not want it published; on the contrary, it seems likely that the leak was fully authorised at the highest level and I don't expect it came from, shall we say, a single rogue circuit judge briefing *The Guardian* from a Hong Kong hotel room.

Were the judges right to leak their paper? Of course they were. This week, I interviewed the justice minister, Lord McNally. When I asked him how many responses he had received in support of his paper—I suspect the answer is none—he had to fall back on the argument that lawyers were defending their own interests. I tried to make the point that the judges had no financial interest in legal aid reforms. Lord McNally was not impressed, of course—he argued that lawyers and judges were all insiders—but it was a valuable piece of evidence to have at my disposal.

Then, yesterday, the views of the Judicial Executive Board mysteriously found their way into the public domain. The *Law Society Gazette* got hold of the senior judges' response to the consultation paper. And somebody sent me a copy after hearing me say on the radio that I had not seen it at the time.

The senior judges' comments on the government's proposals are restrained but no less powerful for that. Here are some extracts:

> Some of the proposed changes are likely to transfer rather than save costs. It cannot be emphasised too strongly that good advocacy reduces cost … Poor advocacy is wasteful of resources; cases are less well prepared and they occupy more court time and take longer to come to a conclusion, while simultaneously increasing the risk of mistakes and miscarriages of justice.
>
> There should be standards of quality and a robust quality review and assurance process in place as an integral part of any price-competitive tendering model. If not, there is a real risk that the firms obtaining contracts will employ those who will take the lowest salary in order to maximise the firm's profits … The task of developing such a system should not be underestimated.
>
> Many young and talented lawyers are no longer choosing to practise in crime. Some who feel trapped in this area of practice may continue because they have no option. However, in the medium term, if the more talented lawyers do not work in crime, the impact will be not only on the quality of the defence, but also on the quality of the prosecution, many of whom are drawn from the same pool … In the long term, there will be a negative impact on the quality of those joining the judiciary.

The Judicial Executive Board also expressed concerns about the increased number of litigants in person, as we can now call them again. They do, of course, add to the length of the case and therefore its cost; although home truths such as that do not seem to impress the Government.

Time to pull together some threads. It is not easy to be a judge in the modern world. You need quiet fortitude, as Lord Judge rightly said. You need to understand modern methods of communication, but you must not use them to bypass the judge's traditional role. You need to know when to stay silent and when to speak out, while remembering that speaking out may cause more problems than it solves.

When you were appointed a judge, you were looking forward to a comfortable pension. Now, you are beginning to wonder whether you made the right choice. If you are still relatively young, maybe you are thinking the unthinkable and looking for a way back to advocacy.

If you are a circuit judge sitting in crime, perhaps you look around you and ask how it is that one of your colleagues who was still at the bar eighteen months ago is going to become the most senior judge at the Old Bailey in eighteen months' time. If you are a High Court judge you wonder why, when an unprecedented ten vacancies in the Court of Appeal were filled the other day, your name was not on the list and others with less seniority were promoted.

If you are already in the Court of Appeal, you may rue the day you were asked by a well-meaning Chief Justice to take on the high-profile public inquiry that has scuppered your chances of taking the job he is about to vacate. If you are a less high-profile but more senior male judge in the Court of Appeal, you wonder whether those responsible for that appointment have decided that it should go to a woman.

If you are one of the judges responsible for selecting the new Lord Chief Justice you look back with relief at the fact that you have escaped from the Supreme Court and returned to the Court of Appeal. If you are the other of those two judges, you wonder whether it might have been more congenial to have stayed there.

If you are a family judge, you know you may be overruled in no uncertain terms by two commercial judges sitting in the Court of Appeal. If you are one of those commercial judges, you will have noticed yesterday that an argument you dismissed as worthless was found to be decisive by seven members of the Supreme Court, led by a judge who used to appear before you until a couple of years ago.

As a judge, you have to take decisions—something the rest of us prefer to avoid. You have to stick to the speed limit while driving and take care not to lose your temper when you are shopping, just in case somebody recognises you. All the time, the press and public are watching, waiting for you to slip up. Being a judge in the modern world is not easy. Those who do the job deserve our admiration and respect.

6

Judges and the Modern Media

Alan Rusbridger

This lecture was delivered at the University of Leeds on 18 February 2015.

George Bernard Shaw wrote: 'At present, the papers are twenty years behind the times because editors are recluses. Lighthouse keepers with wireless sets know far more of what is going on in the world'.[1] And I sometimes think there is something in that. As a statement of the obvious, journalism can be astonishingly shallow and ephemeral and cruel and silly. Even worse, sometimes it can be inaccurate and misleading and intrusive, but thankfully we now have a retired High Court judge to put all that right.[2] But one of the reasons I think that some people feel so helpless in dealing with the press is that there is some journalism which bears little relation to any kind of truth, not because it tells outright lies, because it seems to operate to a different set of rules which can be unfathomable to outsiders. So I am not here tonight to defend that sort of journalism or even particularly to talk about it. *The Guardian*, in exposing the worst excesses of illegal phone hacking, has, I hope, played its part in trying to clean up some of the most corrupt practices in what used to be called Fleet Street. So that seems to be a whole other story involving another High Court judge and much water under assorted bridges.

But as I began to think about this talk, I wondered what the problem was that I was supposed to address. So I did a bit of modest research

---

[1] Cited in Alan Rusbridger, *Play It Again* (Vintage Books, 2014), at 83.
[2] Moses LJ was appointed first chairman of the Independent Press Standards Organization on his retirement from the Court of Appeal in May 2014.

myself amongst reporters who sit in court. I made one or two phone calls and met a couple of retired judges and I got back a mixture of consistent grumbles and suggestions. Nothing, I have to say is terribly dramatic, and I would like to come back to those later. But then I saw a survey carried out by University College London and published earlier this month and there, buried on page 53, was a very sad statistic that judges feel very unloved by the media.[3] Only 4 per cent of you—I am going to say 'you'—only 4 per cent of you feel valued by journalists, compared with the feeling that about half the public in general value you, and only 2 per cent of you feel valued by Government. But happily this was made up by the fact that nine out of ten of you feel valued by your fellow professionals, your fellow judges! So clearly you feel unloved by my colleagues, possibly misunderstood and possibly frustrated that, like the Royal Family, you cannot really answer back. I will come back to my colleagues' feelings about this a bit later, and I will also talk a little about what judges could do to help themselves. But since this talk is about judges and the media, I thought it might be instructive to begin by talking about what has happened to the media. Because I do not think you can talk about the subject of judges and the media unless you understand the enormous changes that have affected probably both you the judges, and we the media, over the last, let us say, twenty years. That twenty years is exactly the spell—I just celebrated it last week—of time that I've been editing *The Guardian*.[4]

I joined *The Guardian* in 1979. I thought, especially for the students who probably have no concept of how a newspaper was produced twenty years ago, I would bring in a little clip of film which shows how *The Guardian* was produced when I joined it in 1979. This film was actually made in 1960 about *The Guardian*, but nothing about the production of the paper then had changed at the time when I became a junior reporter.

Sometimes, just when we seem to be running nicely to time, late news comes in. If it is not important, you can fit it in easily. But if it is something big, and breaks at this time of the evening, the chief sub has got to make some quick decisions. The front page, the last to be

---

[3] UK Judicial Attitudes Survey 2014 by Professor Cheryl Thomas, UCL, at www.laws.ucl.ac.uk/news-article/first-ever-survey-uk-judges-highlights-declining-working-conditions-threat-future-judiciary.

[4] Alan Rusbrdger is no longer editor of *The Guardian* having taken up the post in 2015 of Principal of Lady Margaret Hall, Oxford.

made up, has to be on its way by 9.20 p.m. at the latest, if the edition is going to catch the train. You may have to break up page 1, if you are leading with a new story. And a new story will never fit exactly into the hole left by an old one. Column 2 is a bit long so we'll have to cut a few lines. So the maker-up cuts a line with his clippers. That line where they get a pair of pliers and just chop a sentence in half, that happened to me a lot.

Of course, by 1995, when I took over as editor, we had computers, but we were still printing in black and white: our picture editor believed that colour news pictures were a bit vulgar, and many things about the job that I began twenty years ago are the same, but I would say that more things are different. And it may be that both judges and editors have quite a lot in common in the sense that the technology that affects our lives has disrupted and changed what we do and that technology explains or maybe masks even deeper changes which are about attitudes to respect, institutions, knowledge and authority.

When I look back now at the first issue of *The Guardian* that I edited, I see how easy it all was then. It was above all a newspaper. There was essentially one deadline a day. We had deadlines in the evening, but as you saw from that clip of film, nothing much had to be done before nine o'clock in the evening. It was printed text. The medium we were dealing with was words, there were pictures, and there was lots of advertising. There was a finite amount of space to fill. We knew the price of paper and ink and the cost of an advertisement so the economic modelling was comparatively simple. And so was the relationship with readers. They could respond if they liked to, by writing a letter to us, but we got to decide whether the letter was printed or not.

C. P. Scott, who was the famous editor of *The Guardian* for fifty-seven years, a record that is unlikely now to be beaten, wrote a wonderful essay about newspapers in 1921 that is famous for the sentence that 'comment is free but facts are sacred'.[5] But he also wrote in that essay that a newspaper is something of a necessity, something of a monopoly, and because he was editor of *The Guardian* rather than Rupert Murdoch, he added quickly, 'and the first duty is to shun the temptations of monopoly'.

---

[5] C.P. Scott, 'A Hundred Years', *The Guardian*, 5 May 1921.

But he was right in both halves of that sentence; we had the megaphone and the public did not. Radio and television had begun to change things, of course, but collectively, as professional journalists, we were the main channel of information between the rulers and the ruled, the informed and the less informed. And if you were to draw a diagram of how news worked back in 1995, you would have a top-down diagram in which the journalists were up here on an elevated platform and we were passing information down to the readers, who were very grateful and below us. That is how it felt because we had the unique access to information and I think at some point we confused this access with authority.

So along came the digital revolution—the ability to distribute words and pictures at virtually no cost—to enormous audiences worldwide, and this was a violent time of change of newspapers. The economics of what we did, gigantic cathedral printing halls, lorries trundling through the dark, wholesalers in the middle of the night, 17,000 newsagents who had to be reached, little boys on their paper rounds—all that began to shift. And advertisers in particular realized that they could bypass newspapers and market their houses or cars or jobs online. We had the traumatic experience of £40m worth of advertising walking out of *The Guardian* within two years, and we were not alone. The *Sunday Times*, which had been a money-making machine for Rupert Murdoch (reputed to make a profit of £1m per issue at one stage), fell into loss. And the regional press was hit particularly viciously, losing much of its advertising income very dramatically.

Now, much of it was due to a man called Craig Newmark, who founded something called Craig's List in 1995, from his 'global head-quarters' in which he in fact remained, until 2010. He only had a staff of about ten, none of them wanted to be rich, and he did not have very high overheads. It was a model that was essentially one that was impossible to beat. It printed advertisements which it put on its website, and they were largely free to the seller and free to the buyer, which is a difficult economic model to compete with. And thus from the building in San Francisco, Craig Newmark and his small band of colleagues decimated the newspaper business. Newspaper companies responded by cutting back on costs; newsrooms shrank and so began a kind of death spiral. The papers became less interesting because the quality of the editorial content fell off. Fewer people therefore bought newspapers, which meant there was less money coming in, which meant it was time for management to cut costs again, and so on. And if you judges here wonder why there are so few court reporters in your court nowadays, that is the reason.

This phase of digital disruption, which became known as Web 1.0, of course, confounded many newspaper managements. Would it catch on? How could it possibly make sense? Newspapers had withstood the advent of radio and television; was this different? Why would anyone give away journalism for free? It would simply cannibalize the print product. But companies, of course, began grudgingly to put some of their stories online, after they had appeared in print. And, of course, the relationship with the reader changed quite a bit; they could now respond to what we published and they didn't have to go through the filter of a letters' editor in order to do so. Power began to shift subtly.

The next wave of the technological revolution, the so-called Web 2.0, or now called social media, happened at the worst possible time, shortly before the Lehman Brothers collapse in September 2008, with all the economic turmoil that accompanied that. Twitter was two years old at the time, Facebook was four years old, Instagram had not been invented, Wikipedia was just seven years old. So Web 2.0 made publishers of everyone in the sense that everyone could now write, photograph, film and comment without having to go through the old mediators, i.e. us (the media). Not only could you all create these new words and images (content is a deadening but efficient way of describing the output) but you could distribute and share it rapidly and enormously widely.

Newspapers were caught flat-footed and most of them were still entirely unwilling to believe that something was happening that was in fact as significant and as radical as the invention of the printing press by Gutenberg in the mid-fifteenth century. Our readers were now freely associating with each other—how dare they—and forming networks of interest without going via us (the media). And you have got these new communities of subjects and discussion, unaffected by geography, which rapidly developed. Also, the public could often access the same sources as we had, sometimes more quickly than we could digest and report the news ourselves. And there grew up schools of new media theory around this with titles and aphorisms that told their own story—'Here comes everybody', our readers know more than we do!'; the 'wisdom of crowds'; people talking about the 'former audience'; and there was something in all that. Take 'our readers know more than we do'. When most reporters heard that for the first time they were affronted and dismissive of the comment—it was written by a West Coast journalist, Dan Gillmor, in 2004—only just over ten years ago. Never mind that it was a statement of the obvious.[6]

A good medical correspondent may be reasonably expert in many fields, but she has never been a surgeon, or worked in an Accident and Emergency department, late at night, or treated a cancer victim. Her readers will indeed often know more than she does. So what happened was that blogs started up in which professionals began to write more expertly than most newspapers could ever aspire to. We have got good media correspondents and a good legal editor, but if you want really detailed authoritative coverage of media law, you are now more likely to be a devotee of the INFORMM website, which has been going for about three years, against *The Guardian*'s 193 years, and says it has around 1,400 posts in that period.[7] Most of these blogs did not earn much, if any, money; on the other hand, like Craig's List, they had an entirely different cost base to old media. In most cases, people wrote for the love of it.

Hugh Tomlinson QC, who runs this website, tells me that virtually no one ever gets paid for writing for INFORMM. So the implications of this new ecosystem began to be acutely felt together with the sharp questions it raised. Who counted as a journalist in this new world? Could we limit the definition of 'journalist' to people with appropriate training or people who derive sufficient income from writing or publishing? Those definitions seemed wholly artificial.

What about bloggers like Glen Grunwald, who broke the Snowden story? He was a trained lawyer with his own community of around a million regular readers that he brought to *The Guardian* when he came to us. So he brought his readers and he has certainly got strong political views, but then so do many journalists on the *Daily Mail*. Should his activism disqualify him from being thought of as a journalist?

And what would become of newspapers if all these specialists helped themselves to great chunks of what we did, as they soon did, sometimes doing it rather better than we could, both technically and in terms of their specialist knowledge and focus? For sports

---

[6] *We the Media*, by Dan Gillmor, was published in California in 2004 by O'Reilly. In this book Gillmor discusses how the proliferation of grass-roots Internet journalists (bloggers) had changed the way news was handled. One of the book's main points was that a few big media corporations could no longer control what 'news' was available, now that news was being published in real time, and was available to everybody, via the Internet.

[7] INFORMM, the International Forum for Responsible Media.

obsessives would find plenty of immensely deep, authoritative coverage of football, cricket, or baseball online, often compiled by fans. The same was true of culture, science, fashion, food, weather, you name it. Not many people did the expensive, hard bit—the actual news. Still less the really expensive, really hard bit, investigative reporting, war corresponding, sustained specialist reporting or paying to have experienced correspondents living and working abroad. So there was an obvious danger for papers like *The Guardian* that we would be left doing the stuff that no one else wanted to do because there was no obvious business model that could possibly sustain the difficult bits.

And court reporting became a major casualty. Who could now afford to cover numerous courts in the way we did when I first worked on a local paper? Or even follow one complex case through from beginning to end, doing justice to all sides of the case? Sometimes it felt as if we were in a classic disaster movie; the plane you were flying was, I have mixed my metaphors, losing circulation at about 10 per cent a year, and would certainly crash into the ground at some point in the next ten years, and yet we could not afford not to fly the plane because it still generated the cash to stay airborne. So somehow you had to rebuild the plane in mid-flight.

But what would be the new economic model even if we succeeded in doing that? Some, like *The Times* of London, erected paywalls, so that no one can read a word of *The Times* content without forking out some money. We did the opposite, making most of our digital content free so that it could be read and shared around the world. As of now, *The Times* is read on a daily basis by about 180,000 readers, mostly in the United Kingdom. And normally today we *The Guardian* are read by an audience of about 6,000,000 unique browsers a day, two-thirds of them abroad. That's a huge difference now between two different business models, and yet at the same we are both losing about the same amount of money. I like our model better because we have a vastly greater readership than *The Times*, which, I think, leads to more influence editorially, as well as to much greater digital revenues. And if you are a journalist on *The Times*, you don't much like their model because their work is so hidden—no one, or a tiny, a tiny number of people, relatively, shares, discusses, or even accesses their stories. But in truth no one yet knows whether either model is sustainable.

We were all slow to see how younger audiences would see some of the new digital upstarts as players in the news space. I joined Twitter relatively early in January 2009, but I remember being extremely sceptical when our head of digital, Emily Bell, told me a few months later that Twitter would soon be better than most newsrooms at many forms of news: always faster; always more distributed, openly; more profusely sourced; and usually more widely linked. It was one of those things that Emily used to announce that usually turned out to be somewhat true. Just like the occasion when she told me the news story is dead. That was not wholly true either, but it was not wholly untrue.

Of course, people still write news stories but she was onto something in two senses. One is that the live blog, as a way of keeping up a narrative on the news, is often the most effective way of telling a story. And the advantage of a live blog is that it can pull in multiple other sources: it can incorporate reaction; it is not like a story, which fixes an event at a moment in time. And, of course, that is the second respect in which a story is not quite dead, but changed. When I was a young reporter, a story usually began and ended with the moment of publication. Now it is more of a continuum. You can announce in advance to your audience that you are writing a story and ask for help, or witnesses, or expertise, or sources, and once you press the button to publish, the life of the story is, in a sense, just beginning. Unless the story is very boring and insignificant—in which case, why are you writing?—there will be a reaction. People may contest parts of it; they want to add to it, correct it, clarify it, complain about it, give context, deny it, praise it. They may do so in comments underneath the piece or they may do it on Twitter or Facebook or Reddit.

So what do you do as a news organization about that response to a story because actually some of that response would make it a better account of the thing you are trying to describe? Or do you say, life is too short for that, that is not what journalism is, we are just going to ignore that? We have published the story, if somebody else wants to take that on, that is up to somebody else. But Emily was largely right about Twitter, I think. It is a quite extraordinary medium and for news, for conversation, for debate, for community, it is the most viral form of distribution. It is where things happen first. As a search engine it rivals Google; it is a formidable aggregation and reporting tool. It changes the tone of writing because it requires listening, as well as talking. It levels the playing field between participants in a public space.

The energy on Twitter gathers around people who can say things crisply and entertainingly, even though they may be 'unknown'. It has different news values from many newspapers. People think it has a short attention span. Actually it has an immensely long attention span, sticking with issues and subjects long after the caravan of professional journalists has moved on. It creates communities; it changes notions of authority. A twenty-one-year-old student is quite likely to be more drawn to the opinions and preferences of people who look and talk like her. It is an agent of social change. So this thing that started so recently, when people had no idea of what it was going to be or do, suddenly moved right into the space of news in ways that we still cannot work out. *The Guardian* is obviously very different from Twitter; that is, *The Guardian* rather inelegantly chopped up into little pieces to reflect how you have to design a website if it is going to fit on a mobile phone. It is very different from Twitter, just as it is different from Buzzfeed or Vice or Facebook. But these are all now players in the same news space and in many respects they understand the techniques, expectations, values, and rhythms of digital communication better than we do.

And I have not even mentioned the biggest player of all, Google, nor the hardware. Where were you when you first held an iPhone in your hand? Maybe the younger students in the audience cannot remember. I remember mine in the sitting room of a friend who had just come back from New York, shortly after the initial release in June 2007. I remember the hot excitement of flipping from app to app and the extraordinary sensation of navigating through or over London via Google Maps and Google Earth. But did you ever imagine in 2007 that people would watch films, or read books, on a screen not much bigger than a box of matches? But of course they do, and now 40 per cent of people who access *The Guardian* digitally (now) read it on that size screen.

Much of our journalism is read on Facebook. We go where the audience is, rather than trying to say everybody must come to us. We struggle to compete with YouTube as a platform for video. Twitter beats us on much breaking news. We have a few hundred reporters; Twitter has, if you like, millions. And the significance of mobile readership has huge implications for the scheduling of the day. If we do not begin our day at 7 a.m., it is too late because people pick up their phones when they get out of bed, and they want to see that the day is up and running, and if we are not there, they will go to somebody else. And if we do not file news as it is happening, that is too late, because mobile users return repeatedly throughout the day for updates. And yet we still have to have the same team producing a newspaper, starting at 9 p.m. in the evening and going on until 2 a.m., because that's where the cash is, and in the 24/7 world, with over 16 million unique browsers a month outside the UK, we have to edit out of New York and Sydney, too.

I am not complaining about any of this; it has actually been rather good for *The Guardian*. We are still the ninth-biggest paper in the UK in print. In the world, we are now as big as, if not bigger than, the *New York Times*. It changes from month to month, but we are the biggest English-language serious paper, not including the *Daily Mail*, in the world. And while we have done that, we have not cut a single foreign correspondent because we believe the world is difficult to understand without international context. Our investigations over the past four years: Wikileaks, rendition and torture, phone hacking, Edward Snowden and surveillance, HSBC and (only last week) tax avoidance, are staying true to what a newspaper should be. But along with virtually everyone else, we have not yet cracked the numbers.

Now, I am going to come back to the possible lessons of this new world for judges at the end, but since I have talked a bit about Twitter, that may allow me to segue seamlessly into the sandwich of this talk, the filling in the middle, which was the response of reporters when I said I was going to come and talk to a few judges about the courts. So, here is what some of them said, and quite a lot of them are around Twitter. I do not know how much this is apparent, it is partly why I wanted to talk about this today, but if you are a reporter in court, you live in this new world and, and you sometimes feel frustrated that courts do not feel very well set up for you. Here they are, I am just going to quote them.

Here is one:

> Lord Judge's decision to allow tweeting and laptops in court has transformed court reporting for the better. I think all judges have to be aware of just how instant news is today. Most seem to be, though I am sure there are still some less familiar with Twitter. A lack of Wi-Fi or even a phone signal in many courts, however, does impede and it's very frustrating.

Another reporter:

> The way we present news today is totally different, with video, audio, picture galleries all very important. In my experience there can be a reluctance by the Crown Prosecution Service (CPS) to release to the

media evidence which has been put before a jury—photographs, videos, photocopies of documents such as letters, diaries, etc. Sometimes such material is given to us, but on an ad hoc basis, and often on the whim of the CPS. Ideally for us the default position would be that such material is automatically released on request, unless good reason can be given for not doing so. After all, it has been put in front of a jury; it's part of the evidence on which they have reached their verdict and it would be good to have a debate and proper guidelines on this, rather than leaving it up to the CPS. I am sure much more could be released than currently is, and we should press for it.

There were more like that:

I guess the big thing from my perspective is that they sort out the making of, logging and distribution of reporting restriction orders. Judges should make these in writing; they should be sent to a central place where those with authority should be able to check applications. And you do not need telling about how some of them fail to appreciate the viral, worldwide nature of postings on the Internet.

A less happy reporter wrote as follows:

Not enough judges or counsel, defence and prosecution, take account of Twitter. There have been times when prosecutors have sought to impose restrictions after a verdict or a key ruling has been tweeted. Live tweeting has been permitted since 2011 so it would be good if all judges and counsel familiarize themselves with the practice of tweeting.

Another reporter complained that the press are an afterthought:

The press really appreciate judges who proactively seek and listen to their views at the time reporting restrictions are raised. It would be good if reporting restrictions were considered routinely at the beginning of cases and hearings, if it is likely to be an issue. It can be exceptionally difficult to attract a judge's attention. You can find yourself standing up to challenge a direction and the judge has already turned his back and walked out of the room. Sometimes a journalist is not even in the line of sight of a judge and it is difficult for them to make themselves visible or heard. In some courts, the press are behind the dock, as in Southwark, which has a lot of high-profile cases. It would be good if judges were reminded to involve the press as a matter of routine. Mr Justice Saunders is terrific at this. He always seeks out the press, invites them to contribute on the spot, if they so wish. Asking journalists to make submissions in writing, as some judges do, means that orders can take hours, if not a day, to emerge.

And here is another view, again on the theme of helping reporters with access to the information being revealed in a case:

> The systemic issue that concerns me about the courts, who do they think that the wealth of information that flows through the courts belongs to? Maybe they can be challenged about why the assumption in courts is still—why should this information be given to the media? Be it stuff to be heard in an open court, in criminal cases, or pleading skeleton arguments in civil cases. How can they, as leaders of the criminal justice system, change the culture so that the assumption is—why should information not be made available to the media? Can judges help the system enter the late twentieth century?

And finally, as I was coming up on the train today, a colleague emailed me this morning from court:

> They should automatically give the judges' directions, printed out and then handed to the jurors, to the press. I am currently sitting in the Old Bailey with a very fast-speaking judge, summing up. His directions are of particular interest given the ongoing debate around the trial of public officials. There are just three journalists in court. Everyone has the speech except us.

And then she emailed later in the day to say that she had just been denied a written version of what the judge had said.

So those are the feelings from reporters about about what it is like to work in court.

And then there is my much smaller sample of judges where I met a fair degree of frustration over how they were occasionally, it must be said, portrayed. And how difficult it was for judges to set the record straight, when they felt they had been misrepresented or were being unfairly criticized. There seems to be a strong feeling that while the spirit of Kilmuir still rules, most people seem to believe it is a positive development that senior judges can and do make speeches, and they thought it was good that some of you are now dipping a toe in the waters of BBC Radio 4, to appear on *Law in Action*, or Clive Anderson's programme, *Unreliable Evidence*. But what to do when a judge is getting the hairdryer treatment from the *Daily Mail* over a report of sentencing remarks? And what can be done more generally to help people understand about the courts, about the independence of the judiciary, about access to justice? About the relationship between English and Strasbourg law about sentencing, about human rights, about adequate funding for justice, about how judges are appointed, or, to use a topical example, about who gets to decide who sits in a particular case?

Well, I think that takes us back to the beginning of this talk and maybe the title of Clay Shirky's 2009 book about this new democracy of the Internet, *Here Comes Everybody*.[8] And I think everybody includes you.

I remember another new media guru, Jeff Jarvis, telling me at least ten years ago that, in future, every organization or business would be a media company, and like Emily Bell of the death of the news story, or the significance of Twitter, I did not really know what he meant, I was sceptical, but of course it is true. Everybody today has a website, and that includes just about every company, non-government organization (NGO), academic institution, government department, school, charity, and sports club in the country. And of course judges. You do have your own website and are therefore, in a sense, a media organization. Why would anybody want to be a media organization? I think it is terribly simple. Why would anybody in their right mind want to be mediated by others when they can mediate themselves? Publish your own content and you do not have to rely on anyone else to be the intermediary for anything you say or do. And the courts, tribunals, judiciary website is clearly attempting to do something of that order. It has sections on what the judiciary is, how it works, what is involved in going to court; it even has a section on how to address a judge if you happen to meet one or write to one or speak to one or be sentenced by one. You can find out which judges have retired, who has made a speech, and there is a section containing some judgments. It is not a lavish site; it is not comprehensive. I am told that the judicial communications office has a staff, to cover 4,000 judges and 20,000 magistrates, of just three. And whether that is an appropriate budget and level of staffing for the court system in England and Wales is, as your lordships sometimes say, entirely a matter for you to decide. As a journalist, the website operation does look a bit patchy and under-resourced. And I sometimes wonder whether, if you are going to invite people like me to come along and speak to you, it might not be a good idea to invite some reporters, people who spend their lives in courts and would tell you what would be most useful from their point of view.

---

[8] Clay Shirky, *Here Comes Everybody: How Change Happens When People Come Together* (Allen Lane, 2009).

And then there is the question of whether it could be used more imaginatively when the judiciary is under attack singly or collectively, or both. Let us take a single, recent example when a judge came under a lot of criticism, rightly or wrongly, and this is where it seems to me that the judiciary is missing a trick. We had this case in mid-January when a judge was splattered all over the front pages for reportedly criticizing a sixteen-year-old girl for grooming a teacher, who went on to have an affair with her. And that story launched a hundred columns, mostly lambasting the judge and, more generally, the judiciary. One headline on a piece of commentary read: 'Judges lacking knowledge of popular culture is one thing, but ignorance of human relationships is truly disturbing', so, to some extent, you all get tarred by the brush when one of you is in the headlines. I am very glad that I did not have to write a column or editorial on those sentencing remarks, because I have no idea how I would have come to form a balanced view of how the judge decided on her sentence. There is just nowhere you can go in most of these cases. In most other walks of life an organization under that kind of attack would at least want to put the facts out into the open. But the absence of court reporters with verbatim shorthand would suggest making available a transcript of the remarks not tomorrow or next week, but instantly, because news, for better or worse, now works on an instant, rolling cycle. It is no longer something that will wait until nine o'clock tonight, or a deadline for tomorrow's paper. So if you want to get in before the inevitable cycle of story, outraged commentary, and denunciation gets into full swing, then you have to operate on the rules of the media. Well, that is impossible, I was told. There are only three press officers for 4,000 judges and 20,000 magistrates and so on. Who is going to make the transcript and how could it possibly be made available so fast? Well, up to a point, because most judges and court clerks these days have smartphones and most have some kind of recording device on the smartphone. And so it would be relatively simple, if this is what you wanted to do, to record every sentencing remark, and it is relatively simple to email to a drop box for a central database of sentencing remarks. So, in theory, there could quite easily be a complete database of recordings of every single sentencing remark of every single judge or magistrate on the courts, a website for each day of the week.

It would take a bit of investment, but then Sir Brian Leveson's report has recommended that all courts should be kitted out with high-quality digital recording equipment.[9] So it could be done, but it is only likely to be done if judges care enough about communicating what they do and about the general public standing and understanding of the judiciary and the courts.

So in all this talk of institutions and people becoming their own media organizations, bypassing intermediaries, I do not want in any way to minimize the skill, importance, influence, or, I would think, necessity of the press, the professionals, who may sometimes frustrate you, exasperate you, even anger you. But good reporting at its best has always seemed to me completely necessary to any kind of civilized society. And as the economics conspire against newspapers some people may begin to understand what it could mean to have centres of power which go relatively unchallenged and unexamined by an independent force in society, without the the independent standpoint and vigorous reporting of a decent news organization. But that is a different speech.

My suspicion is that the courts will want to take this role of communication more and more seriously over time. And that in the course of doing so you will begin to face many of the challenges that are inherent in good journalism. The Supreme Court now publishes condensed summaries of all its judgments for general consumption; there is the press summary there and then you have got the judgment. That is a form of journalism. Anyone who has tried to write such a summary, particularly against the clock, will know that it is harder than it looks. Your own website, as I say, is admirable in many ways. It has even got a kind of video game in which we can try our hands at being a judge. But overall it looks a bit random and is frankly a bit dull if the purpose is to engage people more widely in thinking about the things that are doubtless dear to your hearts to do with the importance of an independent justice system in this country.

So it may be that over time judges will have to think a bit more like journalists in communicating what they view, what they say, and what they care about. I think they could do worse than read Lord Denning's memoirs,[10] and no speech at the Judicial College is complete without a reference to Lord Denning, but I read them again this week and they

---

[9] Review of Efficiency in Criminal Proceedings by the Rt Hon Sir Brian Leveson, President of the Queen's Bench Division, January 2015, Ministry of Justice.

[10] These amount to several volumes written over three decades and include *Freedom under the Law* (Hamlyn Lecture Series, 1949), *The Road to Justice* (Stevens, 1955), *The Discipline of Law* (Butterworths, 1979), and *The Due Process of Law* (Butterworths, 1980).

are written in just beautiful, plain English. He needed no executive summary to explain what his judgments were about. They could run, unedited, in a mid-market tabloid in the best sense of the word.

I have spoken enough tonight. I hope there are some questions and so I am just going to end with two things. One is a quote, which again I think has shown how much things have changed, how the world has changed, since I came into the business, and the second is a very short clip of film. The quote is from the memoirs of Lord Devlin in 1979, in which he wrote:

> The criticism of the English judiciary comes from progressive intellectuals. Progressives are often intellectual and none the worse for that. But it is important to note that there is virtually no popular criticism of the judiciary.[11]

So I don't know what *The Sun* and the *Daily Mail* were up to in 1979, but it was a more kindly, gentler world then.

---

[11] Patrick Devlin, *The Judge* (Oxford University Press, 1979).

7

Being a Judge in the Modern World

A View from the Caribbean

Mrs Justice Desirée Bernard

This lecture was delivered at the Royal Courts of Justice, London,
25 November 2013.

In addressing this topic the first question to be answered is, what is
meant by the modern world, and from whose perspective? A modern world depends on a period of time and also stages of development and economic growth in a particular country. One has to have
regard to the fact that there are varying degrees of modernity between
developed and developing societies. Invariably one associates modernity with development and the availability of modern conveniences,
goods, and services. We tend to forget or overlook the fact that the
vast majority of the world is underdeveloped or not developed at all.

However, for the purpose of this discussion we can accept the
modern world from the perspective of development with functioning
democratic institutions and accessibility to required services for comfortable living. Since the topic concerns judging in a modern world,
we can assume that we mean judging in the twenty-first century and
possibly in the latter part of the twentieth century.

I speak mainly from a personal perspective, and in doing so I have
to cast my mind back to the time when I became a judge in my home-
land of Guyana. Although geographically located in South America
and bordered by Brazil, Venezuela and Suriname, Guyana was the
only British colony in that continent. As a result, our ties culturally
and traditionally have been with the English-speaking Caribbean.
Being a former colony within the British Empire we inherited the

English legal system and the common law. Our procedural rules and legislation were copied wholesale from the English system, sometimes producing peculiar results; in fact some procedures and legislation which have been repealed here in the United Kingdom are still on our statute books and followed without regard to changing circumstances.

We also inherited judicial wear and courtesies which continued and still continue even after independence. One aspect of judicial wear which was abolished in 1970 was the use of wigs, which, however, are still used in some Caribbean countries. Along with the wigs, Guyana abolished appeals to the Privy Council, and maintained our Court of Appeal as our final court until 2005, when we joined the Caribbean Court of Justice. The rest of the Caribbean has been slow in replacing the Privy Council as the court of last resort. So far only two others apart from Guyana have accepted the Caribbean Court of Justice as their final court—Barbados and Belize. The reason for this has more to do with politics in some instances than with a reluctance to sever the umbilical cord.

I shall at this point speak briefly about the Caribbean Court of Justice, which was inaugurated in April 2005 with seven judges and two jurisdictions—Original and Appellate. The main purpose for establishing the Court was to interpret and implement an economic treaty entered into by members of the Caribbean Community— the Revised Treaty of Chaguaramas—in much the same way as the European Court of Justice and the European Union. The Caribbean Community comprises states of the English-speaking Caribbean together with Suriname and Haiti. The original jurisdiction of the Court is devoted to hearing disputes concerning the Treaty. These are brought by member states against each other or by private individuals or entities against the member states. The Appellate jurisdiction covers appeals from the National Courts of Appeal and operates as the court of last resort, as mentioned earlier, for three of the member states.

Membership of the Court is open to any judge or academic with a common law background, and a civil law one with qualifications in international law. Judges sit in their individual capacities and not as representatives of their country of birth—for example, we have an English and a Dutch judge.

I now return to the topic under discussion. As stated earlier, Guyana and the other former colonies of the Caribbean have adopted the English procedure and legislation. Although much reliance is placed on English cases as precedents, the Caribbean courts as a whole are endeavouring to develop their own jurisprudence based on Caribbean customs and traditions and, wherever appropriate, local decisions are cited with approval.

There are some new and emerging issues with which a judge in the world today may be confronted and which never arose for judicial consideration thirty or forty years ago. One such issue is computer crime, which is increasing exponentially, since the electronic industry is developing at such a rapid rate that what is new today is likely to be out of date within a few weeks. An increasing number of computer crimes are being committed both domestically and internationally. A personal computer connected to the Internet may be infected with malicious software within a very short space of time. There are different types of attacks on computers, some in an attempt to access stored information which may have a saleable value, e.g. corporate espionage; other attacks may be made by seeking to control a computer to send spam or host illegal content.

Here in England I am informed that legislation has been enacted to control these crimes. Cases have been brought requiring judicial representation and familiarity with such crimes in order to impose appropriate penalties. This type of crime presents new challenges for judges with the advent of the World Wide Web. In my part of the world, legislation has not as yet been passed to combat computer crime, but I am sure that in the near future this will become necessary.

The subject of surrogacy is another new issue which judges in the Caribbean now have to adjudicate upon. This arises when a woman carries a baby for another woman who is unable to do so, or to conceive. Several legal issues could arise apart from the medical ones, and these could be monumental, leading possibly to extensive litigation when disagreements arise. Rights of custody, visitation, inheritance, adoption, emotional attachments, are only a few of the problems which may flow from surrogacy, if not properly addressed at the initial stages of this new form of parenting. Judges have to be sensitive to the issues involved and make decisions which are fair and within the boundaries of the law, being at all times mindful that the welfare of the child or children involved is the paramount consideration.

I believe that under English law the mother of a child born through surrogacy is always the surrogate mother, as the law regards the woman who gives birth to a child as the lawful mother. There are also issues which may arise through international surrogacy; that is, mothers giving birth to children through surrogacy arrangements with foreign women or couples or vice versa. Laws may also be broken by advertising surrogacy. All of these impose obligations on modern-day judges.

Of even greater significance is the issue of same-sex marriages and all of the legal problems which can arise from such unions. The issues arising may be capable of early resolution as the same laws applicable to other marital unions may apply, e.g. adoption and custody of children, maintenance, and division of marital assets, the parties being the only difference. So far, in my part of the world, we have not had to deal with this issue, but I am certain that we shall have to do so within the not too distant future. In like manner is the issue of surrogacy. We have to be prepared to deal with the issues when they arise.

We now live in a world which has shrunk in terms of travel and access to information which can be easily obtained through the Internet and social networking. This has made the commission of criminal offences much easier to perpetrate and slower to detect. Although crimes such as human trafficking were committed in the past, the number of victims smuggled across borders and forced into prostitution and other sexual crimes has increased worldwide. Human trafficking has become a problem for both developed and developing countries. Caribbean countries have not escaped the international network, and our courts, out of necessity, are grappling with the ever-increasing incidents of minors being forcefully abducted from their homelands.

Moving away from new criminal offences and other world-changing issues, the delivery of justice has been expedited in developed and some developing countries. The filing of court documents and all of the procedures connected with hearing cases have been made considerably easier and faster. In the past, hearings were delayed by cumbersome recording of evidence, often handwritten, or transcribed by shorthand reporters. Now such evidence can be made available instantly and transcripts delivered immediately. The work of judges has been made much easier, including the research required for the delivery of judgments. One just has to enter the name of a relevant case into a computer and the answer is at your fingertips. Our Court is the beneficiary of modern technology, for which we are indeed grateful, and for which we have been commended repeatedly.

Of course, all of this leads back to my opening remarks about the developed and developing world. We have to be cognisant of the fact that there are parts of the world where modern technology is still a distant dream, and courts and judicial personnel (including magistrates) continue to dispense justice without the assistance of modern technology. Justice must be administered whether the evidence is recorded by hand or by machine, and whether the research is obtained through legal tomes or a search engine. It is conceded that the lack of advanced technology reduces the capacity of courts to deliver justice in a timely manner. Developing countries continue to be plagued by ever-increasing backlogs of cases. In some countries with weak economies the choice between improving the judicial system and constructing a hospital or school is easy to make, with the judicial system being relegated to the bottom of the list of priorities.

Another development within the judiciary at this point in time is the large number of women who are entering the legal profession, compared with the numbers several years ago. Within the Caribbean women are graduating from law schools in considerably higher percentages than men. I am sure this is not confined to the Caribbean and may be so in other jurisdictions. It will certainly have implications for women joining the judiciary eventually, although at present we see them at the lower end of the judicial spectrum, e.g. as magistrates. The number of female judges, particularly in the higher echelons of the judicial system, is still much lower than men. I include myself here as the only female judge among six males. Hopefully the tide will change as women ascend the ladder and break the proverbial glass ceiling.

One important aspect of being a judge in today's world is transparency. Judicial decisions and the reasoning which informs those decisions are more publicly scrutinized than in an earlier era. Formerly judges tended to work with greater privacy and virtually no accountability; they did not feel obliged to disclose their thought processes in arriving at decisions except through published law reports; in fact judges never interacted with the press. Today in some jurisdictions, through an active press and other media, the judiciary has come under a microscope, with detailed inquiries being made of the circumstances which informed their rulings. Although judicial interaction with the media is still restricted to some extent, it is less rigid, and some jurisdictions have public relations personnel attached to the courts, thereby shielding the judiciary from media exposure. Nevertheless, the whole aspect of judicial accountability has assumed importance. Some current views reveal that the judiciary should no longer be cloistered, but be more transparent, particularly in relation to decisions that arouse public interest. The effects of this may have implications for a significant majority of citizens.

Similarly, judicial conduct attracts far more media attention than it did in past decades. Of course, we now live in a very open society where privacy is limited and one's actions come under severe public scrutiny. In these circumstances the adoption of judicial codes of conduct has become necessary, with guidelines on how judges should conduct themselves. This was unheard of years ago. No one would have thought that there was need to lay out rules on how judges ought to comport themselves. Sadly today this is necessary, as discussed by the Bangalore Principles of Judicial Conduct in India early this century, later adopted by Chief Justices and senior judicial officers from around the world. They promulgated such principles as integrity, impartiality, equality, propriety, independence, competence, and diligence. These principles have been accepted by judiciaries of the Commonwealth and elsewhere and have given rise to the acceptance of codes of conduct for judges and magistrates. In most instances these codes are merely advisory rather than punitive, operating as guidelines on the type of conduct that is expected from office holders of trust, and from whom the public demands higher standards of behaviour.

A recent addition to codes of judicial conduct in some countries is advice on dealing with social networking and the placing of information on websites likely to have an adverse effect on matters before the courts. This is certainly a new phenomenon which has implications for the judiciary, if not handled carefully. Discretion and caution in deciding what a judge personally posts on social network sites are important factors to be considered in order to preserve the integrity of judges, and to avoid compromising the administration of justice generally.

Several examples of abuse of the process have surfaced, with judges being utilized as pawns in contested cases either by unwittingly accepting social invitations from persons or friends involved in proceedings before them or contacts being made through their relatives, friends, and sometimes judicial staff. Judges have to be on their guard constantly when interacting socially or accepting invitations which appear ostensibly innocuous. This is particularly so in small jurisdictions where judicial personnel are well known. The problem may not be so acute in large jurisdictions where it is easier for judges to be anonymous, with such anonymity being a blessing in disguise.

What has become a worldwide concern within recent times is preservation and protection of the environment, with legislative measures being taken to avoid its pollution and destruction. Judges may now find that their dockets include cases concerning restraint on destruction and excavation of heritage sites and forests mainly for mining and other forms of development. It cannot be denied that destruction and exploitation of our natural resources have been and continue to be effected in the name of rapid urbanization; aggressive modernization thereby creates imbalances within our ecosystems. Some jurisdictions have established environmental agencies and courts to handle the plethora of cases concerning destruction of the environment which in former years was not as extensive or which was overlooked in the name of progress.

I end by referring to the most significant issue which has arisen during this century and which a judge in these modern times may have to confront in the future. It is the new and developing concept of cloning; that is, producing an identical clone of another animal or maybe futuristically another human being. Cloning has started with animals, and sometime in years ahead the skill may be perfected to produce a human clone. The legal issues which may arise from this concept are mind-boggling, and laws will have to be formulated to deal with the problems from this experiment with nature if and when it becomes a reality. Let us hope that we are well prepared to deal with it if it ever arises.

These are just a few issues which from my perspective a judge in the present state of world events and advancement may have to confront in the day-to-day administration of justice. I am certain there are several others which may arise depending on the jurisdiction within which a judge is required to serve and the level of attention which is given by governments to these issues either as priorities or as issues which, depending on their economies, do not require urgent attention and could be deferred to some futuristic date.

8

The New World of Tribunals

A Quiet Revolution

Professor Jeremy Cooper

A version of this chapter was first delivered as a public lecture at
the Medway Campus of Kent University, 22 March 2012.

Tribunals in one form or another have existed for a very long time in
this country. Tribunals are established by statute to deal with disputes
between an individual and the state. Some tribunals also deal with
inter-party disputes, for example the Employment Tribunal, which
arbitrates between employers and employees. There is no special
magic in the word 'tribunal', which has its origins in the Latin word
tribunus, meaning simply 'a seat of judgment'. Thus in France, and
many other southern European countries, the word 'tribunal' is the
same as the word for court. No distinction is made. However, despite
the common root of the word used to describe most types of adjudication in continental Europe, tribunals have, over time in the United
Kingdom, developed their own special identity, different from courts.
It is the evolution of this identity that I will be exploring in the course
of this chapter.

Prior to the twenty-first century, tribunals in the United Kingdom
developed in a random, chaotic, and haphazard way. Typically, a new
piece of legislation would be introduced creating a new entitlement—
a financial benefit, a property right, a vehicle or parking regulation.
Over time, disputes would develop between individuals and the state
regarding the enforcement of this new entitlement. The government
department that established the entitlement would then respond by
creating a tribunal, funded and regulated by that department. Thus

the Department of Trade and Industry established the Employment Tribunal, the Department of Health established the Mental Health Tribunal, the Department of Work and Pensions established the Social Security Tribunal, the Home Office established the Immigration and Asylum Tribunal, and so on. It was very ad hoc and vaguely incestuous.

The consequence of this topsy-turvy approach to tribunal development was that by the year 2000 almost 100 separate tribunal jurisdictions were operating across the United Kingdom. There was no central regulation, each tribunal administered in its own way, with its own set of rules and procedures, its own methods of appointing its panel members, its own hearing locations, and its own ways of reaching and disseminating its decisions. And this adjudication industry was very big business, determining in the order of half a million cases a year, handing down many millions of pounds of compensation and defining countless individual rights against the state: rights to social security payments, rights to tax rebates, rights to special education, rights to reinstatement in employment or not to suffer discrimination in a whole host of settings, rights to stay in the United Kingdom, rights to be discharged from a mental hospital, and so on.

And the list of 100 certainly included some rum-sounding tribunals! I particularly like the sound of the Sea Fish Licence Tribunal, the Mines and Quarries Tribunal, the Antarctic Tribunal, and the Chemical Weapons Licence Appeal Tribunal, none of whom ever appear to have sat! And what about the Meat Hygiene Appeals Tribunal, set up to deal with

> refusals to license premises, or in respect of unacceptable conditions in a licence of or the revocation of a licence issued to the occupier of premises, pursuant to the Fresh Meat (Hygiene and Inspection) Regulations 1992, the Poultry Meat (Hygiene) Regulations 1976 and the Poultry Meat (Hygiene) (Scotland) Regulations 1976.

This tribunal existed for a full twenty years, and appointed its own chairman, deputy chairman, and panelists, with its own regulations approved by Parliament. In the course of those twenty years it sat on two occasions!

Small wonder, then, that when Sir Andrew Leggatt was tasked in May 2000, by the government of the day, to investigate the fitness for purpose of the United Kingdom tribunal system he found it generally wanting and concluded his lengthy investigation with a set of radical reform proposals. In his view, the country needed nothing less than a revamped, reconstructed national tribunal system that was independent, coherent, professional, cost-effective, and user-friendly. His vision was for a coordinated network of tribunals in which every individual tribunal user would both understand and feel central to the adjudication process.

So let us investigate what has happened since. First, a little history. As I have indicated, in their earliest manifestation tribunals were not judicial bodies independent of the Executive, but rather administrative extensions of government departments. Then in 1908 the Liberal Prime Minister David Lloyd George created a tribunal to adjudicate pension disputes. This was the first example of a truly judicial tribunal, separate from the Executive and properly part of the judiciary. But although this model was replicated in form in other government settings throughout the course of the next fifty years there was little sense that these tribunals were in substance truly independent of the Executive. The adjudicators were often civil servants, hearings might be paper hearings only, the involvement of the applicant in the adjudication process was usually minimal, and the decision of the tribunal might be only advisory to the decision maker, rather than determinative. They remained in most respects a wing of government.

In 1957 the first comprehensive study of the United Kingdom tribunal system was conducted. The study was the work of a committee chaired by the Rt Hon. Sir Oliver Franks (hereafter 'Franks'). Its most significant contribution to the evolution of tribunals was its laying down for the first time the principle that as tribunals perform a judicial role, they should never be seen as part of executive government, but always as independent of it. This was a robust restatement of the principle of the separation of powers, first articulated in the seventeenth century by the French philosopher Charles Secondat, better known as the Baron de Montesquieu. The theory of the separation of powers maintains that fully mature democratic government is made up of three equal but separate components: the Executive, the Legislature, and the Courts (in effect the judiciary). Government can only operate effectively and free of the threat of tyranny if these three components are kept robustly independent and separate from one another. The crucial point about Franks is that it expanded the third component of government—the Courts—to include tribunals. But although Franks laid down this important benchmark as a statement of tribunal independence, enforcement of the principle remained patchy over the subsequent forty years and many observers would say that the principle was honoured more in its breach than in its enforcement. So when Sir Andrew Leggatt published in 2001 the results of his investigation into the state of tribunals,[1] he reached the stark conclusion that tribunals are not independent of the departments that sponsor them.[2] 'For most tribunals [their sponsoring] departments provide administrative support, pay the salaries of members, pay their expenses, provide accommodation, provide IT support often in the form of access to departmental systems, are responsible for some appointments, and promote the legislation which prescribes the procedures to be followed'.[3] He added, 'our research study revealed how the arrangements can still lead to a perception that tribunals are not independent'.[4] He also concluded that although tribunals collectively constituted a substantial part of the system of justice in this country, too often their methods were old-fashioned and they were daunting to users. Furthermore, because tribunals at that time were 'many and disparate', there was a considerable waste of resources in managing them. 'Tribunals are intended to provide a simple, accessible system of justice where users can represent themselves. So it is discouraging to note the growing perception that they cannot'.[5]

So despite the formal statement of Franks in 1957 of the core underlying principle of independence for tribunals, Leggatt concluded in 2001 that it had not yet been achieved.

Leggatt's Review of Tribunals was undertaken between May 2000 and March 2001 and in the process assimilated the views of over 300 consultees, a phenomenal achievement in its own right given the short time it took to complete. In commissioning the Review the then Lord Chancellor, Lord Irvine, wrote as follows:

> The Tribunals system has for too long been ignored. Significant steps have been taken to modernise the civil and criminal justice systems. It is high time that we also look afresh at the whole system of administrative justice, which has a colossal impact on the lives of well over 470,000 people every year.[6]

The Leggatt Review was root-and-branch and far-reaching. Altogether it made 361 recommendations concerning tribunals, but two were key. First, Leggatt advocated the replacement of the myriad mix of 100 or

---

[1] Sir Andrew Leggatt, *'Tribunals for Users: One System, One Service': Report of the Review of Tribunals* (HMSO, March 2001).
[2] Ibid., para. 3.   [3] Ibid., para. 2.20.   [4] Ibid.
[5] Ibid., p. 7, para. 7.   [6] LCD Press Notice 158/00, 18 May 2000.

so separate tribunals by a composite, two-tier tribunal system (one First Tier Tribunal, and one Upper Tier Tribunal, each tier divided into jurisdictional chambers for administrative purposes, and each with its own chamber president who would be a senior judge). The two-tier system would be overseen by an Appeal Court judge, nominated by the Lord Chancellor and the Lord Chief Justice for this purpose, who would be known as the Senior President of Tribunals. In other words, the 100 tribunals should become two! Second, Leggatt advocated the creation of a new independent Tribunal Service to take over the management and administration of the tribunals from their sponsoring departments. In this way it was anticipated that tribunals would acquire (to quote Leggatt): 'A collective standing to match that of the Court System and a collective power to fulfil the needs of users in the way that was originally intended.'[7] The Review was generally well received and was swiftly followed by a Government White Paper entitled 'Transforming Public Services: Complaints, Redress and Tribunal' (2004).[8] This White Paper not only accepted the general thrust of Leggatt's recommendations, but it went some distance further, linking the format of tribunal hearings to the Government's more general desire to improve the handling of complaints by developing a range of innovative dispute resolution methods. Thus, the White Paper envisaged that the unified tribunals system would become a new type of organization, not just a federation of existing tribunals that would create a system with a 'collective commitment to improvement and innovation for the benefit of the public it serves.'[9]

Now, bear in mind the complexities this reform had to embrace. Tribunals cover a vast range of disputes. The Social Security and Child Support jurisdiction deals with hundreds of thousands of applications amounting to about one-third of all tribunal cases. At the other extreme, there are some tribunals which rarely sit. The subjects tribunals deal with cover the whole range of political and social life, including social security benefits, health, education, tax, agriculture, land disputes, criminal injuries compensation, freedom-of-information challenges, immigration and asylum claims, rents, transport haulier licences, estate agent disputes, and the regulation of consumer credit agencies.

---

[7] Ibid., p. 7, para. 8.
[8] White Paper Cm. 6243, July 2004.
[9] Leggatt, para. 9.

Let me give a few examples to illustrate the range of tribunal work. Let me start with the Tax Tribunal. The range, weight, and difficulty of tax appeals is probably unique within the tribunal system. At one extreme are challenges to tax returns, default penalties for late submissions, and so on. For these cases, whilst some understanding of tax law is necessary, in-depth knowledge of tax law is not. At the other end lie cases of untold magnitude and complexity, involving vast sums of money. The United Kingdom's tax law alone extends to several thousand pages of small type. In addition, almost every big tax case involves some element of European or Human Rights law, or both, and in many cases it is necessary to understand other aspects of the law, since the incidence of tax liability cannot be determined without a proper understanding of the underlying transaction or situation. That may require some knowledge of, for example, the law of trusts, of banking, of derivatives trading, or of the construction industry.

What about the Mental Health Tribunal, the jurisdiction I know best? At any one time over 45,000 individuals are detained (or sectioned) in the United Kingdom under the Mental Health Act. Well over 50 per cent of these detained patients annually exercise their right to appeal to the Mental Health Tribunal hoping for discharge, and in around 12 per cent of these cases discharge is granted by the tribunal. These patients range from young people with bipolar disorder, depression or drug-induced psychosis, to patients with dementia, to serial killers in high-security hospitals, some of whom may also have a severe psychiatric condition.

Or the Employment Tribunal, which currently receives around 61,000 claims a year.[10] These include many thousands of allegations of race, sex or age discrimination (a female employee announces her pregnancy and loses her job, or wants promotion and is told that favours of a personal nature might strengthen her chances; a middle-aged employee is passed over for promotion in favour of a younger,

---

[10] The number of claims submitted to the Employment Tribunal has declined fairly dramatically over the past few years from a peak in 2011 of *c.*125,000 claims to 106,000 claims in 2013–14, and now the current figure. The main reason given for the reduction in the number of claims is the introduction by the Government on 29 July 2013 of claimant fees. There are, however, other factors to consider, including the advent of early conciliation, the economic recovery, and changes to substantive employment law. For further analysis see Doug Pyper and Feargal McGuiness, 'Employment Tribunal Fees' (House of Commons Library, Briefing Paper No 7081, September 2015), and *Fairer Fees: Fixing the Employment Tribunal System* (Citizens Advice Bureau, 2015).

less qualified employee, etc.—the list is long, and depressing). These are small cases, but for the individual in question their significance is huge and the outcome of the case may change their lives for ever, for better or for worse. Holiday pay, the comparative rights of part-time workers, the rights of disabled employees to receive reasonable adjustments to their workplace to enable them to carry out their duties, and pension rights cases are all examples of issues that are regularly litigated before this tribunal.

Employment cases also reflect regional employment issues—in London and the South East a concentration of service-industry workers often seek remedies and redress; in East Anglia, it is agricultural workers; and in north-east England there are many workers trying to enforce their rights to a minimum wage. The cases traced through their geography paint an accurate economic profile of the nation's employment patterns. And occasionally the Employment Tribunal will deliver a blockbuster of a decision on a truly massive scale. In 2009, for example an Employment Tribunal in Northumbria considered a challenge to a job evaluation study which affected more than one million jobs in the NHS. It was argued that jobs done mainly by men had been deliberately weighted, but there were also several technical challenges and the tribunal had to decide the principles according to which the viability of the study should be assessed. Having heard evidence over several weeks and been presented with more than 25,000 pages of documents, the Tribunal upheld the job evaluation study in a 233-page judgment, and the reforms went ahead.

Perhaps the busiest of all the tribunal jurisdictions is the Social Security and Child Support Tribunal, which deals with a whole range of social security and other benefit entitlements.[11] These may be small decisions in money terms—a few pounds extra benefit here, an extra entitlement there—but to the individual in question they can mean the difference between getting out of the house or complete social isolation, providing the opportunity to make friends and become part of normal society. That little bit of extra benefit can make all the difference.

---

[11] The Social Security and Child Support Tribunal has experienced in recent years even more dramatic fluctuations in its workload following the Government's various welfare reforms, and will continue to do so. The number of applications has fallen from its peak of 507,000 in 2012–13 to 108,000 in 2014–15.

Take MPs' expenses. Most people think the whole exposure of the expenses scandal was down to the *Daily Telegraph* using an inside source in the House of Commons Accounts Office. But this is only part of the story. It was in fact the Information Rights Tribunal that initially gave the newspapers the right to access and then publish the information about MPs' expenses, following a freedom-of-information request.

So, in summary, tribunals now handle over 300,000 cases a year, sitting in hundreds of different locations across the country ranging from purpose-built state-of-the-art hearing centres to hotel meeting rooms or hospital wards. In this activity the HMCTS currently employs *c.*3,000 administrative staff, supporting *c.*6,000 judicial office holders—judges, doctors, social workers, accountants, surveyors, trade unionists, nurses. The annual cost of the operation, excluding the salaries of the judicial office holders, is now very substantial.[12]

So what is the quiet revolution? The revolution has been the moulding, in a few short years, of the mass of disparate, disorganized adjudicatory bodes known as 'the tribunals' into a single judicial structure run by a coherent, streamlined, and highly efficient agency, the Tribunal Service, now as part of HMCTS.

But before expanding this notion further, let me set the wider context. The emergence of tribunals as a new, coherent, unified force is part of wider constitutional changes which have penetrated the justice system over the course of the past decade. In June 2003, in the wake of the White Paper to which I made earlier reference, Prime Minister Tony Blair announced without warning a radical new programme of constitutional reform designed to cement an institutional separation between the Government and the judiciary. This involved, (1) the abolition of the Lord Chancellor's historic role as head of the judiciary and the transfer of most of his judicial leadership functions (in England and Wales) to the Lord Chief Justice; (2) the transfer of the process for appointing all judicial officer holders, including the great majority of tribunal office holders, from the Lord Chancellor to a new independent body, the Judicial Appointments Commission; and (3) the transfer of the functions of the highest court in the land (the Judicial Committee of the House of Lords) to a new judicial body, the

---

[12] See www.gov.uk/government/uploads/system/uploads/attachment_data/file/433948/hmcts-annual-report-accounts-2014-15.pdf.

Supreme Court. The new Court was to be symbolically housed outside the Houses of Parliament, in a restored building on the opposite side of Parliament Square. These ideas were rapidly progressed through Parliament and found their statutory basis in the Constitutional Reform Act 2005. And it was this process that laid the building blocks within which the quiet revolution could now take place.

By spring 2006, the Lord Chancellor Lord Falconer had publically resolved that tribunals were 'a distinctive part of the justice system separate from the courts judiciary, with a special responsibility to provide speedy, expert and accessible justice in specialist areas of law'. So what did he mean, what do we mean, by 'distinctive'? How do tribunals differ from courts? In some ways tribunals perform very similar functions to courts: magistrates', civil and Crown courts. They receive evidence, they listen to the views of the parties, and they reach a decision as to who wins, in many cases with further powers to order compensation.

On the other hand, they are quite distinctive from courts in a number of key ways.

- Tribunal proceedings are normally handled more quickly and efficiently in tribunals than in courts, indeed part of the responsibility of the Senior President of Tribunals (SPT) is to ensure that proceedings are handled quickly. There is no equivalent duty in the courts' system.

- Unlike courts, tribunals rely heavily upon the specialist expertise of their members, including both lawyers and non-lawyers (such as doctors, nurses, disability specialists, surveyors, tax experts, accountants, or others with relevant experience). In courts judges are judges first, experts second.

- Tribunals use flexible procedures designed to suit the needs of the particular client group. By flexibility I mean (a) trying to be responsive to the level of understanding of the proceedings possessed by the parties and arranging the order of the hearing to accommodate the level of understanding, (b) a willingness to adapt the level of formality to reduce the anxiety levels of parties, and (c) flexibility as to the layout of the hearing room.

- Tribunals seek to put the tribunal user as central to the adjudication by being accessible and 'inquisitorial'. This is sometimes described as the 'enabling approach', supporting the parties in ways which give them confidence in their own abilities to participate in the process and in the tribunal's capacity to compensate for the appellant's lack of skills or knowledge. This was described to me by one appellant as 'wanting the tribunal members to play an active role towards me, showing a sympathetic understanding of my problem, by listening, asking relevant questions, drawing me out, and generally sorting out my case'. The Leggatt Report specifically referred to the need for tribunals to 'be alert for factual or legal aspects of the case which appellants may not bring out, adequately or at all, but which may have a bearing on possible outcomes'.[13]

To reflect these differences tribunals try to develop rules and procedures that are both simple and simply expressed. As Leggatt himself stated:

> It should never be forgotten that tribunals exist for users, not the other way round. No matter how good tribunals may be they do not fulfil their function unless they are accessible by the people who want to use them, and unless the users receive the help they need to prepare and present their cases.[14]

The reforms unleashed by this series of historic declarations have been extensive and the momentum continues at a breathless pace. The new organizational structure that has been put in place to develop and protect tribunals as distinctive, independent judicial bodies is achieving its goal as the quiet revolution progresses. There are essentially five key factors at work driving this revolution, as follows: leadership, constitutional protection, independence from sponsoring departments, the independent jurisdiction of the Upper Tribunal, the Judicial College.

LEADERSHIP

Crucial to the strengthening of tribunals as distinct and different has been leadership. Since 2007 tribunals have been fortunate indeed to have been led with outstanding skill by the three Senior Presidents of Tribunals, the first being Lord Justice Carnwath (now Lord Carnwath), then judge of the Court of Appeal, ex-chairman of the Law Commission. In 2012 he relinquished the post to become a

---

[13] Leggatt, para. 7.4.   [14] Ibid., para. 6.

Justice of the Supreme Court, and was replaced by the equally able Lord Justice Sullivan, who was in turn replaced in 2015 by the dynamic incumbent Lord Justice Ryder. The creation of the new post of Senior President of Tribunals (SPT) provided unified leadership to the tribunals judiciary and bridged the gap between courts and tribunals. How? Statute requires the SPT to be a member of the Court of Appeal. There is also a statutory duty of cooperation between the SPT, the Lord Chief Justices of England and Wales and Northern Ireland, and the Lord President of Scotland, in relation to judicial training, guidance, and welfare in the tribunals. In addition, the SPT has important powers and duties in relation to matters such as the assignment and deployment of judges and members to chambers, the making of practice directions, and the membership of the Tribunal Procedure Committee, which approves, monitors, and oversees all the tribunal rules and procedures. Thus, he or she has the status and the powers to truly make things happen. He is also a member of the Judicial Executive Board.

CONSTITUTIONAL PROTECTION

The Constitutional Reform Act 2005 now imposes a statutory duty on the Lord Chancellor and other ministers of the Crown to uphold the continued independence of the judiciary, and section 1 of the Tribunals, Courts and Enforcement Act 2007 extends the definition of 'judiciary' to include all those judiciary sitting in tribunals administered by the Lord Chancellor. This independence has been reflected in awarding the title of 'judge' to all tribunal judges, who also now take the same judicial oath as court judges ('to do right to all manner of people after the laws and usages of this Realm without fear or favour, affection or ill will').

INDEPENDENCE FROM THE SPONSORING GOVERNMENT DEPARTMENT

Administration of the tribunal and courts system is now the responsibility of a single Ministry of Justice (MOJ) agency, the HMCTS, and tribunal administration has once and for all been taken away (except in some aspects of the Northern Ireland system) from the sponsoring government departments. This has not only led to a more robust independence, in the sense that the sponsoring departments' power to influence the approach of a tribunal through drafting its rules etc. is largely curtailed, but also to a more robust rationalization of MOJ estate, sharing of hearing centres, the slow bringing together of disparate IT systems, sharing of clerking facilities, and further developing the use of telephone directions hearings and the use of video links and so on.

INDEPENDENT JURISDICTION OF THE UPPER TRIBUNAL

The creation of the Upper Tribunal as a Superior Court of record and binding authority gives all parties in the majority of First Tier cases for the very first time a right of appeal to a specially constituted tribunal, on a point of law. Procedures are quick and relatively informal, and decisions normally delivered shortly after the hearings. The Upper Tribunal is thus already making its mark, developing its own distinctive style, and publishing its own law reports. Monetary awards by tribunals are directly enforceable and contempt powers are also available.

THE JUDICIAL COLLEGE

The big development in judicial training over the past two years was the coming into being on 2 April 2011 of the Judicial College. The college brought the training of all judicial office holders in England and Wales (and also many tribunal office holders in Scotland)—c.32,000 in total—into a single training organization which is now the central professional learning and development institution for the judiciary and tribunal members (collectively described hereafter as 'judicial office holders' (JOHs)). The idea underpinning this project is simple: a single training college will both enhance judicial independence and promote public confidence by providing reassurance that all judicial office holders are trained to common standards, receive up-to-date specialist training, and are able to benefit from cross-fertilization of ideas within a common training forum. Other positive features of a unified training organization include the provision of an enhanced capacity to create administrative efficiencies and more effective use of resources and the opportunities the College can provide to strengthen collaboration with other bodies both across the UK and into Europe and the wider common law world. The College also intends to develop an academic programme to complement its specific training activities. The overarching vision of the project is to create a Judicial College that will 'become and be recognized as a world leader in judicial education'.[15]

In 2014–15 the Judicial College provided training in thirty-four separate jurisdictions across the United Kingdom, including 292 courses in both residential and non-residential settings for tribunal JOHs. Training includes bespoke specialist courses designed and delivered within jurisdictions; cross-jurisdictional training in judicial skills, delivered since 2016 though the College's newly created Faculty; training programmes in leadership and management, in stress management, and in working with litigants in person; and a comprehensive programme for training trainers using the most advanced contemporary training methodologies, including extensive use of e-learning via the College's Moodle-platformed Learning Management System.

The College's pragmatic approach to judicial training and the built-in flexibility of its training philosophy has created a key cornerstone enabling all JOHs to respond positively to the many challenges the contemporary judicial world continues to lay down.

WHAT ARE THE FUTURE CHALLENGES?

The tribunal network has expanded at an exhausting rate, and is set to expand still further as more and more tribunals currently outside the service express interest in 'joining the club': the Residential Property Tribunal joined the First Tier Tribunal in the spring of 2013 and the Valuation Tribunals (Rates and Council Tax), School Appeals, Parole Board, Parking and Traffic Adjudicators, Traffic Commissioners, are all possible future candidates for membership should they so choose.

---

[15] European Commission Final Report Tender JUST/2012/JUTR/PR/0064/A4—Implementation of the Pilot Project—European Judicial Training provides evidence of such recognition.

Fluctuations in caseload in response to new government legislation and recession are the first major challenge to highlight. The unpredictable impact on the system of new legislation—some planned (Human Rights Act and Equalities Act), some not, e.g. the impact of recession and fees introduction on the caseload of the Employment and Social Security Tribunals—is very hard to plan for and subsequently to manage. In some cases the effect of new legislation is to increase exponentially the costs of the tribunal system as more and more people challenge the decisions brought about by the cuts, which leads to a need for more judges, more hearings, and associated costs, which may end up costing more than the savings made by benefit cuts! In other cases, the opposite (and often unpredicted) occurs with sudden dramatic reductions in caseloads, as in the Employment and the Social Security and Child Support Tribunals.[16]

The possible effects of the devolution movement provide a second uncharted challenge to the tribunal system. Large numbers of tribunals located in Scotland, Wales, and Northern Ireland remain within the United Kingdom tribunal family under HMCTS, with cross-border sitting arrangements, funding and recruitment from a common pool, and centrally developed training, regionally delivered. But the wider political moves in the three regions (Wales, Northern Ireland, and, most prominently, Scotland) towards differing degrees of devolution carry with them potential new tensions in the cross-border relationships and the inevitable talk of independent tribunal services within each of the three jurisdictions. Scotland is well advanced down this route, Wales is talking about it, and Northern Ireland may not be far behind.

Perhaps the biggest challenge of all is how do tribunals retain their distinctiveness at a time of multi-ticketing and common judicial training as they move closer to the European concept of the career judge? Herein lies the paradox, and one that needs careful nurturing over the coming years. For might it be that, as the tribunals come of age and courts and tribunals work more and more closely together, with judges sitting in a number of different court and tribunal jurisdictions in the course of their careers, the distinctive tribunal approach that we value and uphold as special will slowly fade away? Will tribunals eventually become indistinguishable from courts? This potential

---

[16] See above at footnotes 10 and 11.

problem will require both rigour and vigilance among those charged with vouchsafing the future of the tribunal system. But we must not allow the solution to become the problem.

So finally let me return to my earlier quotation from the Leggatt Review and the aspiration that tribunals should achieve a collective standing to match that of the court system and a collective power to fulfil the needs of users in the way that was originally intended.

How far have we got? The tribunal system as a whole now has coherence, with an excellent administrative infrastructure; the Judicial Appointments Commission continues to appoint high-quality tribunal judges and members (sometimes hundreds of applicants competing for a handful of positions), who all have constitutionally guaranteed independence. Excellent training is provided for all tribunal JOHs, within the new Judicial College. Much has been done to establish in the eyes of the general public that the justice tribunals deliver is as significant as that delivered in the courts. HMCTS is able to absorb new tribunals into the system, in response to the creation of new rights and entitlements. Above all, tribunals strive continuously to put the user first in all their deliberations, and research amongst users suggests that generally they are succeeding in this endeavour. It is work in progress, and the revolution is far from complete, but we are getting there.

9

Reflections on the Tribunal Reform Project

Lord Carnwath of Notting Hill

This lecture was first delivered at the College of Law, Chancery Lane, London, on 16 January 2013.

Two questions are posed on the home page of the judiciary website. The first is 'Do judges use gavels?' The other is 'Why do people bow when they come into court?' These are offered as tasters to encourage the reader to explore '1,000 years of evolution' and to 'find out how our justice system developed'. Presumably they are thought to be the sort of thing about judges which interest the public. In case you are curious, the answers are:

- 'Although they are often seen in cartoons and TV programmes and mentioned in also everything else involving judges, the one place you will not see a gavel is in an English or Welsh court.'
- 'The presence of the Royal Arms explains why lawyers and court officials bow to the judge or magistrates' bench when they enter the room. They are not bowing to the judge—they are bowing to the coat of arms, to show respect for the Queen's justice.'

Next to these helpful questions, you will find some typical images of judges: a circuit judge in criminal robes—formal wig and gown and red sash, a rear view of assorted judges processing from the Abbey Service in full-bottom wigs and purple gowns. Much more down to earth, and I would hope of more genuine interest, is another section of the website, which gives a series of pen portraits (anonymous, but very personal) of what different judges actually do—under the heading 'a day in the life of … '. The district judge, for example, tells us that contrary to ordinary perceptions of a judge in a crowded courtroom with 'clerks and police officers and phalanxes of court staff', most of the time is spent working alone: 'The same room has to double as chambers for private hearings and a court for public hearings. My only protection is the desk in front of me and a panic button.' The district judge has a lot of ground to cover: practice and procedure affecting civil disputes (contract, negligence, personal injury, property disputes, civil injunctions, etc.), family disputes (divorce, nullity, disputes over children and finances, domestic violence, etc.), bankruptcy, and winding up, and then:

> Thursdays are usually Possession Day when I will deal with either landlord and tenant claims, both public and private, or mortgage possessions. We tend to deal with local authority and Registered Social Landlord cases in bulk so it is not unusual to find oneself facing a cause list of 60–75 cases on one day.

Crucial to the job is said to be 'people management':

> Most of the individuals who appear in front of me do not have the benefit of legal representation and they range from one end of the spectrum to the other, from the supremely lucid to the mentally incapable; from the polite to the downright nasty; from the highly-clued to the clueless.
>
> With no-one else to support me and with minimal protection, I am required to be not just a knowledgeable lawyer but a social worker, psychologist and therapist as well. I will be dealing one-on-one with all strata of society from incredibly diverse backgrounds with only occasional help from legal representatives.

This, you may think, is a commendably frank and realistic picture of what everyday judicial life for many is really like.

As significant as the contents of the judiciary website is the fact that it exists at all—that there is a website devoted to the judiciary; that it includes not just court judges, but the tribunals judiciary and magistrates; and that it is seen as part of its function to explain to the public what judges do. These are all incidents of a major change, of which the public may be only dimly aware, that has taken place over the last decade in the constitutional position of the judiciary and, with it, in their appreciation of their own role in society.

The big changes date from June 2003. I still remember the sense of shock that afternoon when I heard on the BBC news that the government had decided, without any previous discussion, to launch a constitutional revolution, the most striking feature being the proposed abolition of the historic office of Lord Chancellor, and with it the removal of the present incumbent, Lord Irvine. Ten years on we are still working out the consequences of those dramatic events.

One of the avowed aims of the changes was to strengthen judicial independence—actual and perceived. At the time I was unconvinced by what seemed a mere pretext for political action. Independence as such, in the sense of freedom from political interference, had never been a real issue. There was no practical risk of political interference in judicial decision-making. Nor, at least in the post-war period, had politics been allowed to play any significant role in the appointment of judges. Even before the Judicial Appointments Commission (JAC) there was little complaint that judicial appointments were made other than on merit. If anything, the historic role of the Lord Chancellor as a senior member of government with responsibility for defending and promoting the interests of justice was a source of strength.

In retrospect, however, I believe there has been a profound change, but it has been of a rather different and more subtle kind. Institutional independence in itself meant little. But over time it has brought a new sense of collective identity and with it of collective responsibility.

The seeds of change were already there. For a growing sense of collective judicial responsibility I would look back to the introduction of the Human Rights Act in 1998. That was a major jurisprudential development which would affect courts and tribunals at all levels. Two years were left before implementation to allow time for preparation. That opportunity was taken. It stimulated an unprecedented collective exercise, led by the judges themselves with the Judicial Studies Board, to prepare for the new challenges. For the first time, judges at all levels, from the House of Lords down, succumbed to a common programme of judicial training. They found themselves not merely sitting together in judicial seminars, but struggling together with the complexities of case studies under the convention. Often it was the judges closer to the coal face, from the lower courts and tribunals, who showed a better and more flexible grasp of the conflicting practical and human issues at stake than their appellate colleagues.

At about the same time, Sir Andrew Leggatt was preparing his innovative report on the tribunal system—'Tribunals for Users'. His recommendations were underpinned by two simple ideas: first, that tribunals existed for their users, not the other way round; and second, that tribunals were, and should be recognized as, an integral part of the independent judicial system. They should be separated from their sponsoring departments and brought within the justice system. They should have 'a collective standing to match that of the Court System and a collective power to fulfil the needs of users in the way that was originally intended.'[1]

Since then, ironically and unhappily, the issue which perhaps has done most to give us a sense of collective identity as a judicial family has been the continuing saga of judicial pensions. When I was first appointed as Senior President and the judges were in negotiations with Lord Falconer,[2] it came, I think, as a surprise to my senior judicial colleagues to learn that there were many salaried tribunal judges who were affected in exactly the same way as the court judges. By the time of the most recent disputes, the tribunal interest was taken for granted and tribunal judges were strongly represented on the Chancellor's pensions committee.

The legal and structural changes introduced by the Constitutional Reform Act (CRA) 2005 were far-reaching. At the highest level, judicial independence was exemplified by the creation of a new Supreme Court to take over the appellate functions of the House of Lords. I was not an enthusiast at the time. Like many others, I found it difficult to see the point of what seemed to be a very expensive way of doing not very much—a change of form, not substance.

However, having a little experience of how it looks from the inside, I am now persuaded that I was wrong. The change was well described by Lord Hope, not initially an advocate of the move, but who became one of the principal architects of the new Court. In a lecture given a year after the establishment of the Court, he spoke of the sense of empowerment which came from cutting free from the practices and traditions of the House of Lords:

> The most significant force for change, as it has turned out, was the fact that the Supreme Court was released from the many rules and conventions of the House of Lords and the justices were free to develop new rules and conventions for themselves. The rules and conventions of the House, always carefully observed by the Clerk to the Judicial Office, gave dignity to the proceedings. They also gave rise to something that characterizes any society whose traditions depend on ceremony and the ever watchful eye of officials who have been trained to ensure that they are adhered to—the feeling that because everything has always been done that way, it must be right ...[3]

---

[1] Sir Andrew Leggatt, '*Tribunals for Users: One System, One Service*': *Report of the Review of Tribunals* (HMSO, March 2001).

[2] Lord Chancellor at the time.

[3] Lord Hope, 'Do We Really Need a Supreme Court?', Newcastle Law School, 25 November 2010.

We may have lost some of the pomp and circumstance of the old location but we have gained much in terms of the convenience of the public and the lawyers who work in our Court, and have been able to devise rules for ourselves which suit the purpose of doing justice as an independent function rather than as part of an essentially legislative organization.

In the House of Lords it was the Law Lords who came first. Everyone else was there, one felt, on sufferance. In the Supreme Court the reverse is true. Democracy has taken over. Access to the building is very simple. The public are made to feel that they are welcome and—as it is a public building—to appreciate that in that sense it is their Court.

Some may feel that we have a little way to go to achieve complete user-friendliness. I have every confidence that under our new president, Lord Neuberger, more changes will come. However, as a member of the Court I am now much more aware than I was of the sheer volume of work, energy, and imagination required from both the justices and administrative staff, simply to create the new Court and its processes.

At the lower levels, the sense of empowerment has come not so much from breaking free as from coming together, under strengthened and unified judicial leadership. The CRA established the Lord Chief Justice in England and Wales as President of the Courts and Head of the judiciary (section 7). Neither of these concepts was very fully worked out in the statute. His duties as President were to represent the views of the judiciary to Parliament and Government, to maintain appropriate arrangements for their welfare, training, and guidance, and for their deployment and the allocation of work within the courts. The Lord Chancellor's office was retained but without any leadership role in relation to judges. He acquired a new statutory duty to uphold judicial independence,[4] and retained his responsibility for administration—the duty to ensure 'an efficient and effective system' to support the carrying on of the business of the courts.[5] Appointment of judges was entrusted to a new Judicial Appointments Commission, and discipline to a new office for judicial complaints.

---

[4] Constitutional Reform Act 2005, section 3.
[5] Courts Act 2003, section1.

These changes were complemented two years later by the even more striking changes to the tribunals system. In line with Leggatt's proposals they were reformed into a unified two-tier system, divided into chambers representing different specializations, each led by a chamber president. Their members were given the same status as court judges, and they were required to take the judicial oath (a major logistical exercise, involving more than 6,000 tribunal judges and members). They were protected by the same guarantee of judicial independence as their court colleagues. Overall leadership was entrusted to a Senior President of Tribunals.[6] The Lord Chancellor was again given the duty to ensure an efficient and effective system to support the tribunals.

The office of Senior President of Tribunals was an interesting constitutional creation. It was an entirely new autonomous office, not subject to direction from the Lord Chief Justice (LCJ), the Lord Chancellor, or anyone else. Its functions were modelled on those of the LCJ, including responsibility for welfare, training, and guidance. But there was more. The Senior President of Tribunals was required by statute to have regard to defined objectives: the need for tribunals to be 'accessible', for proceedings before them to be 'fair and to be handled quickly and efficiently', and for members of tribunals to be experts in the subject matter or law of the cases before them. The explanatory notes to the bill said that these criteria were intended simply to reflect 'the long-standing principles underlying the jurisdiction of tribunals', as recognized since the 1957 Franks report. (No great surprises there, although one would like to think that accessibility, fairness, and efficiency are not peculiar to tribunals.)

But then there was something much more radical. The Senior President of Tribunals was required to have regard to 'the need to develop innovative methods of resolving disputes that are of a type that may be brought before tribunals'. This was a new one. I have no idea where it came from. It was not in the bill as originally published, I believe it was unprecedented. As far as I know, the Senior President of Tribunals is the only judicial officer—possibly anywhere in the world—with an express duty to innovate. Note: not just the desirability of thinking about innovation, but the *need* to do it.

---

[6] Tribunals, Courts and Enforcement Act 2007, section 2.

An important feature of the new scheme was flexibility of deployment—the ability to assign tribunal judges and members from one chamber to another, subject to ensuring the necessary expertise and training. This had been very valuable in enabling the service to meet fluctuating demands in the different jurisdictions without extra recruitment. For example, it enabled us to create a completely new environmental jurisdiction from scratch to deal with demands in that field expected to arise from new regulatory legislation, but at a time when we had no real idea what the scale of the demand would be. We were able to assemble an impressive panel of judges and specialist members, simply by inviting applications from those with established expertise within our existing 6,000 members.

Another important development was the designation of court judges at all levels up to the Court of Appeal, as *ex officio* tribunal judges, able to sit by request of the Senior President. This has led, for example, to High Court judges (from throughout the United Kingdom) sitting regularly in the Upper Tribunal on immigration cases. The powers of the LCJ and Senior President in relation to the deployment and cross-assignment of judges both within and between the courts and tribunals will be extended significantly if and when the Crime and Courts Bill becomes law.

I give one perhaps unusual illustration of what this can mean in practice. I was sitting in the Court of Appeal in an immigration case, which raised a significant issue of European law. It was clear to us that the issue needed wider investigation than had been given so far by the Upper Tribunal. I gave the leading judgment, setting aside their decision and remitting the case to the Upper Tribunal, inviting the parties to submit further evidence on practice in other European countries. I did not want to leave it there. Putting on my hat as Senior President, I was able to request myself to sit in the Upper Tribunal on the remitted appeal, which I heard with two senior immigration judges. Although this course was perhaps unconventional, no one could say it was inconsistent with my duty to innovate. It seemed to me to give us the best of all worlds: the specialist expertise of the senior tribunal judges, combined with broader legal perspective and perhaps the added clout of a Court of Appeal judge. Happily our judgment was subsequently upheld by other colleagues in the Court of Appeal.

The new judicial leadership structure for both courts and tribunals was reflected in strong roles for the Judicial Executive Board, and the Tribunal Judges' Executive Board, which brought together the senior judicial leadership in each body to take a central role in policy decisions. The Senior President provides the link by sitting on both. At the same time the Judges' Council was reshaped to include representatives from all levels, including tribunals and magistrates, thus giving a better collective voice across the judicial community.

The 2005 Act made a reasonably effective job of dividing up the various functions which had formerly been exercised by the Lord Chancellor. But it said little about how they were to be made to work together, or who was to have overall responsibility for developing them as an integrated system for the benefit of users. To take an obvious example, it makes no sense for judicial leaders to talk about planning for improvements in judicial performance without relating them to infrastructure, buildings, IT services, and support staff, responsibility for which rests with the Lord Chancellor.

For the courts this separation of responsibility between judges and administrators was reinforced by the establishment of the LCJ's judicial office as a separate organization from HM Court Service, each with its own chief executive. Although there was a Court Service Management Board, on which judges were represented, under an independent chairman, its authority and reporting lines, and its relationship to the LCJ and the Lord Chancellor, were somewhat obscure.

Personally I was happier with the tribunal model of a single organization for judges and administrators. This had been the tradition in the constituent tribunals, and we saw no reason to change it. Perhaps because a much larger proportion of tribunal judges came from a solicitor background (over 65 per cent), judicial leaders seemed more ready to treat the task of administration, and working closely with the administrative staff, as an ordinary part of their job. In agreement with our first chief executive, Peter Handcock, I decided that we would carry the single-organization model into the new tribunal structure. As I explained in an early note to the senior judges, while my general position was that 'judges should judge and administrators should administer', the boundaries were blurred, and the only real answer was a partnership between them.

Things have moved on since then. The more that tribunals and their judges were assimilated to their court counterparts, the less easy it became to defend the logic of a tribunal administration completely separate from that of the courts. Financial stringency also played its part. In early 2010 the government decided to bring the two together in a combined HM Courts and Tribunal Service. This had the inevitable consequence that the office of the Senior President had to be separated from the rest of the tribunals administration, and assimilated in practice to that of the Lord Chief Justice, although formally distinct as the statute required. My initial misgivings were much allayed by the appointment of Peter Handcock as the first chief executive of the combined service. Equally important was the creation of a new Courts' and Tribunals' Board, under a strong independent chairman, and with equal representation of judges and senior administrators. The first chairman, Bob Ayling, rightly insisted on clear authority from the LCJ and the Lord Chancellor before he would accept the post. It is too early to judge the success of this model, but from my early experience as a member of the board (before I moved to the Supreme Court) I am very optimistic.

The assimilation of the offices of the LCJ and the Senior President has had other positive consequences. One, of course, was the creation of the Judicial College, which offers great opportunities by combining the educational experience and the financial resources of the two constituent bodies. Another was the establishment of a much stronger and professional human resources team within the judicial office, whose work includes fulfilling the statutory welfare responsibilities of the LCJ and Senior President. There are many areas in which the functions of court and tribunal judges overlap, and it makes sense to provide joint services. I was in the end fully persuaded of the merits of combining our forces and resources.

Going back to the tribunal reform project, I would emphasize that it was judge-led from the outset. We were helped by the enthusiastic support of successive Lord Chancellors, and generally the lack of any serious political controversy. It started with the initial report of Sir Andrew Leggatt, and the government White Paper, which revealed the strong influence of Lord Justice Henry Brooke as judge in charge of modernization. After my appointment, I established a series of working groups led by senior tribunal judges, working closely with the MOJ officials, to develop the statutory framework in the bill, and then when it was enacted to fill in the details of the new structure. I find it hard to think of any feature of the final package which did not accord with judicial thinking (except possibly the separation of the War Pensions jurisdiction into a single chamber, resulting from a late rebellion by some military leaders in the House of Lords. Even that, I think in retrospect, worked out for the best).

The sense of partnership between judges and administrators was important in helping to give a sense of cohesion and shared purpose to the new organization. Not everyone had been convinced of the merits of bringing such an apparently disparate collection of jurisdictions into a single organization. But as Leggatt had envisaged, it brought collective strength and a sense of common purpose to our dealings both with the courts and with the MOJ and other government departments, and a shared determination to work together for the improvement of the service for our users.

The chambers' structure has proved very effective, and could perhaps be replicated elsewhere in the judicial system. It gave the chamber presidents the power and authority to look in detail at the workings of their different jurisdictions, and to develop innovative ways of improving things. You can see plenty of examples in the Senior President annual reports. Although issued in my name, these were largely compilations of reports from the chamber presidents. This was not just laziness on my part. I was keen that the chamber presidents should take responsibility, and credit, for what they had achieved. It has also resulted in a valuable and personal historical record of how much has been done to strengthen and reform the different sections of the new tribunal system.

Let me take two examples. An obvious priority for action was the Mental Health Review Tribunal, now part of the Health, Education, and Social Care Chamber (HESC). It had been inherited from the Department of Health in a depressingly dysfunctional condition, evidenced by the regularity and volume of complaints to the Council on Tribunals. The client base was unusual—some of the most vulnerable people in society, but also some of the most dangerous. Unusual also was the need to bring the tribunal to the appellants, rather than the other way round. On the plus side were a very strong force of part-time judges and specialist members, and the availability of legal aid, and in consequence a small body of experienced and dedicated professional representatives.

What was needed was much better organization and leadership on both judicial and administrative sides. Both were quickly addressed, and the service has, I believe, been transformed. The ineffective and demoralized London-based administration was replaced in Leicester, where there was already a highly skilled and much more stable team of administrative staff dealing with a number of other tribunal jurisdictions. On the judicial side, the new chamber president, Judge Phillip Sycamore, identified the need for a core team of full-time specialist judges, to work with the administrators to improve direction, efficiency, and case management. This was not to diminish the importance of the part-timers, but to provide better coordination. The economic case was made to the Lord Chancellor, and with the active cooperation of the Judicial Appointments Commission a core group of salaried judges has been appointed, all of very high quality.

A duty-judge scheme was also introduced whereby salaried judges would base themselves on two to three days a week with the administration in Leicester. As Judge Sycamore says in the 2011 annual report:

> Duty judges deal more swiftly and efficiently with queries and case manage in situ with listing and booking teams … Another benefit … is the training opportunity provided to administrative staff as the duty judge is on hand to explain queries leading to a broader understanding of the work of the tribunal …[7]

There was a quite different challenge in another part of the tribunal system, again serving clients from the most vulnerable and needy sections of society. These were the former social security tribunals, now incorporated into the new Social Entitlement Chamber of the First Tier Tribunal. In numbers of cases it is one of the most important parts of the justice system, handling several hundred thousand cases a year, nearly all small in monetary terms, but of critical and often urgent importance to the appellants. Unlike the mental health jurisdictions, legal representation is the exception. The challenge for the judges and specialist members is very great. They need to be on top of some fairly complex regulations, and, to get through the numbers, cases must be dealt with quickly and economically, but fairly and sympathetically.

Shortly after the establishment of the new chamber, the new chamber president, Judge Robert Martin, was faced with an unprecedented rise in the volume of projected appeals—from 240,000 in 2008–9 to over 400,000 in 2010–11, and increasing thereafter. This was largely attributable to legislative change, notably the introduction of Employment and Support Allowance (ESA), to replace incapacity benefit, leading to the need for many redeterminations and many more appeals.

---

[7] The Senior President of Tribunals' Annual Report 2011, at 45.

In this case our most important client, apart from the individual claimants, was the Department for Work and Pensions (DWP). We needed their active cooperation not only to make reliable estimates of the likely demand, but if possible to stem the flow. Accurate projections were vital for recruitment. We needed to work with the JAC to expand rapidly our force of judges and specialist members, particularly doctors, and to train them. As Robert Martin explains in the 2012 annual report, the combined strategy of expanding judicial capacity, and improving productivity, has enabled the chamber to increase its disposals from 245,000 in 2008–9 to a projected 460,000 in 2011–12. I would be surprised if there is any other part of the judicial system (here or indeed anywhere in the world) which has coped so successfully with expanding demand of this scale, without loss of judicial quality.

At the other end, to encourage better decision-making and reconsideration with the Department, and so diminish the flow of appeals, the chamber president, with my agreement, was instrumental in helping to set up a working group, including representatives of the department, the Tribunal Service, and the judges. Some thought that the direct involvement of judges in an exercise of this kind might compromise judicial independence. To me it was common sense. We could not sit back and let ourselves be engulfed in the flood while our claimants were left to struggle without rights or redress. In response, the DWP started a number of programmes designed to improve decision-making, including a 'super-reconsideration' initiative which led to some 7,000 cases under appeal being revised in the appellant's favour without the need for a hearing.

You may think I have gone on too long about tribunals. But the challenges are essentially the same in all parts, and at all levels, of the judicial system. Institutional independence has given us both the freedom and the responsibility to rethink our own roles as judges, and the way we are serving the public. It is no longer enough for us simply to sit back and decide cases that are put in front of us by the administration. We are providing a varied service for a varied market. It is for us as judges to identify the needs of that market and to work with the administrators to ensure that our service meets those needs, and to make sure that the public understand what we are doing.

Let me end by a reference to another important section of the civil judiciary catering for a very different market—those now accommodated in the ultra-modern Rolls Building. In October 2011 Mr Justice

Vos (now Lord Justice Vos) gave a characteristically powerful lecture under the title 'The Role of UK Judges in the Success of UK plc'. His theme was the vital importance to the commercial success and standing of this country, nationally and internationally, of the quality of our justice system, and the central role of the judges in protecting and improving it. As he put it:

> Judges are not—contrary to popular belief—just lawyers that are past their sell-by-date. I like to think they hold, not only an extremely privileged, but also an extremely important, position as the guardians of our legal system. It is the judges' responsibility to ensure that our legal system is fit-for-purpose ... The judges have significant influence on the regulation of both lawyers and other professionals. They can do much to make and keep the legal system the envy of the world.

I would like to think that our legal system can be the envy of the world at all levels—not just in the way it deals with Russian billionaires, but in the way it deals with all sections of the community. It is our job as modern judges to make sure that happens.

10

Improving the Delivery of Justice in the Shadow of Magna Carta

*Lord Justice Ryder**

This chapter is based upon a speech first delivered in Washington, DC on 13 November 2015.

Alfred North Whitehead, a Cambridge philosopher, once said: 'The safest general characterization of the European philosophical tradition is that it consists of a series of footnotes to Plato.'[1] And Plato's works? They have been said to be nothing more than footnotes to Homer.[2]

While some historians would no doubt say that Magna Carta is of little practical relevance today, I think it can safely be said, as generalisations go, that the development of the Anglo-American common law has been carried out in the shadow of—if not as footnotes to—Magna Carta.

No doubt a judge faced today with an argument based on the provisions in Magna Carta would take Chief Justice Roberts's approach. Last November he noted, 'If you're citing Magna Carta in a brief before the Supreme Court of the United States, or in an argument, you're in pretty bad shape ... We like our authorities a little more current.'[3] The same is true in England and Wales. The common law, however,

---

* I wish to thank Dr John Sorabji for all his help in preparing this lecture.

[1] Alfred North Whitehead, *Process and Reality: An Essay in Cosmology* (1929), Part II, Chapter 1, section 1.
[2] D. Hall, 'Whitehead, Rorty, and the Return of the Exiled Poets', in J. Polanowski and D. Sherburne, eds., *Whitehead's Philosophy: A Documentary History* (2004), at 83.
[3] J. Roberts cited in J. Bravin, 'Chief Justice Roberts Wishes Magna Carta an Early Happy 800th Birthday', *Wall Street Journal Law Blog*, 5 November 2014, at http://blogs.wsj.com/law/2014/11/05/justice-roberts-wishes-magna-carta-an-early-happy-800th-birthday.

is wider than cases and authorities. It rests on common values, a common tradition, and a common jurisprudential approach—the common law method of precedent arrived at through an adversarial process.

Magna Carta gives one of the earliest expressions of those common values: of our belief in the idea that no one is above the law, that a just society is one governed by the rule of law (if I can borrow from John Adams that we live under a government of laws, just laws, not men[4]); of our belief in representative government—its chapter 14 foreshadowing a famous demand made here that taxation rests upon representation; and of our belief in open markets. The last may surprise you. I do not suggest that its draftsman and John's barons were adherents of a nascent Chicago school approach to economic liberalism, i.e. that they were early incarnations of Milton Friedman. If we pay attention, however, to chapters 25 and 33, 41 and 42, and their emphasis on ensuring the free movement of trade goods within and across borders, the free movement of tradesmen (businesses) through prohibiting the application of tolls on them upon entry into the state, we can certainly see an early essay into the realms of free trade.

Common values can always find expression in many different ways. A government of laws can take the form of a constitutional republic or a constitutional monarchy. Representative democracy can be presidential in nature or parliamentary. Constitutions can be codified or uncodified. They can have the status of fundamental law, or that idea can be absent, as it is in the United Kingdom. Although here it is worth pausing to consider that at an early stage Magna Carta in one of its versions was accorded a status akin to that which the US Constitution has: that of fundamental law. In 1368 Edward III enacted a statute that confirmed the Charter. It stated, 'The [Magna Carta] … be holden and kept at all points; and if there be any statute made to the contrary, it shall be holden for none.'[5] Statutes enacted inconsistent with Magna Carta would be, in other words, unconstitutional. While that provision remained in force until 1863, the idea that laws could be struck down based upon that provision or the common law did not take hold in England and Wales.

---

[4] J. Adams, *The Works of John Adams* (1851), Vol. 4, Novanglus, Essay no 7, at 106.
[5] 2 Edw. 3, *c*.1.

Despite Chief Justice Sir Edward Coke's attempt in Dr Bonham's Case,[6] the idea that courts could embark upon the judicial review of legislation never became a feature of our constitutional settlement. We never had a *Marbury v Madison*[7] moment. We did not because, as Associate Justice Matthews rightly captured it in an extended discussion of Magna Carta in *Hurtado v California* (1884), the check on Parliamentary supremacy in the United Kingdom was Parliament itself through 'the power of a free public opinion represented by the Commons'.[8]

Common values, different expression, then. And equally, common expression. Both our constitutions secure a rigorous application of the doctrine of separation of powers. Courts and an independent judiciary exercise the judicial power of the state; something to which Magna Carta's demand that only those learned in the law be appointed as judges and that the court should be separated from the King's court provides an early commitment.[9] And the courts? Their approach is governed by a deep-seated commitment to, as the 1354 version of Magna Carta put it, 'due process of law';[10] in US terms, to the Constitution's procedural due-process guarantees.[11] In modern parlance in England and Wales, procedural justice.[12]

But shadows can lengthen; they can become more defined. Equally, they can become fuzzy over time; they can recede. Commitments can fade over time, as we forget their basis or the values they articulate. I think I can safely say that even without celebrating its anniversary this year, the common values that flow through and from Magna Carta remain strong within our two nations. The question is, can we improve the means by which we give life to those values? Our courts, for instance, articulate commitments to equality before the law to effective access to justice.

Can we take steps to better realise them? I believe we have to do so. We cannot but seek to improve how our courts deliver justice. We have to do so because any weakening of our justice systems creates a weakening of our civil society. It starts on the road back before Magna Carta, where men, not laws, governed. As Associate Justice Felix Frankfurter put it, and I am sure we all agree, 'There can be

---

[6] (1610) 8 Co. Rep 113b.   [7] 5 U.S. 137 (1803).
[8] 110 U.S. 516 (1884) 531–2.
[9] 10 Magna Carta 1215, Chapters 17 and 45.   [10] 28 Edw. 3, *c*.3.
[11] US Constitution, 5th and 14th Amendment.
[12] Magna Carta 1215, Chapters 3 and 40.

no free society without law administered through an independent judiciary.'[13] If the law is to be so administered, then the very task of governance that is required necessitates a continuing scrutiny of the efficacy of the institution to assure the respect that it needs to function, with the consequence that we cannot but look to the possibility of reforming our justice systems. In England and Wales we have recently embarked upon such a reform programme. It is not reform for reform's sake. Our aim is clear. We intend to ensure our courts and our tribunals are better equipped to deliver fair and high-quality justice, are better able to realise Magna Carta's values and to secure the rule of law that underpins our free and open society. How do we propose to do so? I will suggest that the reforms should have three limbs: (a) the creation of one system of justice, (b) the development of one judiciary, and (c) the enhancement of access to specialist justice. I want to take the three in turn.

'There can be no equal justice where the kind of trial a man gets depends on the amount of money he has.'[14] So said the US Supreme Court in *Griffin v Illinois*, another case that made specific reference to Magna Carta, noting how it gave expression to the unceasing desire to 'move closer' to the goal of providing 'equal justice for poor and rich, weak and powerful alike'.[15] That goal is given expression in England and Wales in what the common law has long acknowledged to be the constitutional right of access to justice, available to and guaranteed for all citizens.[16]

It is, of course, one thing to proclaim your commitment to equal access to justice. It is another to transform that formal commitment into a substantive, lived, reality. Effecting the transformation requires there to be clarity and certainty in the law; access to independent legal advice, which is both readily available and affordable; and access to a first-class system of readily accessible courts and tribunals. A complete answer would, however, need to take account of all three issues. I can only focus on the last of the three today.

In England and Wales our court system—county court, High Court, and Court of Appeal—is, bar one recent formalistic and one substantive change, the product of reforms carried out in the

---

[13]   *United States v United Mine Workers* 330 U.S. 258; [1947] 312.
[14]   351 U.S. 12 (1956), 19.   [15]   351 U.S. 12 (1956), 16.
[16]   *Bremer Vulkan Schiffbau und Maschinenfabrik v South India Shipping Corp. Ltd* [1981] AC 909, 977.

nineteenth century. The formalistic change was the merger in 2013 of the various county courts into a single county court for England and Wales. The substantive change was the creation of a new single Family Court in the same year. We live with a Victorian and post-Victorian superstructure, one which not only applies to the court structure but equally to court processes, buildings, and the nature of hearings.

Things are more modern in the tribunals, which is to say the Upper and First Tier Tribunal. Unlike the courts, their jurisdiction is primarily United Kingdom-wide. The reason for this is that they have, in the present form, only been in existence since 2007. Prior to that the United Kingdom had what could best be described as a patchwork quilt of many specialist tribunals, each of which had their own jurisdiction, and differing origins in substance, time, and personnel.[17] They can be traced to 1908, and the creation of what was then the local pension committee established under the Old Age Pensions Act of that year.[18]

In legal terms they are a recent innovation. Their procedures differ from those in the courts, with greater flexibility and accessibility, in some cases a more inquisitorial or investigative approach and, for instance, no general expectation that lawyers represent parties. Their jurisdictions are limited in scope, in contrast to courts of general jurisdiction. The Employment Tribunal is, for instance, limited in jurisdiction to employment disputes. Their personnel differ from the courts, as they are not only constituted of the judiciary but also of non-judicial members who are experts from the field for which they have responsibility.

In 2007 the patchwork quilt was rewoven.[19] The various tribunals, with one or two notable exceptions, were merged into a new hierarchical structure. The tribunals became chambers. Greater use of judicial personnel from the courts became the norm, while use of specialists remained at the heart of the system. The office of Senior President of Tribunals was created, with equivalent responsibilities to those of the Lord Chief Justice of England and Wales, to provide leadership for the tribunals judiciary. In essence, as occurred with the courts in the 1870s, out of the many a single tribunals justice system was forged.

---

[17] See Chapter 8 above.
[18] Edward Jacobs, *Tribunal Practice and Procedure* (3rd edn, Legal Action Group, 2014), at 3.
[19] See Chapter 9 above.

Like the courts, however, the tribunals also rely on a post-Victorian superstructure. Their case-management processes remain, primarily, paper-based. Hearings take place in buildings inherited from the recent, and sometimes not so recent, past. In 2015 we thus have two complementary justice systems, both of which are to a significant extent products of our past.

The question, the pressing question, we are faced with today is how to ensure that these justice systems are best able to act as one, to provide one system of first-class justice for all our citizens. It is particularly pressing today because, unlike at any time in our past, this question—and the reforms it will and cannot but necessitate—arise against a recasting of the state subsequent to the financial crisis of 2008. We can answer this question in a number of ways. I will only outline three.

First, we must not only recognise that clarity and simplicity have to be central to court and tribunal processes, we have to achieve it. In the past we have attempted this through rendering rules of procedure as simple as possible. Experience shows that where this succeeds, it does not always last. Rules like substantive law accrete precedent as readily as a ship's hull attracts barnacles. Equally, rules can all too often become an obstacle to justice as they can become the basis for adversarial skirmishing by parties in an attempt to win on procedural grounds. In an era where large numbers of litigants are unable to secure the assistance of lawyers, the need to avoid such eventualities becomes all the more pressing. It does so because complex rules can become a barrier to effective access to those without expert legal advice, obtaining thereby a procedural advantage in litigation for those who are represented unless the court or tribunal is astute to intervene. The result is an absence of equal justice in anything other than the formal sense. How can we overcome this problem?

For those with long memories, Dean Clark famously called for the then recently introduced US Federal Rules of Procedure to be 'the handmaid of justice'.[20] In doing so he consciously echoed Collins MR's earlier comment to the same effect: rules were to be the means by which substantive justice was achieved.[21] Today we seek to achieve this through ensuring that our procedural rules are governed by an

---

[20] C. Clark, 'The Handmaid of Justice' (1938) 23 *Washington University Law Quarterly Review* 297.
[21] *Re Coles* [1907] 1 K.B. 1, 4.

overriding objective—similar in concept to Rule 1 of the Federal Rules, which Dean Clark did so much to devise. That overriding objective calls on the civil courts to do more than secure substantive justice in individual cases. It calls on the courts to manage process with that aim in mind, but equally with the aim of securing economy and efficiency in litigation, of securing equality of arms, consistent with a commitment to proportionality. Not only must the process be proportionate to the cost, complexity, and value, among other things, of an individual case, but also access to the process must be distributed equitably across all those who need to call upon the justice system. Our rules still require process to be the servant of substantive justice, but they require the courts to take account of the need to be that servant in all cases, not just the one in front of the court at any one time. Substantive justice is as much now a function of distributive as of corrective justice.

This instrumentalist aim should lead us to develop our procedure in new ways, and ones that for the first time take full account of developments in information technology. This could be accomplished in a number of ways. At the present time we have a number of different means of commencing proceedings across the courts and tribunals, depending on the relevant rules of procedure. We have different rules on service and due notice, and for filing documents with the court and serving them on other parties. In each case the process is, as I mentioned earlier, primarily paper-based.

These processes are, given their nature, labour-intensive for the courts and tribunal administration. They are equally labour-intensive for litigants, and in the case of lawyer-less litigants they are not as easy to follow as they could be. In order to further the aim of securing greater distributive justice, we could take a step that both Collins MR and Dean Clark would have well understood. We could merge the initial aspects of our various processes into a single, common process just as we once replaced the individual procedures contained in the common law forms of action into a single action. This common process would not be paper-based. It would be IT-based.

Litigants should in the future be able to access a courts and tribunals website, through which they can initiate proceedings and pay the relevant fee, and do so through the use of intuitive, simple-to-use Web forms. This should then form the basis of effective service either by the litigant or by the court, the starting point for the generation of procedural timetables unique to the proceedings, the electronic court file, and e-based case management. As has recently been suggested by Sir Brian Leveson, the President of the Queen's Bench Division of our High Court, assistance should be made available to litigants via the use of digital navigators to help them use the new system.[22]

A single Web-based system, leading into e-filing and management, will help to secure a more efficient and economic system, thus ensuring that the State's resources can be targeted properly across the justice system. It will also ensure that litigants, whether they have lawyers to assist them or not and irrespective of their financial resources, can access the system on an equal footing. The existence of e-prompts, where procedural deadlines are imminent; the use of e-receipts and notification to the court and the parties when procedural obligations have been completed (or remain incomplete); and the use of plain language with easy-to-understand instructions should all go towards minimising the possibility that rules will become tripwires for the unwary or the inexperienced. Greater use of the Internet should enable the justice system to better achieve its objective of securing substantive justice for all those who need to call upon the courts and tribunals.

Greater use of the Internet will make the justice system generally more accessible in another way. Going to court can be a daunting prospect for many of our citizens. The daunting can translate into inaction; into rights not being vindicated, into abuse of private and public rights remaining unchallenged and effectively unchallengeable. Process in the court system should not contribute to citizens failing to seek redress when their rights are interfered with. The growth of the Internet has meant that more and more of us are familiar with buying, selling, and complaining online. Whether we are buying through a Web supplier or direct from businesses, selling via eBay or similar Web platforms, writing reviews or emailing our complaints about a service direct to the source, most of us are at home on the Net. That we are suggests to me that an Internet-based process to initiate and manage proceedings will be something that individuals will be at home with, to a far greater extent than the previous paper-based process. Greater use of the Internet can thus be harnessed to increase access to justice.

This leads me to my second point. Increasing use of the Internet and information technology generally should enable us to reform another aspect of our post-Victorian superstructure: our court estate.

---

[22] Brian Leveson, *Justice in the 21st Century* (9 October 2015), at [46]; see www.judiciary.gov.uk/wpcontent/uploads/2015/10/pqbd-caroline-weatherill-lecture-2.pdf.

It could do so in at least two ways. First, the replacement of paper filing systems with e-filing should enable a reduction in the need for back-office space. We can thus modernise our court buildings, making better use of our space. As importantly, we can reduce the number of times when litigants and their lawyers have to physically attend court. Moving a significant amount of pre-trial (not trial) process online, while promoting the use of technology to enable hearings to be virtual, will arguably reduce the need to maintain some of our post-Victorian court estate. Use of the Internet should in itself, through greater familiarity with it among the public, open up access, and just as importantly, through reducing the cost and time spent on court appearances, bring the price of justice within the reach of more citizens than has historically been the case.

This is intrinsically linked with my third point. Increasing use of technology will enable us to realise an expansion of justice in more than the formal sense. It will enable the court system to create a multi-door courthouse—again, an idea first developed here in the United States. Procedural reforms across our justice system—whether it is the promotion of mediation and conciliation in civil and family proceedings, or the promotion of the more accessible means of dispute resolution through the tribunals justice system—have been moving us towards this idea for the last thirty years. Effective use of technology will enable us to assess claims when they are issued to determine whether they are suitable for resolution by means other than formal adjudication, to assist the parties to select the appropriate method of resolution and manage the claim appropriately. Equally, it will enable us to direct those claims that are unsuitable for non-formal adjudication to the appropriate litigation track with the procedure tailored to the claim's needs, while also enabling claims to move back to that track if consensual resolution is not achieved. In this way we could expand access to justice through facilitating an expansion in our concept of justice, and ensure that the justice system's resources are targeted proportionately.

Taken together—modernisation of process, greater use of technology, the expansion of justice opportunities—should, with careful planning and proper implementation, enable us to provide a system of justice that is first-class, accessible, and appropriate in nature for all citizens. It will enable us to replace our present structures, physical and procedural, with ones fit for the Information Age of the twenty-first century in just the same way as we replaced a justice system that evolved to serve a medieval agrarian society with one fit for the Industrial Age in the nineteenth century. Means and method may change, but the aim remains to forge a system that is best able to secure the rule of law.

This leads me to my second substantive subject: one judiciary. The structure of our judiciary is again a product of a long inheritance. As such it has developed what can only be described as true complexity. This is characterised in a number of ways. One way to categorise our judiciary is by reference to the courts and tribunals. In the former courts, judges sit. In the latter, judges of the First Tier and Upper Tribunals sit, as do non-legal members of the tribunals. On the surface a straightforward distinction. But courts' judges are also judges of the tribunals, although they can only sit there in accordance with directions given by me, as Senior President of Tribunals, and under arrangements made by the Lord Chief Justice. Tribunals' judges can sit as judges in some of the courts, again in accordance with various deployment and assignment procedures.

Another way to categorise the judiciary is hierarchically. In the courts, the Lord Chief Justice, Master of the Rolls and other heads of division, and Lord and Lady Justices of Appeal are judges of the Court of Appeal. More than that, we are the Court of Appeal and vice versa. The same is the case for High Court judges and the High Court. In our county court sit circuit judges and district judges sitting as judges of that court. They are not the court. Fairly straightforward. To a degree. The seeming simplicity is undone by the fact that some, but not all, of the heads of division are also judges of the High Court: they too are the High Court and vice versa. All the Court of Appeal and High Court judges are also—among a whole host of other types of judge, including tribunals' judges, judges of the county court.

A similar pattern can be seen in the tribunals. Again a superficial straightforward hierarchy is underpinned by a complex web that enables certain judges to sit in all levels of the structure.

A third way in which the structure could be characterised is by reference to the various statutory provisions that enable judges to be authorised to sit in different courts and tribunals to those to which they were appointed. In some cases these authorisations are horizontal, for example to enable a circuit judge whose primary appointment is to sit in the county court to sit in the Family Court. In other cases it enables the judge to sit in a higher court, for instance a circuit judge can sit, if authorised, in the Crown Court (our superior criminal court), the High Court, and the Court of Appeal Criminal Division.

So far I have only concentrated on the judges. In addition, we have High Court officers—the Queen's Bench and chancery masters and the registrars: officers who exercise judicial functions, the inspiration for United States special masters and magistrates. When they sit in the High Court they are officers of the court, but when they sit—as they can in the county court—they are judges of the county court. And then there are multiple types of deputy judge, practitioners who sit as judges on a part-time, fee-paid basis in a variety of different courts and tribunals.

This picture is less than ideal, which is not to suggest that it does not work. It does. What it does, though, is carry with it a number of practical problems. First, it requires an otherwise unnecessarily complex set of arrangements to be put in place and carefully maintained to ensure that judges are properly authorised to sit in various courts and tribunals.

Second, it carries with it limitations on sitting arrangements that are a product of history. The Master of the Rolls, for instance, unlike the High Court heads of division, is not a judge of the High Court. He can only sit in that court if specifically authorised to do so by the Lord Chief Justice. The rationale for this was Sir George Jessel MR, a dominating figure in the courts in the late nineteenth century. As Master of the Rolls he was both a judge of the High Court and Court of Appeal. He preferred the High Court, and from 1873 to 1881 he sat there rather than in the Court of Appeal. In 1881, when Lord Justice James died, the remaining Lords Justice of Appeal did not feel up to sitting on appeals from Jessel MR's decisions.[23]

The answer was provided by Parliament when it enacted the Supreme Court of Judicature Act 1881. One of its provisions transformed the office of Master of the Rolls into one that is solely as a judge of the Court of Appeal. No longer would other Court of Appeal judges worry about having to pass judgment on his decisions. Less picturesque examples of restrictions that lack any real modern necessity exist in abundance.

If we are to improve the delivery of justice, one contribution to that aim might be a reconsideration of this complex web of judicial offices. We could look to rationalising the number of offices. What justification can there be, for instance, to continue to appoint different types

---

[23] Lord Evershed, *The Court of Appeal in England* (1950), at 12.

of judge who can sit in the same level of court and tribunal? A modern system ought not to maintain artificial distinctions, particularly if they serve no proper purpose and if they arguably hinder deployment and inhibit the individual judge's career opportunities.

Our starting point ought to be one of principle: we need to maintain our commitment to an independent and impartial judiciary, one appointed on merit, and with the right mix of abilities, knowledge, and skills. We should aim for as simple a structure as is consistent with that aim. We should be looking to maintain a judicial hierarchy, one that maintains the constitutional role of the senior judiciary—the Court of Appeal and High Court judges—while developing a structure of judges below that level who are capable of sitting as judges across courts and tribunals of comparable level. A framework that enables flexible deployment to maximise opportunity and efficiency and facilitate those judges with leadership responsibilities being able to plan, allocate and distribute work between judges; to plan future recruitment; and to better implement judicial training to improve skills and facilitate merit-based promotions.

Magna Carta called for judges to 'know the law of the realm'.[24] We need to work towards creating one judiciary, capable of enabling the right judge to be able to sit in the right court or tribunal on the right case. In this way, we can ensure that those judges who know the law of the realm are always able to deliver justice in as efficient and effective a manner as possible.

But reform is only part of the story. It must be complemented by quality; that is, a drive to ensure that our judiciary is capable of recognising and applying good practice and innovating and developing their specialist knowledge.

Innovation and the judiciary are perhaps two things which are not ordinarily seen as going hand in hand. The legal profession and the judiciary are typically understood to be conservative forces, in the sense that they resist change. The extent to which this is true is, of course, a matter of debate. But as stereotypes go it is one that persists.

Our duty to secure the rule of law, it seems to me, more than suggests that we have to be capable of innovation. We cannot simply assume that our duty is discharged by deciding cases, as central as that is to the judicial role. The judicial power of the state requires more. Sitting back and adjudicating on issues and evidence presented

---

[24] Magna Carta 1215, Chapter 45.

by well-briefed, skilled advocates is one thing. Such situations are not always the case. All too often we are called upon to determine disputes where one or more parties are without legal representation. As such we have to be more than the referee in an adversarial process. We may need to be more investigative; we may need to take active steps to secure equality of arms. Within the arena of family justice in England and Wales we have been developing such techniques. We have had to innovate, to learn from other jurisdictions. We have had to change to a problem-solving approach, so that we are able to undertake the proper identification of the issues in dispute, control the evidence needed, and in certain cases question witnesses.

Such innovation is only the starting point. If we are to see the justice system become an IT-based, multi-door system, we will need to develop the necessary skills and techniques to ensure it works as best it can. A problem-solving approach in court will have to be matched by a problem-solving approach to case management.

The development and use of specialist knowledge has always been a hallmark of the tribunals judiciary. It is an ever-present feature of the courts judiciary. This is of crucial importance for two reasons.

First, harnessing specialist knowledge is a key means by which we can foster innovation. Knowledge of approaches from other jurisdictions underpins the development of collaborative justice in the family courts, such that the court-controlled inquisition becomes a collaborative inquisition between the judge and other professionals and the parties themselves. What we learn in one area or from one source can be applied creatively in others.

Second, as we develop new techniques and new ways of delivering justice, new demands will be placed on the judiciary. Judges will have to understand their caseload to a greater extent than in the past; be able to identify features of cases that are out of the ordinary; and be able to predict, react to, and actively direct cases in order to try and achieve the best-quality outcome in each case. That outcome may or may not be an adjudicated judgment.

That will depend on the nature of the case. We will need specialist skills and knowledge to best achieve such results for litigants and the state.

My starting point in this chapter was Magna Carta. I have strayed far from it. In doing so, however, I have tried to sketch out a number of ways in which we are trying to reshape our justice system in order to better realise its commitment to equality before the law, to better enable us to secure the rule of law. At the start of his famous treatise *A Theory of Justice*, John Rawls commented that 'laws and institutions, no matter how efficient and well-arranged, must be reformed or abolished if they are unjust',[25] or, as he might have gone on to say, if they produced injustice.

The reforms and potential reforms I have outlined will no doubt embed greater efficiency in our justice system. Equally, they aim at ensuring that the system is as 'well arranged' as it can be in the Internet Age. We seek these reforms not because efficiency and a more robust structure are our aims. We do so in order that our courts and tribunals are better able to deliver justice. 'Justice the first virtue of our social institutions' is a living virtue that has to be available to all substantively and not merely formally.[26] We seek it so that Magna Carta's shadow remains strong in the twenty-first century.

---

[25] John Rawls, *A Theory of Justice* (revised edition, 1999), at 3, 18.
[26] Ibid., 25.

11

The Modernization of Access to Justice in Times of Austerity

*Lord Justice Ryder**

This chapter is based upon a speech first delivered at the University of Bolton on 3 March 2016.

Back in the autumn of 2012, when the country was basking in its Olympic glories, I spoke about the importance of respect for the autonomy of our citizens and the opportunities then before us to modernize our family justice system.[1] Since then, reports and speeches (in particular about public—including legal—policy) have become ever more sombre in focus. The word 'austerity' seems to creep into the titles and text of most major addresses we now hear. Following Sartre, I will follow the crowd in order to be different.

I take this approach for a very important reason. It is one that I expect the Lord Chancellor and his colleagues in Cabinet would recognize and I would like to explore the point with you. It is in many ways a simple reason. The point about 'austerity' is this. What is right, is right; what is fair, is fair; and what is just, is just. Justice has no second class: even in an age of austerity.

Too often, though, we tend to continue with the established, the traditional, way of realizing these aims and objectives because they are the established, the traditional, ways. We may tweak systems. We may revise aspects of our approach in the face of individual problems, but we tend to do so within an established frame of reference. We tend

---

* I wish to thank Dr John Sorabji for all his help in preparing this lecture.
[1] Lecture delivered at Bolton University on 12 November 2012.

to examine fundamental questions only in the face of a crisis. In the nineteenth century we reappraised our court structure—one that had evolved over some 700 to 800 years—in the face of a fifty-year-long crisis of access to justice. We took what on anyone's view was a bold step then, a radical step. We swept away our inheritance and created a single High Court and Court of Appeal for England and Wales.

Austerity, the product of the 2007–8 financial crisis, provides a basis upon which we have had to scrutinize the ways in which we secure the rule of law and the citizen's access to justice as part of that. It provides the spur to rethink our approach from first principles. As such we should not see austerity as the driver of reform. It is not a question of cutting our cloth. It is a question of austerity forcing us to do what it took fifty years of failure in the 1800s to do. To look at our systems, our procedures, our courts, and our tribunals, and ask whether they are the best they can be, and if not, how they can be improved.

Our goal, our objective, remains constant. Austerity has no impact on that, nor could it properly do so. A properly functioning justice system to which citizens have effective access in order to determine and vindicate their rights is a mark of a liberal democracy committed to the rule of law. That is as true now as it was when Lord Diplock articulated the point in the famous *Bremer Vulkan* decision.[2] That is our goal now, as it has always been. Austerity makes us ask the question, how do we better achieve it? That is what I want to focus upon in this chapter.

I have been heavily engaged in reforms being effected to the family justice system. Rather than focusing once more on those reforms, which are now implemented and embedded, I want instead to focus on another, wider-reaching programme of modernization. I am now the Senior President of Tribunals, and my primary focus is the tribunal system, and its reform programme, which exists in a broader change programme affecting all courts and tribunals and which is the largest programme of change in any justice system in the world.

---

[2] *Bremer Vulkan Schiffbau und Maschinenfabrik v South India Shipping Corp. Ltd* [1981] AC 909 at 979: 'Every civilised system of government requires that the state should make available to all its citizens a means for the just and peaceful settlement of disputes between them as to their respective legal rights. The means provided are courts of justice to which every citizen has a constitutional right of access in the role of plaintiff to obtain the remedy which he claims to be entitled to in consequence of an alleged breach of his legal or equitable rights by some other citizen, the defendant.'

In one sense the tribunals provide a very modern system of justice, having evolved over the past hundred years, and having been substantively restructured in 2007 as a result of the Tribunals, Courts and Enforcement Act of that year.[3] Until that time, the tribunals' 'system' (such as it was) represented a veritable patchwork quilt of specialist legal fora managed by departments and agencies across the public sector. Today, it is unified in one First Tier Tribunal and a senior Upper Tribunal, with administrative and executive support from the agency also responsible for running the courts: HM Courts & Tribunals Service.

Tribunals within that unified structure (and in some that are not, for example the Employment Tribunal), fall under the judicial leadership of the Senior President, in which office I am the third incumbent. Within that structure there are some five and a half thousand office holders, judges, and an extraordinary range of expert professional and lay members. To put things in context, across the courts in England and Wales, and excluding for one moment the magistracy, there are around 3,200 judges. Tribunals, therefore, are neither minnows nor in a minority.

The tribunals' systems is, by statutory design as well as of necessity, specialist, innovative, and (by comparison with most of the courts), where appropriate, less formal. Its processes are often inquisitorial or investigative, rather than the traditional model of adversarial justice. It was designed so that individuals can pursue their claims without having to resort to lawyers, although this is not to say that lawyers are absent from the system or that we seek to have a lawyer-free zone. Far from it, lawyers will have an increasingly important role to play in design, development, and facilitation.

Tribunals deal with claims, cases and appeals which enable citizens to hold the state to account for the daily decisions taken across a broad and diverse terrain. These are decisions which have a significant impact on people's lives, be they about welfare rights, immigration status, tax decisions, or otherwise.

Tribunals deal with appeals about disability payments, special educational needs for children in schools, compensation for victims of crime, compensating those injured while protecting our country on

---

[3] Edward Jacobs, *Tribunal Practice and Procedure* (2nd edn, Legal Action Group, 2011), at 3. See also Chapters 8 and 9 above.

military service, the determination of rents and charges by landlords in the rental sector, information being held back from public scrutiny, and detention in mental health institutions where vulnerable people lack the capacity to understand why.

In addition to our administrative-law workload, we also determine private-law disputes, for example between employers and their workers, which can involve claims for unpaid wages, accusations of discrimination, or compensation for redundancy or unfair dismissal. Our property and land jurisdictions deal with major infrastructure projects often involving millions of pounds, for example on compulsory purchase.

Tribunals form an integral part of our country's justice system. They are and will continue to be an essential component of the rule of law, and must remain as accessible as possible. Accessibility is, however, not an unchanging construct. As society modernizes, so must the institutions that serve it if they are not to degrade or fall into disuse.

One of the causes of the nineteenth-century crisis in our courts, setting to one side their outdated structure and forms of procedure, was that they failed to respond to changes in society. They were courts that had evolved as part of a largely agrarian society. As we all know, the eighteenth and nineteenth centuries saw massive social changes across the United Kingdom: industrialization and urbanization—the dark satanic mills of Blake's vision, the growth of Cottonpolis in and around Manchester, and of Spindleton, as Bolton was once described[4]—of new forms of business structure, the limited-liability company, widespread use of partnerships, and so on.

Those changes, married to population growth, placed pressures on the courts that simply could not have been met at the pace at which they were then evolving. They called for a different, a better, way of delivering justice, one that was suitable for the Victorian Age. Broadly speaking, we live today with, and within, the terms of that Victorian inheritance. Yet we do not live in a Victorian Age. We live in the Internet Age. Our justice system—and this is as apposite for the tribunals' system notwithstanding the differences that exist between it and the courts' system—needs to evolve. We need a Victorian approach to innovation to move us beyond our Victorian legacy.

---

[4] M. Williams and D. Farnie, *Cotton Mills in Greater Manchester* (Carnegie Publishing Ltd, 1992), at 20.

What, then, are the hallmarks of reform? Coming into my senior presidency, now five months ago, I recognized hallmarks with which no interference was needed: specialist decision making, using innovative and informal techniques, to provide effective and accessible justice for our users.

Without damaging those hallmarks, we can simplify the ways in which justice is done, empowering citizens to put their case forward when they think the state has got it wrong. If a citizen comes to the system, they should be able to negotiate it at their convenience, using the tools and technology they apply in other parts of their life.

We can at the same time improve and modernize the working environment for our judges and specialist members, creating a judiciary which is responsive to the varied and specialist nature of the diverse problems presented. The judiciary should have modern, flexible, digital tools and problem-solving techniques to help them get to the heart of their cases quickly, resolving wrong decisions or weeding out the hopeless case. We should not forget that access to justice is an indivisible right: it is one that applies as much to defendants as it does to claimants. It is as important to ensure that meritorious claims are brought and rights are vindicated, as to ensure that unmeritorious claims are resolved quickly and correctly so as to ensure the least interference with or disruption to the substantive rights of defendants.

Like the citizens it serves, justice can be delivered in many ways— by the most appropriate decision maker; in modern hearing rooms, or in mental health hospital units, community halls, or remote locations; by video link, on laptops, tablets, and smartphones, online, with the citizen and decision maker coming together virtually. It might be said that the idea of delivering justice in such settings is in some sense wrong, that it traduces the majesty of the law. Such potential criticism misses one very important point: justice does not stand outside or above the citizen. To return to an earlier theme, the right to effective access to justice is an important corollary of the autonomy of the citizen and that citizen's responsibilities to and place in society.

Citizens, whether litigants or not, are not supplicants coming to the high hand of judgment. They are rights' bearers. And our justice system should be capable of ensuring that as such they are able to access those rights in an appropriate setting. Justice, and access to it, should lie at the heart of the community. In this it is not the Victorians' legacy we need to learn from, but rather their predecessors who through the development of local justice in local courts, often involving—as it then did—local juries—ensured that the delivery of justice was a feature of the community. Do not get me wrong—this is not about local buildings or the court and tribunal estate—that would be an entirely superficial and simplistic way of characterizing access to justice. This is about recognizing the way that we live in a digital society and responding accordingly. With modern methods, effective use of IT, we ought to be creating—re-creating—local justice. This will be a justice system where many sizes fit all; not one size for all. A much simpler system of justice, with the judiciary at its heart, citizens empowered to access it, using innovation and digital tools to resolve these cases quickly, authoritatively and efficiently.

That is our aim and I would like to talk to you about the detail that underpins that vision, and demonstrate that progress towards it is not only possible, but also necessary, whether we live in times of austerity or not.

Since becoming Senior President, I have explored the potential for modernization under three key themes: one coherent and seamless justice system, one flexible and efficient judiciary, and a focus on better outcomes for users. The aim is to ensure that cases which end up before the system are dealt with fairly by the right person or people, with the right expertise, in a timely and efficient fashion. Let me take each point in turn.

ONE SYSTEM

To serve the needs of a twenty-first-century society, the justice system must be digital by default and design. Some progress has been made towards digitizing elements of process already. In Employment Tribunals, the vast majority of new claims are now commenced online. Our Immigration and Asylum Appeals can also be issued through an online portal. There are portals for users in the courts, too: Money Claims Online has been in operation since 2001 and has over 180,000 users annually. But once the 'submit' button is pressed by the user or their representative, a civil servant at the other end has to print the e-form, and make up a paper file. From that point on, we are back to square one: almost back to the Dickensian model of justice via the quill pen.

The creation of online justice cannot therefore simply be a matter of digitizing what might be called the frontline processes. It must go further than that. It must properly embrace what is described as online dispute resolution. This concept can cover two distinct, but linked, ideas. On the one hand it can refer to the creation of an online means to facilitate the settlement of disputes by agreement. Online mediation or negotiation. Such a system exists, for instance, in the Netherlands: the Rechtwijzer 2.0.[5]

It can also refer to an online court or tribunal. Lord Justice Briggs is currently looking at this latter idea as part of his Civil Courts Review. It has been tried before. As I understand it the first such court was created in the United States. It was known as the Michigan Cyber Court, and it was created in 2002. It was to be entirely digital or online. The entire process would take place online. It was also a relatively inexpensive court to set up. It was not, however, a success.[6] Its funding was withdrawn. Let me say straight away, that will not happen to us and there is good reason why it will not.

Michigan's Cyber Court was a development ahead of its time. It is strange to think now—as I imagine you all have a smartphone sitting in your pocket, that you are frequent visitors to Amazon, that you download music rather than buy CDs—that in 2002 the iPhone and the revolution it began were five years away. In 2002 the idea of a digital—a cyber—court was something more at home in Star Wars or Star Trek. The view from today is markedly different. It is an idea that is in tune with the zeitgeist. I doubt that any such court today would meet the same fate as that of Michigan's. It is a concept that will, I suspect, save money by requiring fewer court or tribunal buildings, fewer but better-qualified support staff, and reduced costs for litigants.

I am equally convinced that such an approach will improve the way we do justice. I have seen it do exactly that. There are examples that already work. Goods and services today are transacted virtually. Meetings are facilitated by technology, making the globe seem a much smaller place. And documentation can be shared and revised online between multiple parties, at times convenient to them, without 'opening hours' and the physical constraints of our existing systems and buildings. We are exploring an application of this idea in the tribunals system. It is a concept known as the online continuous hearings. I will soon be trialling this in my Social Entitlement Chamber, which deals with appeals against welfare decisions.

---

[5] See www.hiil.org/project/rechtwijzer.
[6] See http://www.jurist.org/dateline/2012/03/tony-niescier-personal-jurisdiction.php.

It works like this. Change your view of litigation from an adversarial dispute to a problem to be solved. All participants—the appellant, the respondent Government department, which in this case is the Department of Work and Pensions and the tribunal judge—are able to iterate and comment upon the basic case papers online, over a reasonable window of time, so that the issues in dispute can be clarified and explored. There is no need for all the parties to be together in a court or building at the same time. There is no single trial or hearing in the traditional sense. Our new approach is similar to that already used in other jurisdictions, where the trial process is an iterative one that stretches over a number of stages that are linked together. In our model, however, we will not need those stages to take place in separate hearings or indeed, unless it is necessary, any physical, face-to-face hearing at all. We will have a single, digital hearing that is continuous over an extended period of time.

Again, and similar to the practice in other countries and the traditional approach of the tribunals, the judge will take an inquisitorial and problem-solving approach, guiding the parties to explain and understand their respective positions. Once concluded, this iterative approach may allow the judge to make a decision there and then, without the need for a physical hearing, the traditional model to which the system defaults at present. If such a 'hearing' is required, for example to determine a credibility issue, technology could facilitate that too. It may be a virtual hearing.

Digitizing the system is a necessary but, on its own, not sufficient step. If we simply digitized our existing courts and tribunals, and their processes, all we would do is to digitally replicate our existing system. Such an approach would fossilize our Victorian legacy. It would embed and continue into the future the systems of the past, and in so doing carry with it the prospect that we would simply carry forward the problems inherent in those systems.

Digitization presents an opportunity to break with processes that are no longer optimal or relevant and at the same time to build on the best that we have to eliminate structural design flaws and perhaps even the less attractive aspects of a litigation culture. It also provides us with the opportunity to create one system of justice, a seamless system. I firmly believe that a digital-by-default system should not just strive to deliver something that is physically more accessible but also something that is better at solving problems; that is, the 'one-stop shop'. If a litigant, party, or user has a problem, they should be able to come to the system to have that problem resolved. They should not have to compartmentalize their own problem, and run to different parts of the system with each bit. In the 1870s the Victorians swept away the idea that a litigant had to use a distinct form of procedure, unique to each type of claim, each in a different court, some of which had overlapping jurisdictions and different remedies. It is time to complete their work and provide the user with the legal equivalent of a 'one-stop shop'.

Let me elaborate. At the present time different forms and processes apply across courts and tribunals. There are overlapping jurisdictions in a number of areas. The courts and the Employment Tribunal have jurisdiction over employment disputes. The courts and the First Tier Tribunals' Property Chamber have overlapping jurisdiction for certain property disputes. Protected and vulnerable people often need the help of the family courts, the Court of Protection, and Mental Health Tribunals. There are other examples in other jurisdictions.

Such a situation is patently inefficient and a less than ideal way of delivering justice, both for the courts and tribunals and for those who need to have their disputes resolved. Digitization and the development of online courts and tribunals ought to provide the means to eliminate such deficiencies. It should enable the creation of a single point of entry to the justice system. It should facilitate the direction of claims to the right part of the system, which should be shorn of unnecessary duplication. Resources and expertise should be directed to the right part of the system for a particular type of claim, rather than spread across different aspects of it. Rules and processes should be simplified as far as possible; they should be common to all parts of the system where that is justified, and they should be different and specifically tailored where that is necessary. Not one size fits all—but the right size for the right case—delivered through the right process.

ONE JUDICIARY

Systems design is not simply a matter of the best use of technology. It also requires the best use of the judiciary. By this I do not suggest that we should marry technology and the judiciary together and create an algorithm: the digital judge in a digital court. What do I mean?

Across the courts and tribunals we have a breadth and depth of judicial expertise that is in very many ways of unrivalled quality. Our judiciary is widely and rightly respected across the world: for its ability and expertise, its judgment and strength of character. It is something we are rightly proud of.

The question, though, is whether we are making the best use of it. Are we ensuring that the right judge, with the right experience, is able to hear the right case? The power exists to enable this to happen. The Tribunals, Courts and Enforcement Act 2007 and the Crime and Courts Act 2013 provide wide-ranging powers to the Lord Chief Justice and Senior President of Tribunals to enable this to happen. We are working on devising, and testing, the means to best use those powers.

I should stress here the need to test, as this applies across the board. One of the great flaws of our historic approach to reform has been to identify a problem, alight on a perceived solution and then implement it. No one group of people—judiciary, civil servants, or even ministers—should believe that they have the monopoly on what works in a change programme. We must engage our users and our judges to ensure that we have identified the right problems and the sources of the same. We should scrutinize the range of solutions together and evaluate our strategy and our plan to ensure that in their implementation we achieve an effective and efficient system. We are taking this approach to reform. In terms of developing a system for the effective deployment of the judiciary, we are testing what we have discussed. We are, for instance, part way through the development and use of a pilot scheme that will enable the deployment of a number of judges from the Employment Tribunals into the county court. We await the outcome of the scheme to see what we can learn, and what improvements are necessary.

The pilot scheme is not simply an example of ensuring that we are able to use our powers to ensure that judges are deployed to the right court or tribunal. It is more than that. It is a means by which we can enhance judicial expertise. A judge who, on the basis of business need, is deployed from what could be called their home jurisdiction— the court or tribunal in which they normally sit—to a jurisdiction elsewhere will gain valuable experience. They may be deployed into, say, the Property Chamber from the county court, because of their knowledge of property disputes, or be concurrently authorized to sit in all employment jurisdictions or in both mental health and mental capacity jurisdictions.

Flexible deployment and concurrent authorization will provide the opportunity to the user for a 'one-stop-shop' approach to problem solving and to the judiciary for career development by the enhancement of skills, knowledge, and experience as judges deal with a broader range of litigation and take back the good practice they find being used by their colleagues to their home jurisdiction. If expanded across the courts and tribunals system as a whole, such an approach will create—to use the language of human resources—significant 'up-skilling'. Put more simply, we will produce a better-qualified and experienced judiciary, one better able to deliver justice.

So far I have concentrated on the salaried judiciary, those that have permanent positions. The tribunals, and the courts, make significant use of part-time, fee-paid judges. Individuals who, for instance, remain in practice as lawyers, or as practitioners in specialist areas. A more holistic approach to the utilization of such fee-paid judiciary ought to facilitate the development of greater skills and experience both within individual jurisdictions and through multi-jurisdictional specialist groups.

In addition to the better use of both salaried and fee-paid judiciary, we have started to develop and evaluate another feature of the tribunals: the assistance that can be provided to judges by legally qualified registrars and specially trained case officers to whom supervised functions can be delegated. Those familiar with the enhanced role of legal advisers in the family court will know of the benefits that delegated process monitoring can bring to speed and consistency. That is also our experience in the tribunals. But case management is not simply a matter of ensuring that a claim is ready for trial. Lord Justice Briggs has noted that our approach to case management should be one aimed at managing a dispute resolution process, and not one of managing to trial.[7]

That is surely right. Better use of skilled and appropriately trained registrars and case officers will help us to implement such an approach. Their use, for instance, will facilitate access to justice by those who simply cannot access it at the moment any more than they will be able to access it in a digital system—and that is important. They can help facilitate effective triage of claims so that each claim is allocated to the right process, and the litigants are given appropriate support to move towards an appropriate resolution. It will also enable far greater use of a so far underutilized dispute resolution technique: early neutral evaluation (ENE).

In broad terms, the idea is simple. At an early stage of any claim, the parties outline their claim to a neutral third party, who then gives an assessment of the merits of the claim. The assessment is

---

[7] M. Briggs, *Chancery Modernisation Review* [2013] at para. 5.9.

not binding (although the possibility always exists for the parties to agree to be bound by it). In general, the assessment is a means—and in many cases an effective one—to enable the parties to approach a settlement negotiation having received an objective, neutral view on the strengths and weaknesses of their respective positions. If the claim does not settle, and it proceeds to trial, the individual who carried out the assessment has no further role to play.

ENE is found in the family justice system, where it is known as family dispute resolution. It has been around in the Commercial Court, the Admiralty Court, and the Technology and Construction Court for some time now, and more recently the High Court's Chancery Division has started to promote its use. The greater use of skilled registrars, case officers, and fee-paid judges ought to enable ENE to become an embedded part of the system, assisting parties to properly assess their positions. In so far as it promotes settlement, it secures a benefit to the parties through early resolution of their dispute. It equally enables the more efficient use of judicial resources, by enabling them to be concentrated on those claims that genuinely cannot be resolved consensually. And where the claim doesn't settle, it facilitates better use of both court and party resources, promoting better case management by enabling the parties to narrow the issues in dispute.

Of course, this comes at a price, although I do not mean that it calls for significant investment. The price is greater judicial training. If judges are to be deployed more widely than at present, and are to deal with a broader range of disputes, they will need appropriate training. A key focus, therefore, of moulding one judiciary will be the work carried out by the Judicial College. Training will have to be matched by a commitment across the judiciary to implementing the new approach effectively. We will need to get the culture right, and will need to do so across the whole of the judiciary.

A new basis for developing real career progression across the judiciary will help secure for the medium and long term a more diverse judiciary, one better able to reflect society and maintain the confidence of society as a whole. The tribunals are assiduous caretakers of the most diverse part of the judiciary. We want to share what works with everyone.

QUALITY-ASSURED OUTCOMES

Finally, I want to touch on the idea of quality-assured outcomes. How are we to ensure that we improve decision making while also ensuring that the new deployment measures are carried out effectively? This has a number of aspects.

First, it will require the judiciary to share best practice across tribunals and courts. Different approaches are taken in different chambers in the tribunals, just as they are taken in different courts, in just the same way that different countries take different approaches to their court structures and procedures. We often examine best practices in other jurisdictions. Both Lord Woolf and Lord Justice Jackson, for instance, examined other common law jurisdictions when carrying out their civil justice reviews. We are presently learning from the Netherlands, as well as British Columbia and the United States, about the development of Online Dispute Resolution.

Best practice is not, however, just a matter of what goes on in other countries. It is something which arises much closer to home. We will examine and learn from best practice across our own jurisdictions, and our systems will be better for it. By sharing the best of what we know, we will all be better judges and our ability to deliver quality justice—the ultimate test—will improve.

Quality assurance is more than learning. It is a matter of putting knowledge into practice. I am sure that you have all heard the phrase 'practice makes perfect'. It does not. To make perfect assumes that you can identify the perfect to start with. It is one thing to teach new techniques, to broaden experience—but again the real test is in the delivery. Quality assurance therefore calls for appraisal. We must ensure that what has been learnt translates into practice, that practice is not embedding the imperfect. And by 'we' I mean the judiciary; appraisals carried out by anyone other than the judiciary would be a stark infringement of judicial independence. Judicial appraisal is already embedded in tribunals' practice as an important personal and career development mechanism that helps improve quality.

And, finally, moving to the strategic and the practical, effective planning and forecasting systems need to be implemented to support effective deployment. They will be necessary to identify: how many of what kind of judges do we need in which places doing what and with what support? We need better data and analytics to understand the business need if we are to deliver and administer effective justice by ensuring that the right judge is in the right place for the right case. We need to be able to forecast workloads to be able to plan for the deployment, recruitment, and training of the judiciary. An effective justice system requires effective strategic and operational planning for the future.

Our vision is of one system of justice, supporting the needs of all our diverse users, without consigning any to a second-class service; one judiciary, with specialist expertise, deployable across jurisdictions, flexibly and responsively, as caseloads require, supporting service delivery as well as career progression; and better-quality outcomes, facilitated through innovative problem solving and inquisitorial dispute resolution, supported by modern infrastructure, and backed by performance monitoring and appraisal.

Austerity has provided the impetus to develop and realize that vision, to take the necessary steps to modernize our justice system and bring it into the twenty-first century. But not just the twenty-first century. In 1912, a Chief Justice—of Wisconsin, not of England and Wales—said this: 'Equal justice ... has been the dream of the philosopher, the aim of the lawgiver, the endeavour of the judge, the ultimate test of every government and every civilization.'[8] As a judge and as a member of what that Chief Justice would have described as a branch of the governance of the state, it is my intention that—as far as we possibly can—the reforms that flow from the vision for reform I have outlined this evening help secure equal access to justice, to a justice that is the right of all.

---

[8] Chief Justice Winslow, cited in D. Rhode, *Access to Justice* (2004), at 185.

12

The Centrality of Justice

Its Contribution to Society and Its Delivery

Lord Thomas of Cwmgiedd*

This chapter is based upon a lecture delivered in memory of
Lord Williams of Mostyn on 10 November 2015.

It is a privilege and honour to give this lecture in memory of Lord
Williams of Mostyn. It is made possible by the generosity of Farrar's
Buildings (where I was pupil as a barrister to His Honour Judge Monro
Davies QC and of which my judicial pupil master, His Honour Judge
Sir Robin David QC, was a door tenant). It is a privilege, as although
Lord Williams and I never practised in the same area of the law, he
was always most generous in his encouragement, wise advice, and
counsel. It is an honour as Lord Williams's career spanned both the
Bar (for he was successively leader of the Wales and Chester Circuit
and chairman of the Bar) and the House of Lords (he was successively an undersecretary of state, minister of state and deputy leader
of the House of Lords, Attorney General and leader of the House of
Lords). More importantly he was, as Lord Falconer described in the
Dictionary of National Biography, a 'committed reformer. He wanted
to change the institutions of which he had been so successful a member. But he never lost the support of the two institutions where he
achieved pre-eminence—the Lords and the Bar'.

It is with these words in mind that I turn to the subject of this
lecture: explaining the centrality of justice in our nation state and
addressing the urgent need for radical reform to safeguard and

* I would like to thank Dr John Sorabji for all his help in preparing this lecture.

enhance that centrality through the better delivery of justice. This is a reform that must be achieved with the support of those engaged in the justice system and others.

It is appropriate to take democracy as my starting point. In particular it is to the reflections of the second President of the United States, John Adams, one of the great US presidents and of Welsh descent.[1] In a moment of pessimism, he said: 'Democracy never lasts long. It soon wastes, exhausts and murders itself. There never was a democracy yet that did not commit suicide.' Adams's observation is of continuing relevance. The commitment to democracy is a living commitment which must be secured by two pillars: the strength of its institutional pillars (the Executive, Parliament, and the judiciary) and the assent and confidence in the institutions by those who are governed by them.[2]

In this lecture, I want to focus on one aspect of the first pillar—the judiciary and the justice system—and its central role in our democracy. The warning of Adams is equally applicable to the justice system. We all know of the barbarity of the criminal justice system and the appalling delays and expense of our civil justice system before the reforms of the nineteenth century. These were good examples of how a system of justice can waste and exhaust itself. But although we rightly pride ourselves as having one of the finest judicial systems in the world, there are serious dangers to our system which demand reforms perhaps as radical as those of the nineteenth century. I want, therefore, to look at what reforms must be made to preserve public confidence in our system of justice and, more importantly, to enhance it, so that Adams's pessimism does not become a prophecy applied to that institutional pillar of the state.

Let me first turn to say something of the centrality of justice and the nature of our judicial system. You may wonder why I do so. There is an emerging view that our judicial system is simply nothing more than the provider of an adjudication service either between the citizen and the state, or between citizens. The view gains currency as it is perceived that individuals, businesses, and local and central government

---

[1] 'Welshmen as Factors in the Formation and Development of the US Republic'— the successful prize essay at the International Eisteddfod at the World's Columbia Exhibition, the Chicago World Fair of 1893.

[2] K. O'Regan, 'A Pillar of Democracy: Reflections on the Role and Work of the Constitutional Court of South Africa' [2013] 81 *Fordham Law Review* 1169.

come to the courts to use them as an adjudication service, just as they would go to a mediator, arbitrator, or ombudsman or other private provider of such services.

Differences, of course, do exist between the justice system and these other dispute resolution services. The justice system would, for instance, be viewed as a state monopoly, although it would no doubt be possible to conceive of an ombudsman service as a monopoly provider within the ambit of its jurisdiction. Equally, the justice system could be seen as providing an adjudicatory dispute resolution service, unlike the more facilitative process provided by mediator. But then again, arbitration and, to a certain degree, ombudsman services provide an adjudicatory process. Differences, and similarities, can be multiplied.

If the judiciary were looked on in this way as simply a provider of adjudication services, it would be impossible to see how the judiciary and the justice system could be conceived as a pillar of democracy. Conceived of as a service, and one that does no more than resolve disputes—whether civil, family, criminal, public law, or private law— there is little, perhaps, to differentiate it from various forms of alternative dispute resolution. Any distinction between formal and informal justice begins—if it is not already, on this view—to be lost. Worse than that, formal justice collapses into informal justice. Looked at this way, the fears expressed by writers such as Professor Trevor Farrow that the common law is in danger of privatizing justice can seem all too patent.[3]

The idea that the justice system does no more than provide a dispute resolution service, that in doing so it provides merely private benefits to litigating parties, is fallacious. I agree with Chief Justice French of the High Court of Australia that 'courts are not and should not be seen to be providers of a spectrum of consensual and non-consensual dispute resolution services'.[4] The idea is fallacious because it undermines our constitutional settlement. A democratic state secures justice, in the widest sense, for its citizens through representative institutions of government—Parliament and the Executive—and

---

[3] See, for instance, T. Farrow, *Civil Justice, Privatization and Democracy* (University of Toronto Press, 2014).

[4] R. French, 'Essential and Defining Characteristics of Courts in an Age of Institutional Change' (Supreme and Federal Court Judges Conference, Adelaide, 21 January 2013), at 3. See www.hcourt.gov.au/assets/publications/speeches/current-justices/frenchcj/frenchcj21jan13.pdf. Discussed in P. Spender, 'Wavering Alternations of Valour and Caution: Commercial and Regulatory Litigation in the French CJ High Court', [2013] 2 *J. Civ. LP* 111 at 116 ff.

through an independent judiciary and justice system. The latter ensures that those institutions, just as much as the state's citizens, act within the law. A consumer service merely resolving disputes cannot play such a role. Mediation, for all its rightly recognized virtues, cannot do so. Nor can arbitration, nor any ombudsman.

If we conceive of the justice system as no more than a service provider, we plant the seeds for Professor Farrow's feared privatization. If the justice system is no more than a state monopoly providing exactly the same benefits to individuals as the London Court of International Arbitration, one of any number of mediation services, or, for instance, the Furniture Ombudsman,[5] then the next logical question is why should the state maintain that monopoly? Its danger lies equally in the fact that it might facilitate the false belief that the justice system is in the same category of public services as education and the health service. It is not. It is in the same category as Parliament and the Executive. It forms part of the institutional framework which safeguards the rule of law and underpins democracy.

There is no suggestion that the justice system is to be privatized. But, as Professor Dame Hazel Genn has cogently and forcefully argued, the suggestion is there that the courts do no more than provide services that confer private benefits on litigants has more than found its way into the mainstream.[6] The position was perhaps best summed up in an article by Dingwall and Cloatre, who concluded:

> Successive U.K. governments have decided that, although civil justice may be a public service, it is not a public good in the sense that Lord Woolf asserted in his first report. Although, as Lord Woolf notes, governments have been reluctant to defend the policy in public, their communications with the Civil Justice Council made it clear that they see the system as providing only private benefits for individuals rather than collective benefits for the society as a whole.[7]

Institutions that simply confer private benefits on individuals are not one of the pillars of democracy and cannot safeguard the rule of law or the prosperity of our nation state.

---

[5] An independent not-for-profit organization established in 1992. It specializes in providing alternative dispute resolution services for consumers and businesses in the retail, furniture, and home improvement sectors.

[6] See, for instance, H. Genn, *Judging Civil Justice* (Cambridge University Press, 2010); H. Genn, 'Why the Privatisation of Civil Justice Is a Rule of Law Issue' (F. A. Mann lecture, 2012). See www.laws.ucl.ac.uk/wp-content/uploads/2014/08/36th-F-A-Mann-Lecture-19.11.12-Professor-Hazel-Genn.pdf.

[7] R. Dingwall and E. Cloatre, 'Vanishing Trials? An English Perspective' (2006) *Journal of Dispute Resolution* 7, 51 at 67.

Why is the justice system therefore a pillar of democracy? There are a number of reasons. Time will permit me only to mention some of the more important: first, the safeguarding of the rule of law; second, maintaining the certainty of the law while allowing for its development; third, providing public access to the law; fourth, providing openness and accountability; and fifth, making decisions independently of interests.

Let me say a word about each of those I have mentioned.

SAFEGUARDING THE RULE OF LAW

First, the justice system safeguards the rule of law. The means by which it resolves disputes differs qualitatively from the approaches taken by the many mechanisms of informal justice. It does so through providing substantive justice by finding fact and applying it to law. It provides justice according to law. It does so through a fair process, one that guarantees equality of arms between the parties, which is neutral as between them. This plainly has value over and above the individual case. As Professor Fuller rightly noted, the means by which the courts, through hearing and testing evidence and reasoned argument presented by disputing parties, is a fundamental means through which the rule of law is made real.[8] It is the essence of the democratic state.

MAINTAINING THE CERTAINTY OF THE LAW WHILST ALLOWING FOR ITS DEVELOPMENT

Second, the provision of substantive justice is not simply an end in itself. Its reach goes far beyond the immediate parties. In this respect, and unlike any aspect of informal justice, it is a continuous process that affects the other pillars of democracy just as it does all citizens.[9]

Decisions in individual cases clarify the law where it is obscure. They provide certainty where there has been doubt. They ensure that

[8] L. Fuller, 'The Forms and Limits of Adjudication' [1978] 92 *Harvard Law Review* 353.
[9] It does so because, in the words of James Madison, 'law is … a rule of action'. To be effective as such it must be known and fixed. J. Madison in A. Hamilton, J. Madison, and J. Jay, *The Federalist Papers* (C. Kesler ed.) (Signet, 2003), No 62, at 379.

the norms provided by the law truly are norms, and not mere aspirations. They transform bare rules of law into a living framework guiding the lives of citizens; the economic activity of small, medium, and multinational corporations; and Government conduct: 'Protecting legal rights, in other words, has value beyond what those rights are worth to any single [litigant].'[10] The justice system achieves this transformation in two ways. First, through what could be described as the certain application of the law to individual cases. Through deciding cases consistently with precedent and under the guidance of an appellate structure, the judiciary maintains certainty in the law. Individuals, business, and government can order their affairs on a sure legal footing. The consistent application and explication of the law enables all of us to know the legal framework within which we live our lives.

Second, it does so through judges developing the law. Judges can do so in appropriate cases, in accordance with established principle, as explained by Lord Diplock in *Home Office v Dorset Yacht Co. Ltd*[11] and more recently elaborated by Sir John Laws in his Hamlyn lectures.[12] Substantive justice's achievement in any one case can result in the development of novel law. As any first-year law student knows, without this common law approach there would be no *Donoghue v Stephenson*.[13] Equally, there would be no principled— and still developing—law of restitution or unjust enrichment. Without the court's ability to develop the law, without its creative function, the tort of negligence would have progressed no further than Esher MR's decision in *Heaven v Pender*,[14] and unjust enrichment would remain swimming in the confused and murky shallows of implied contract.

Individual decisions do not therefore merely provide a service to the litigants; they play an essential part in the maintenance and development of the law. They are a fundamental aspect of our common law constitutional settlement, since they help create the framework of law. The contrast with the methods of informal dispute resolution is clear. No means of securing informal justice could legitimately

---

[10] D. Rhode, *Access to Justice* (Oxford University Press, 2004), at 11.
[11] [1970] AC 1004.
[12] J. Laws, *The Common Law Constitution* (Cambridge University Press, 2014).
[13] [1932] AC 562.
[14] (1883) 11 QBD 503.

play such a role. There are, of course, limits to the justice system's creative role. It is, broadly speaking, incremental. It is evolutionary, not revolutionary. And, most importantly, it is subordinate to Parliament, which is rightly sovereign within our constitution. Subject to these limits, the justice system speaking through individual decisions is an institution of the state, not a mere service provider.

The contrast can again be seen by reference to the impact of arbitration. Up until 1979 a substantial contribution had been made to the development of commercial law by appeals by way of special case (in effect a case stated) from decisions of arbitrators. A substantial amount of my own experience as a young commercial lawyer was to request the arbitrator to state the award in the form of a special case on a point of law; if I lost the arbitration, I could appeal to the Commercial Court.

It is undeniable that the practice, as applied not only to the maritime market but also to the commodities market, produced far too many appeals. So in 1979 an Arbitration Act restricted the right of appeal. That restriction is now embodied in the Arbitration Act 1996. Many have felt that the restrictions are too tight and have stultified the development of English commercial law. As long ago as 2004 in delivering the Sixth Cedric Barclay Lecture, Sir Robert Finch, then the Lord Mayor, called for a widening of the scope of appeals from commercial arbitrations in order to help the modernization of English commercial law so that it kept in tune with the developments of the commercial world. Eleven years on, the need is even greater. One of the central defects of arbitration is that the process by which the law is developed in a way which I shall now turn to describe cannot take place within the privatized system of arbitration. In the words of Lord Nicholls:

> The common law is judge-made law. For centuries judges have been charged with the responsibility of keeping this law abreast of current social conditions and expectations. That is still the position. Continuing but limited development of the common law in this fashion is an integral part of the constitutional function of the judiciary.[15]

---

[15] *National Westminster Bank v Spectrum Plus* [2005] AC 680 at [32].

PROVIDING PUBLIC ACCESS TO THE LAW

A third fundamental aspect of our judicial system is that decisions are made available to all citizens so that they can plan their lives on the basis of the law. Jeremy Bentham once entertained the idea that if we could render law simple, through codification, everyone could be their own lawyer.[16] Codification would in fact never have produced the answer he wanted; codes stand in need of interpretation and explication just as do other forms of law. There is vastly more to German contract law than is found in the Bürgerliches Gesetzbuch (BGB). There is more to the United States Constitution than its bare words.[17]

Bentham had two reasons for thinking that it was important that everyone could be their own lawyer. The first reason would not be popular to some. Bentham considered that making the law simple was a means by which the necessity of resorting to—and having to pay—lawyers could be avoided. Where legal disputes arose everyone could be a litigant-in-person, well versed in the law, and well able to fight their corner before the courts. The second reason was to ensure that, if the law was well understood by all, they could take steps to ensure that legal disputes did not arise. It had a preventative function. Understanding the criminal law, and the penal consequences that flow from breaching it, would play an essential role in ensuring that society would be peaceful. Understanding the operation of contract law, the extent of a duty of care, would enable individuals and businesses to avoid the adverse consequences of breaches.

As disputes are avoided through proper planning, society's resources can be directed in ways which are neither 'wasteful' nor 'disruptive'.[18] Again it is not possible for arbitration or mediation to play such a preventive role. Resolution reached by such methods is necessarily private as between the parties. It is not binding either on other parties to arbitrations or mediation. It cannot clarify or develop the law.

---

[16] J. Bentham cited in P. Schofield, 'Jeremy Bentham: Legislator of the World', in M. Freeman (ed.), *Current Legal Problems 1998* (Oxford University Press, 1998), at 137.

[17] For a discussion see A. R. Amar, *America's Unwritten Constitution* (Basic Books, 2012).

[18] *D v NSPCC* [1987] AC 171, 232.

Insofar as decisions circulate, they often circulate to a narrow range of lawyers who may then gain special knowledge of the way in which groups of arbitrators decide issues. It therefore lacks the features that would enable it to play the wider normative role of decisions reached in litigation before the courts.

Ombudsmen, it might be said, may play a similar function to the courts. As an academic in the Netherlands has pointed out, they and their decisions can both inform and educate.[19] But here too there is a problem. Ombudsmen and their decisions play this role against the background of norms established by the courts. As with arbitration and mediation, it presupposes the framework of law provided by the justice system.[20]

Alternative dispute resolution (ADR) rests upon the robust health of the justice system if it is to play its proper role. Absent the justice system, absent ADR. And that is as true for ombudsmen as it is for mediation, arbitration, and any other form of ADR.

PROVIDING OPENNESS AND ACCOUNTABILITY

Fourth, it is a clear principle of the justice system that justice must be delivered publicly and openly in a court so that what is argued and the evidence on which the court proceeds is known. That members of the public can attend and scrutinize our courts ensures that justice, whenever it is being carried out, is on trial. As Lord Atkin recognized, justice cannot long survive as a cloistered virtue.[21] It must be public and open, save in a very restricted number of circumstances.

Openness also provides for accountability in the application and development of the law. A court is not a deliberative assembly. Not

---

[19] M. Remac, 'Standards of Ombudsman Assessment: A New Normative Concept?' [2013] 9, 3 *Utrecht Law Review* (July) 62 at 73–4.

[20] 'Ultimately the collaborative paradigm falters if not grounded upon an absolute'. Professor Jeffrey Wolfe, 'Across the Ripple of Time: The Future of Alternative (or, Is It "Appropriate?") Dispute Resolution', [2001] 36 *Tulsa Law Journal* 785 at 794.

[21] *Ambard v Attorney-General for Trinidad and Tobago* [1936] AC 322 at 335: 'justice is not a cloistered virtue: she must be allowed to suffer the scrutiny and respectful … comments of ordinary men'.

since the abolition of the Court of Star Chamber has England and Wales had a court of policy.[22]

Our courts are courts of law. This is not to say, however, that the law does not develop, within established and principled boundaries, in the light of changes in social and public policy, as I have explained. The law must evolve in order to remain relevant to society. The extent to which the courts can and do develop the law in these ways is necessarily a matter of debate. This must be done in a manner that is acceptable—a debate primarily between the parties but which is conducted openly so that it can afford the opportunity for wider debate which is facilitated by journalists and court reporters making public the issues which are being debated.

That wider debate informs and is informed by public views. As is evident, they can sometimes have a material effect on the decision on the law. Any particular development by the courts can inform and enable public debate and discussion, and through that political debate. The outcome of that debate can, of course, be corrective steps by the Government and Parliament. The justice system is not itself above the law. As such, just like Parliament and the Government, the justice system is accountable through its reasoned decisions and its appellate process.[23]

Accountability goes further. In a democratic state, institutions of governance must be accountable to citizens. This form of accountability necessarily differs across such states. And it differs within states depending on the pillar of government in question. Here our Parliament is accountable via free and fair general elections now held every five years. Our Executive is accountable through Parliament and through the electoral process. The judiciary, in order to preserve judicial independence and thereby the rule of law, is not directly accountable through elections, but this is not to say that it is not democratically accountable. It is, in ways which neither mediation nor arbitration or an ombudsman could be accountable. I have already mentioned one way: open justice. A second direct accountability comes through direct participation of all citizens in our criminal

---

[22] F. W. Maitland, *The Constitutional History of England* (Cambridge University Press, 1909), at 263.

[23] C. Turpin and A. Tomkins, *British Government and Constitution* (Cambridge University Press, 2011), at 567.

process. Lay juries and lay magistrates (Justices of the Peace) lie at the heart of our criminal justice system.

MAKING DECISIONS INDEPENDENTLY OF INTERESTS

Fifth, decisions made by the judiciary are indisputably independent. Each judge, as you all know, takes an oath that he or she will decide all cases without fear or favour, affection or ill will. That obligation is buttressed by the requirement that the judge must avoid any perception of conflict of interest by any material association with the subject matter in issue. The judge is beholden to no party for payment of salary or for the provision of further work. The judge is in no sense beholden to a trade organization, an industry or a regulatory body. The judge is not therefore at risk of 'capture'. The judge is truly independent.

These five reasons are some of the main reasons why justice provided through our judicial system is an essential feature of a democratic state: it is a manifestation of our commitment to the rule of law; it is not an end in itself, but rather the means by which the framework of law is clarified, developed, and given normative force; it provides the bedrock upon which all forms of ADR rest. It is thus more than the public good argued for by Professor Dame Hazel Genn and others. It is in this way an essential pillar of our democracy.

There can, therefore, in my view be no doubt of the centrality of the justice system to the modern, democratic state. If the state is to carry out its core duty, of securing justice for its citizens through the elaboration, vindication, and execution of their and its rights and duties, it cannot but ensure that the justice system is understood to be as important as Parliament and the Executive, and that it is supported accordingly.

Our society rests on three pillars. Should anyone of them fall, we will all fall with it. I have already made clear the need for radical reform. The question then becomes how we carry out such reform to the delivery of justice that it retains that centrality and its vital role as a pillar of our democracy and does not fall victim to Adams's observation. It is to that I now turn. I do so on the assumption that proper funds will be provided to enable reform to take place.

REFORMING THE DELIVERY OF JUSTICE

The proper basis for reform, as a means of securing the better delivery of justice, must be a principled one. It must be one that is predicated on the understanding that the justice system is a pillar of democracy; that it succeeds only in so far as it secures substantive justice and the concomitants to that, which I outlined earlier; and that it does so consistently with a number of constitutional principles. Those principles, which I am sure you well know, are, to name a few: the constitutional right of access to the courts, to equality before the law, to open justice, and to timely and affordable justice, and its delivery by an independent and impartial judiciary.

These principles are the balance upon which proposed reforms must be weighed. Let me therefore turn to some of the areas in which radical reform is essential.

Technology

Reform to the court infrastructure is essential. There is no way in which the present system can continue. Reform is therefore predicated on the better use of modern technology to provide the basis of a modernized infrastructure.

Part of this will be the increased use of technology as a means to access the court process. However, as reform must proceed in accordance with principle, it will require steps to be taken to ensure that that is accessible. If, for instance, the means to commence a claim are by issuing it online, the technology must not simply have to work, but it must be available to everyone in a simple enough way that it can easily be used. We cannot, in the name of increasing access to justice, create a new barrier to entry. Equally, if we are to move a large number of hearings online we cannot do so at the cost of open justice. If we undermine open justice we reduce judicial accountability and, crucially, an aspect of participatory democracy. Technology must be a means to enhance, not to undermine.

Procedural Reform

This leads me to procedural reform. I need not speak about the reforms that have taken place in the family justice system. Further reform awaits IT. In the criminal justice system, the steps to be taken are clearly laid out in Sir Brian Leveson's report; digitalization is under way.[24]

As to reform of the civil courts, I can well imagine that one not unreasonable response to any suggestion of further procedural reform from those who practise in the civil courts would be, as they say in America, 'stop already'. Constant tinkering undermines certainty, increases satellite litigation, and through that increases litigation cost and delay.

There is, however, no alternative to further and more radical reform. That is because technology-based reforms to administrative processes will necessarily lead to radical procedural reform. If, for instance, the default position becomes that claims are issued and served online, procedural rules must be made that underpin this. But those rules, given sufficient resources and expertise, must enable procedure properly to be simplified in a large number of areas. Anyone who doubts this should read Lord Justice Richards's masterly and magisterial Barnard's Inn Lecture.[25]

Could the use of technology go further than procedural reform to facilitate online hearings and e-process? In two recent reports both the Civil Justice Council[26] and JUSTICE[27] suggest that that is so. Taken together they propose a new online court and the introduction of a new class of quasi-judge, a registrar. This new class of court officer (in the United States they would describe it as a member of the adjunct judiciary) would be able to carry out case management, and to screen claims so that they were allocated to an appropriate dispute resolution mechanism, amongst other things. They would therefore have to be experienced, skilled, and well trained.

The review by Sir Michael Briggs will be considering how far such proposals can properly be taken.[28] For example, it will be necessary to

[24] Leveson LJ, *Report into the Culture, Practices and Ethics of the Press* (29 November 2012).
[25] See www.gresham.ac.uk/sites/default/files/25jun15stephenrichards_civillitigation. docx.
[26] Civil Justice Council, *Online Dispute Resolution for Low Value Claims* (2015), at www. judiciary.gov.uk/wp-content/uploads/2015/02/Online-Dispute-Resolution-Final-Web-Version1.pdf.
[27] JUSTICE, *Delivering Justice in an Age of Austerity* (2015), at http:// 2bquk8cdew6192tsu41lay8t.wpengine.netdna-cdn.com/wp-content/uploads/2015/ 04/JUSTICE-working-party-report-Delivering-Justice-in-an-Age-of-Austerity.pdf.
[28] The review's conclusion were subsequently published as: M. Briggs, *Civil Courts Structure Review: Interim Report* (December 2015), at www.judiciary.gov.uk/wp-content/uploads/2016/01/CCSR-interim-report-dec-15-final-31.pdf; M. Briggs, *Civil Courts Structure Review: Final Report* (July 2016), at www.judiciary.gov.uk/wp-content/uploads/2016/07/civil-courts-structure-review-final-report-jul-16.pdf.

ensure that justice remains open and that the development and clari-
fication of the law will take account of all types of case. Reducing the
number of claims determined by way of judgment could reduce the
courts' ability to develop precedent. Such an approach would have
meant no *Donoghue v Stephenson*.

This is an important consideration. I have already referred to the
effect of the curtailment of appeals from arbitration. The more disputes
that are and have been determined by private forms of adjudication,
the fewer opportunities the courts have had to develop commercial
law. And the consequence of this is that the law can ossify. It cannot
work itself fine, correct errors, make clear the content of rights. Its
ability to provide a sure framework for the development and carrying
out of social relations, business dealings and so on is undermined. It
thus undermines our democracy.

One example of how we can properly effect such reform is the
approach that has recently been taken in the Chancery Division and
the Commercial Court. They have seen the introduction of both a
new Financial List and a Shorter and Flexible Trials Procedure.
I should also add that these courts, together with the Technology and
Construction Court, are also moving fast in the direction of electronic
processing. All three instances provide a model for reform.

The introduction of the Financial List is of particular importance,
as it will provide a more efficient and economical means to resolve
financial disputes. It will thus help to secure greater access to the
courts here. Equally it will provide access to the expertise of specialist High Court judges, thus increasing access to high-quality justice.
And as importantly, it will enable the development of the law through
enabling market test cases to be decided for the benefit of all. It is a
reform that not only enhances our ability to implement constitutional
principle, but it is one that enhances our ability to secure the normative value of the law. It is to be strongly contrasted with the damaging
effect of the use of arbitration in other markets to which I have earlier referred. Perhaps the availability of a test-case procedure for the
financial markets will lead to an urgent reconsideration of the test for
appeals from arbitration in other city-based markets, particularly the
maritime, insurance, and commodities markets, or the provision of a
similar facility for important issues in those markets.

The Shorter and Flexible Trials Procedure is another example of
principled reform. Our historic approach to process is that it is pre-
scriptive. Directions are made within the boundaries set by the rules.

Other jurisdictions have taken the view that procedure should contain the option for parties to opt for greater procedural flexibility—for instance, to agree for their claims to come to trial within a short period of time, to agree to limit certain procedural obligations, such as the extent to which disclosure should apply or the length of time available for trial. The aim remains to secure substantive justice. The parties can, to a certain extent, agree to reach that goal in different ways than previously permitted. Again, such a development, through facilitating access to justice, is one that enhances the courts' ability to act consistently with principle, and secure increased participation through reducing litigation time and cost.

The task for both reform to the court system and the review by Sir Michael Briggs is to consider how best to structure reform within the principles I have outlined, to work out how far we can properly use registrars and how far we can properly create a multi-door courthouse that both promotes appropriate dispute resolution and ensures that the court's adjudicatory function is enhanced rather than undermined.

Court Location

Another essential component of reform is the importance of local justice. The proposals for court closures have, rightly, caused significant concern in many areas, including Wales. As I have said on other occasions, consideration of such closures can only proceed if we use modern technology to put in place a real alternative that can produce proper local justice. I need not repeat what I have said on other occasions, most recently in Cardiff. There is one other aspect to local justice to which it is necessary to refer.

At the core of my description of the centrality of justice is the principle that the system of justice is one of the three powers of the state. While there can be debate about the extent to which the police and the prosecution should be organized and be accountable on a local basis, the same is not true of our system of justice. Not only would it be contrary to constitutional principle and the principles on which our system of justice has been organized for many centuries, but independence of all local interests is essential to maintain the integrity of our system of justice and as importantly to maintain the integrity of local government and its freedom from improper influences.

The Structure of the Courts

Our court structure is the product of the 1870s and the 1970s; the former creating the High Court and Court of Appeal, and the latter creating the Crown Court, and seeing the present three divisions of the High Court come into existence through the creation of the Family Division. More recently we have seen the creation of a new single family court and the consolidation of the county courts into a single county court.

The overall structure of the civil courts has not, however, been subject to detailed scrutiny to ascertain whether it remains appropriate for the twenty-first century. In one sense that this has not happened is remarkable. When the High Court was created it was never intended that its divisions would remain as they were. Bar the early consolidation of the three original common law divisions to create what is now the Queen's Bench Division and the reform of the Probate Division and Admiralty Division to create Family Division, they have. The creation of divisions and the power to revise them was intended to ensure that the High Court's structure would reflect the changing business needs of the courts.

That such scrutiny is long overdue is made all the more pertinent given two further issues. First, since the introduction of the Woolf reforms, and more recently the implementation of the Jackson and the Briggs reforms to the Chancery Division,[29] the boundary between the county court and the High Court's jurisdiction has become increasingly blurred. Work that would traditionally have been reserved, due to its complexity and financial value, is now and increasingly becoming and is the province of the county court. Second, technology. This may now enable us to create what has been described as an online court for certain types of civil claim.

Less dramatically, although of equally far-reaching consequences, proper use of information technology should enable us to put in place fully electronic case-management and progression systems. E-filing, e-bundles, e-issuing of claims, and so on should become the norm, as in a significant number of cases, in virtual case management, and in other procedural hearings.

I await the outcome of the Civil Courts Structure review by Sir Michael Briggs,[30] and its recommendations as to how our civil court structure ought to be reformed in order to best enable it to deliver

---

[29] M. Briggs, *The Chancery Modernisation Review* (December 2013).
[30] See Fn 28.

justice today. Its recommendations will, of necessity, have to be tested by reference to constitutional principle just as much as by reference to how, and the extent to which, they will render the justice system more economical and efficient.

It is also necessary to give further consideration to the relationship between the courts and the tribunals. There can be no doubt about the huge success of the reforms to our system of tribunal and administrative justice that has been brought about as a result of the report of Sir Andrew Leggatt. Over the period since that report was implemented, there has been a gradual coming together of the way in which the judges in the courts and the judges in the tribunals work. For example, a significant amount of judicial review work is carried out in the tribunals; the way in which courts and tribunals deal with cases has been influenced by the respective practices. This influence will only increase as courts and tribunals share the same buildings.

There are many other radical changes that must be made but time does not permit.

Working Together

I must therefore turn to a further principle: to emphasize that this is not reform that can be successfully carried out unless all those interested have a role in carrying forward the reform.

For the criminal justice system to work optimally, interaction between the courts, prisons, the Crown Prosecution Service, and other such bodies needs to run as efficiently as possible. If the courts are to be in a position to deliver timely justice, cases need to come on at the right time, which requires well-briefed and well-prepared lawyers to be present in court, witnesses to be there on time, and defendants to be present at the right time and place. This is the approach that has underpinned the report of Sir Brian Leveson and will underpin carrying it into effect.

The same is true for both the civil and family justice systems. The courts and the judiciary are not islands unto themselves. The delivery of timely and effective justice requires close working between them and a host of external agencies, individuals, and legal representatives.

In answering the question how we ensure that we can improve the delivery of justice we cannot therefore simply focus on the courts and the judiciary. Governments at one time talked about having joined-up policy making. The sentiment was undoubtedly correct: if reform is to work as well as it can, it has to be coherent across the piece. It is no good improving one aspect of a system in order, for instance, to improve its speed if unreformed elements mean you can never attain that improvement.

The delivery of justice needs to be understood as requiring a close working relationship between the courts and the judiciary and a number of other institutions and individuals. Real improvement will come when all aspects of the system can work together more effectively and efficiently. In the delivery of reform we must retain the support of the professions and all others engaged in the system.

The Anticipated Benefit

Taken together, these reforms will not simply prevent the decline and ultimate decay of our system of justice, but will improve the system's ability to operate as a pillar of democracy. That is why I highlight them. In doing so I realize that some may say that it is all well and good to improve access to justice for businesses, that improvements more urgently need to be made to improve access for the less well off. That is undoubtedly the case: principle requires it of us. Equality before the law cannot simply be a matter of form. It must be made real. The justice system must deliver for all within society. That is why the senior judiciary and I are committed to ensuring that this latest stage of reform is carried out as carefully and in as considered a way as possible.

CONCLUSION: THE CENTRALITY OF JUSTICE

I started this lecture with the warning given by one US President of Welsh descent about the vitality of democracy. I should end, therefore, with something that has often been attributed to his sometime friend and rival and another US President of Welsh descent: Thomas Jefferson. He is believed to have once said that 'on matters of style, swim with the current, on matters of principle, stand like a rock'.

The present style, if it could be put that way, is for radical reform. Tomorrow's justice system will, if funds are provided for reform, undoubtedly differ in many ways from the one I knew when I started life as a barrister. How it develops must be shaped by matters of principle. On this we cannot move. That is the bedrock. Those principles are that the justice system is an indispensable pillar of our democracy; that each of our citizens must be provided with equality before the law secured by ready access to a fair process before the courts; that the achievement of substantive justice through adjudication conducted by an independent and impartial judiciary is the *sine qua non* of the rule of law and cannot be equated with or reduced to a mere service akin to that providing by mediation, arbitration, or any other form of alternative dispute resolution process. If we stand by our principles we will shape our justice system so that it can fulfil its proper role, and ensure that our commitment to liberal democracy is never at risk of going out of style.

13

Judicial Independence in a Changing Constitutional Landscape

Lord Thomas of Cwmgiedd

This chapter is based upon a speech to the Commonwealth Magistrates' and Judges' Association, 15 September 2015.

The constitutional landscape of England and Wales is still in the middle of great change. The centrality of justice through an independent judiciary is the basis on which democracy, prosperity, fairness, and the rule of law depend in our increasingly diverse societies.

Before turning to explain, by reference to my own jurisdiction of England and Wales, what I see as the key tasks that face the judiciary in achieving what I have described, I want to outline four key themes that underpin my address.

First, the centrality of justice to our societies and the independence of the judiciary cannot be taken for granted. To all of us the centrality of justice to a state is obvious. The provision of justice is, we all know, a core duty of a state. But that is a view we should not take for granted. As judges we have a great deal to do to explain its importance and relevance. We have a key role as advocates actively to point out and explain the role and function of the judicial branch of the state. Again the necessity for judicial independence is obvious to us all. We know it is central to the rule of law. In each of our nations, to a greater or lesser extent, we have to protect it or to fight for it.

Second, strong judicial leadership and engagement are needed. Judges cannot expect others to do all that is necessary to protect the position of the judiciary and the justice system; a proactive stance led by the judiciary is required. This is entirely compatible with the Latimer House principles and with other ethical duties.

Third, the judiciary must reflect society to maintain legitimacy. The maxim 'Justice should not only be done, but must also be seen to be done' is ordinarily taken to require transparency, impartiality, fairness, and propriety. But in a broader sense, it must also encompass the principle that the public needs to have confidence in the judiciary that serves it, so as to strengthen the legitimacy of the judicial process. It is axiomatic, therefore, that one important way of gaining and maintaining the public's confidence is making sure that the judiciary is reflective of society in its composition and in the issues it takes into account.

Fourth, independence must be safeguarded.

In a changing constitutional landscape, each of the above is essential if the judiciary is to safeguard its independence in a way that enables it to uphold the rule of law for the benefit of each of our respective nations.

Constitutional change has been a long but generally slow process. Although we celebrate the 800th anniversary of Magna Carta, it was a very long time before the clauses to which we attach so much significance had any real effect. It therefore may seem initially strange that after a long period where the UK had seen little by way of constitutional change, it has since 1998 been in a period of rapid and continuing change. I would like to highlight four of those changes which are most relevant to the position of the judiciary.

THE STRUCTURE OF THE UNION OF THE FOUR
NATIONS: THE POSITION OF WALES

Scotland has always had its own court system, as has Northern Ireland. Thus the re-creation of legislatures with full law-making powers in devolved fields could easily be accommodated. Wales has not had its own court system since 1830. Although the effect of the grant of full law-making powers in devolved fields in 2011 has taken some time to work its way through, the unitary court system of England and Wales is having to adapt to administering laws passed by two different legislative bodies, one of which legislates bilingually.

THE STATUS OF FUNDAMENTAL RIGHTS

Although it can be said that the courts of the UK have always recognized through the common law the fundamental nature of some rights, the period since the coming into force of the Human Rights Act has gradually highlighted the difficult role that the courts are called upon to play outside the traditional areas of the protection of personal liberty, protection of property and free speech, and the right to a fair trial.

THE RELATIONSHIP WITH THE EUROPEAN UNION AND ITS COURT OF JUSTICE AND THE EUROPEAN COURT OF HUMAN RIGHTS

Although the United Kingdom has been a member of the European Union (EU) for over forty years and of the Human Rights Convention since its creation, it has taken time for the influence of EU legislation and the interpretation of that legislation and the Union Treaty to have a broad impact outside trade and business law.

THE GOVERNANCE OF THE JUDICIARY AND ITS RELATIONS WITH THE OTHER PARTS OF THE STATE

It is to this fourth topic I must turn in more detail to explain the key themes.

The Tradition in England and Wales

Until 2005, the Lord Chancellor—an ancient office of state that had existed since at least the eleventh century—was the head of the judiciary with extensive powers in relation to the judiciary. With at least nominal disregard for the separation of powers, he was also the Speaker of the House of Lords and a senior member of the Government Cabinet. However anomalous it might have been, the office was the 'buckle or linchpin' between the judiciary and the other two branches of the state.[1] It gave the judiciary a certain degree of comfort and stability. The holder of the office had for some centuries been a lawyer of great distinction who also had significant political experience. Judges could therefore generally leave to him (and it always was a him) the relations with the other branches of state, ensuring the position of the judiciary on issues was understood at the highest levels of government: the delivery of reform, the appointment of judges and their dismissal, and most functions relating to the organization of the justice system and the judicial branch of the state. It was a relatively comfortable position.

However, by the end of the last century, this position was already under strain and all of this changed with the passing of the Constitutional Reform Act 2005,[2] which in addition to other major changes (in particular the creation of the Supreme Court of the United Kingdom in place of the Judicial Committee of the House of Lords[3]) recast the office of Lord Chancellor and the organization of the judiciary.[4] A decade later, even though changes are continuing, it is possible to assess the very different position which the judiciary of England and Wales now has.

The legislation made the Lord Chief Justice the head of the judiciary and president of the courts of England and Wales in place of the Lord Chancellor.[5] Vested in the office of Lord Chief Justice were very considerable powers and responsibilities over discipline, deployment, training, welfare, and duties including making representations to Parliament and government.[6] Having transferred organizing, leading, and representing the judiciary from the Lord Chancellor to the Lord Chief Justice, the Act was otherwise largely silent about *how* these responsibilities should be discharged by the Lord Chief Justice. This was deliberate, at least on the part of the judiciary, as it left to the judiciary the opportunity to create its own leadership and governance structure.

What is evolving is a system under which the general policies of the judiciary are by and large arrived at through the Judicial

---

[1] 1 G. Gee, R. Hazell, K. Malleson, and P. O'Brien, *The Politics of Judicial Independence in the UK's Changing Constitution* (Cambridge University Press, 2015), at 31.
[2] Constitutional Reform Act 2005 (*c*.4).   [3] Ibid., at section 23(1).
[4] Ibid., at Part 2.   [5] Ibid., at section 7(1).
[6] Constitutional Reform Act 2005, ss. 6 and 7.

Executive Board,[7] a group of eight or nine senior judges chaired by the Lord Chief Justice, with the advice of the Judges' Council,[8] a long established body which was recast to bring together the various judicial associations of the different types and levels of judge. The Judicial Executive Board or individual judges who, acting on behalf of the Lord Chief Justice, lead on matters ranging from diversity and relations with the regulator of the legal professions to training and international relations, and implement the policies. Whereas in the past all judges were by and large concerned with discharging their judicial function, at senior levels in particular—but also throughout the various tiers of courts and tribunals' judiciary—the judiciary of England and Wales has had to create and refine a new leadership structure for itself, trying to avoid the clashes that can easily arise given the hierarchy that is the basis of the distribution of court work and the appellate structure. Its own civil service, the Judicial Office of England and Wales, supports the leadership judiciary. The last is essential, as the principal task of all judges is to dispense justice through managing and trying cases or hearing appeals; any activity of an administrative or leadership nature, however important, is time spent away from court. Of course, that is not to say that judges should not undertake such activities—on the contrary, they should and they must—but it must be proportionate and they must be able to rely on the strong support of the Judicial Office to implement matters on their behalf.

In addition to a host of other statutory functions that transferred from the Lord Chancellor to the Lord Chief Justice as a result of these changes, of particular importance for my talk is a statutory duty placed on the Lord Chief Justice in 2013 to take such steps as he or she considers to be appropriate for the purpose of encouraging judicial diversity,[9] a topic to which I will return.

The major changes, however, preserved some of the responsibilities and functions of the Lord Chancellor who is now also Secretary of State for Justice, though they have been the subject of yet further change. For example, judicial discipline is a joint function of the Lord Chief Justice and Lord Chancellor (as representing the public interest); appointments are the function of an independent appointments

---

[7] See www.judiciary.gov.uk/about-the-judiciary/the-judiciary-the-government-and-the-constitution/how-the-judiciary-is-governed/judicial-executive-board.
[8] See Ibid.   [9] Ibid., section 137A.

commission, though appointments to some leadership posts are a joint function of the Lord Chancellor and the Lord Chief Justice; each also has powers to reject candidates for good reason.

One of the most important functions that was preserved was the responsibility of the Lord Chancellor to obtain the funds for the court administration. In a complex agreement reached in 2008 between the judiciary and the Government, the judiciary obtained a small role in the allocation of funds by the Finance Ministry and, more importantly, a joint responsibility for the running of the court administration. The court administration is now operated on a day-to-day basis by a board chaired by an independent person, accountable to both the Lord Chancellor and the Lord Chief Justice. The judiciary therefore takes a far greater role than before. This has been a beneficial change, given that the judiciary can utilize its practical and operational insight. The judiciary has been active in analysing practices, considering, initiating, and evaluating reform proposals and driving the implementation of reform.

Although the Lord Chancellor and other ministers are bound to uphold the rule of law and judicial independence, and indeed the Lord Chancellor's traditional oath has been adapted to reflect those responsibilities,[10] the judiciary now have, of necessity, adopted a much more active role in relation to Government and Parliament.

There are regular meetings between leadership judges and the Government. In addition, informal engagement occurs almost continuously between the civil servants in the Judicial Office and their counterparts in the Ministry of Justice and other government departments. There is formal engagement with Parliament as illustrated by the Lord Chief Justice's Annual Report, which is laid before Parliament,[11] and annual appearances by the Lord Chief Justice before Parliamentary Committees shortly after its publication, as well as ad hoc appearances by other members of the judiciary that also form part of this formal engagement.

The result of these major changes to the position of the judiciary (as Graham Gee, Robert Hazell, Kate Malleson, and Patrick O'Brien have correctly concluded in a recently published study, *The Politics of Judicial Independence in the UK's Changing Constitution*)[12] has

---

[10]   Ibid., section 17, which inserts a new section 6A into the Promissory Oaths Act 1868 (*c.*62).

[11]   See www.judiciary.gov.uk/wp-content/uploads/2014/12/lcj_report_2014-final.pdf.

[12]   See *Civil Justice Statistics Quarterly, England and Wales, April to June 2015* (Ministry of Justice).

produced a paradox. Under the system prior to 2005, judges could rely on the Lord Chancellor, a member of the Executive and the Legislature, to protect their independence, and did not have to engage with those other branches of state. Under the new system, which has produced a clear and formal separation of powers, judicial independence is best served by more, not less, day-to-day engagement with Government and Parliament. It has also necessitated a much more proactive stance by the judiciary in promoting an understanding of the importance of justice and in taking more proactive steps in many areas it might traditionally have left to others.

Thus we can see that, in the changing constitutional landscape, this new approach is necessary to protect judicial independence, particularly in securing adequate resources for the justice system and in explaining to the public why it is a judge's duty to make decisions in accordance with law in a way which might not appear at the time to be in accordance with popular sentiment.

As I have mentioned, as judges and magistrates, we all understand the importance of the system of justice. In Europe, and I can only speak at first hand of this, the public tends to take the provision of justice for granted. Most will never need to rely directly on the system of justice. The court systems by and large seem to work and are perceived to uphold the rule of law. With varying degrees of speed, those who are alleged to have committed crimes are tried and their guilt or innocence is determined. Government is generally held to account by the courts and rights are by and large protected and developed. Judges generally command a very high degree of trust; not only is this evidenced by surveys, but by the fact that politicians often turn to judges when they need an independent public examination of a difficult problem. The public do not readily see the serious problems that face the system of justice, such as the inordinately high cost of using the courts, which puts access to justice out of the reach of most, and a system that has not been modernized so as to meet the needs of ordinary citizens (whether or not as litigants in person) and small and medium sized enterprises.

Across Europe, governments face increasing pressures to curtail expenditure. The competing pressures are well known. In the United Kingdom, as in many other countries, we have since the financial crisis in 2008 lived in a time of austerity and restricted budgets. The inevitable consequence of these measures is a reduction in state expenditure on justice.

Indeed many see the courts and the court administration—its buildings, people, and resources—as yet another public service in the way that schools, medical practices, and infrastructure are public services, rather than as an aspect of the state as central as Parliament and the Government. At a time when the control of expenditure is under pressure, the benefits of spending on education, health, and infrastructure are obvious, but the benefit of spending on justice and its modernization, and the remedying of its problems, are not.

Moreover, the work of the courts, tribunals, and judges remains a mystery to so many. Any understanding is unlikely to be aided by its portrayal, or the portrayal of the legal system more broadly, in the media. However, given that much of the court estate belongs to a different era and court processes and procedures are blighted by often unnecessary convolution, not to mention the complexity of the law, such mystery is perhaps unsurprising.

And it is not only the public at large that is unfamiliar with the work of the judges. There can also be a lack of understanding in both the Legislative and the Executive branches of the state of the important and central role that justice equally plays.

As a result of the changes to the constitutional position, and particularly in these times of reducing budgets, never has it been more important for the judiciary, as an institution, to become more outward looking and play a more educative role within the proper confines of the constitution. In particular, judges in England and Wales have to explain the centrality of justice and what is necessary to ensure that the courts can deliver it. Judges have to be active in relation to decisions concerning the adequate provision of judges and court administration and explaining why these go hand in hand with maintaining judicial independence and defending the rule of law.

Arguments about abstract, albeit important, principles concerning the constitutional significance of an independent judiciary will, without more, likely fall on deaf ears. Justice and judges must be, and must be seen to be, relevant. And it is for the judges to explain their relevance. Let me illustrate this relevance point by reference to a few examples drawn from the United Kingdom.

Relevance to Small Traders

Civil claims with sums in dispute in excess of £10,000 (US$15,000) will, most likely, be heard in England and Wales on the fast track of the county court. Imagine you are a sole trader or small business—a builder, a manufacturer, a supplier of some sort—and you have unpaid debts totalling £15,000 (US$23,000). That sort of debt could have a serious impact on your cash flow and might, in turn, cause you issues with your creditors. A year to resolve the issue through court proceedings might be several months too many.

Relevance to Investment and the Financial Markets

Investment will not be made and financial markets cannot operate without an effective and independent system of justice. In the United Kingdom, there is an additional factor, as the UK legal services market generated £22.6 billion (US$34.5 billion) for the economy in 2013.[13]

Social Relevance

Often when the justice system appears in the media, it is about very, very sensitive issues that are of concern to many: serious crime, taking children into care, eviction, deportation, bankruptcy. Few people would *choose* to have anything to do with the justice system at all, but it is important to make clear that a just and fair society requires an efficient and expeditious system of justice.

Constitutional Relevance

Lastly, the principled arguments must be aired, but not in the abstract. Access to justice matters. It matters because courts and tribunals are the means by which individuals are able to assert their rights against others, and against the Government, for each has equality before the law. An accessible and timely system of dispensing justice is required, otherwise the rights become meaningless. Acting with independence, judges are guardians of the rule of law and serve as a check on the exercise of executive power as part of the complex system of checks and balances that underpins our modern democracy. How is this to be done? By making speeches, engaging with the media through the Judicial Press Office, and bringing those that need to understand the courts into the courts to see the work that judges do. One scheme that

---

[13] *UK Legal Services 2015* (The City, UK, 2015). See www.judiciary.gov.uk/wp-content/uploads/JCO/Documents/Guidance/select_committee_guidance.pdf.

has recently been launched places Members of Parliament in courts or tribunals to observe hearings, with the opportunity of discussing the judicial process with the judge.

Explaining why justice matters is not in itself sufficient, unless the judiciary also ensures that, within the resources provided to it, justice is delivered effectively, and that, where reforms are needed, reforms that judges can initiate are initiated by the judges.

It is not easy to ensure that the courts within a state are acting effectively, but it is, in my view, essential for the leadership judges to monitor closely the time different types of case take, the time that elapses before a case can be tried, the number of interlocutory hearings that take place, the workload individual judges bear, and the time that judges take to deliver judgments.

Inevitably in a time when technology is advancing at an ever-increasing speed, court systems need reform to keep pace and to develop more cost-effective ways of delivering justice and modernizing procedure. The judiciary has taken the initiative in establishing new courts (a planning court and a financial court for international markets) and in making extensive procedural reforms, even though constrained at present by the funds necessary to take proper advantage of modern technology.

All of this assists in instilling confidence in the judiciary and the justice system. In particular, improved awareness of the everyday and constitutional role of the judiciary, of the ability to assert rights, and of how to access justice is itself protective of the rule of law. In addition, as public understanding of the role of the judiciary and the justice system increases, so too will understanding of the need for their independence to be protected.

What about judicial engagement and assistance in reform that is the province of the Government and Parliament? There are many areas of reform that are not for the judiciary, but are properly for the Executive and Legislature. Some might say that once it is accepted that the particular matter is not within the scope of what judges can properly do on their own, then judges should leave matters entirely to the Executive and the Legislature.

I do not agree. The judiciary has a real role to play in offering what I have described as technical advice. There will often be choices that are for the politicians to make, but that is not to say that the technical feasibility of reforms is a matter on which judges should not assist by giving advice. Guidance about assistance to Parliament has been issued,[14] and, as a result of a series of seminars with senior civil servants, further guidance will be issued later this year about appropriate engagement with the government on policy matters.[15]

There are many other illustrations which time does not permit me to give. But you may ask why the judiciary should do this. The answer in my view is clear—our changing constitutional landscape has necessitated this to safeguard and to reinforce the centrality of justice and an independent judiciary in the proper functioning of a state.

But doing all of the above will, in my view, not be enough. We also actively engage in ensuring that the judiciary itself and what it does reflect our increasingly diverse societies.

Judicial Diversity

In the past ten years there have been major changes to the judicial appointments process. An independent Commission that is required to appoint on merit now runs it.[16] The judiciary is working actively with the appointments commission in increasing judicial diversity, in particular to remove the barriers to entry to the judiciary and open up applications to the widest pool of candidates.

In 2013, a Judicial Diversity Committee was established to assist in discharging the duty to encourage diversity of which I have spoken. We have put in place ninety role model judges who undertake outreach and mentoring work; we hold specialist outreach events targeted at under-represented groups; we have organized a specialist mentoring scheme for first-time judicial applicants or those seeking to progress to higher office. We put in place this summer a scheme to encourage, through mentoring, a much wider pool of applicants for appointment as deputy High Court judges and early appointment to the High Court Bench. We are beginning to bring about a change, particularly with appointments of female judges, but there is still a great deal to do. We also have diversity and community relations

---

[14] Judicial Executive Board, Guidance to Judges on Appearances before Select Committees (2012) www.judiciary.gov.uk/wp-content/uploads/JCO/Documents/ Guidance/ select_committee_guidance.pdf.

[15] Subsequently published as Judicial Executive Board, *Guidance to the judiciary on engagement with the Executive* (15 July 2016) https://www.judiciary.gov.uk/wp-content/ uploads/2016/07/guidance-to-the-judiciary-on-engagement-with-the-executive.pdf.

[16] Section 63 (2) Constitutional Reform Act 2005 (*c*.5).

judges across England and Wales. Beyond diversity work with aspirant judges, they actively seek to dispel myths surrounding the judiciary and act as a link between the courts and local communities. In addition, they play an important role in informing and educating people—communities, schools, universities—about the reality of what it is to be a judge, which helps to remove the myths and misconceptions that prevail. We have recently increased the number to 123.

Cultures and Languages

I mentioned at the outset the changes in the union of the nations that form the United Kingdom. May I illustrate this by reference to Wales. Legislative and constitutional changes have given Wales a legislature and restored Welsh as a language of the courts and of legislation after an interval of over 400 years; these changes and other factors have restored Wales as a nation with a more distinct identity within the unitary system of England and Wales. On many different levels, the judiciary has therefore made changes to the operation of the legal system to reflect the constitutional change.

Legal Systems and Common Cultural Problems

I also mentioned the impact of our membership of the EU. This means not only a parallel, though much more occasional, dialogue with the institutions of the EU, but for present purposes a readiness to understand and adapt to cultures and legal methods different from that of the UK and the common law. Of the many examples, may I take victims' rights? Most Continental civil systems have a very different investigative process, but also accord to victims many more rights, such as the right to appeal against the failure of the prosecutor to prosecute. Political decisions were made to try and provide the same minimum rights for victims across Europe. Technically difficult though it was to set minimum rights, what proved to be more difficult was addressing the common cultural problem that each state had—the failure to keep victims informed throughout the whole process of what was happening and to take into account their concerns when dealing with cases. Thus, although we may have to reconcile the diversity of legal systems, it is sometimes common cultural problems that the judiciary and the broader legal system need to address.

So, what conclusions can be drawn?

- Judicial independence must not mean judicial isolation.
- The judiciary must explain the centrality of justice and why it matters. That task cannot be left to others. Transparency and openness are crucial to instilling public confidence in the justice system. In so doing, the emphasis has to be on demonstrating the real-life impact, rather than relying on high-level constitutional principles.
- The judiciary needs to engage with the other two branches of state within the confines of the constitution, and this strengthens, rather than undermines, judicial independence as it increases shared understanding and shared respect.
- Engagement with the public and the other branches of the state is particularly important when it comes to protecting judicial independence and the proper funding of justice.
- The judiciary must be reflective of the society it serves and actively take steps to ensure that the processes of the courts take proper account of our diverse societies.

Although I have spoken of England and Wales, I anticipate that much of what I have said about the need for judicial engagement is of much wider relevance.

14

How Diverse Are Judges?

Lady Hale of Richmond

This chapter is based upon a lecture delivered at Bristol University, 29 October 2015.

'Once we accept that who the judge is matters, then it matters who our judges are'. So says Professor Erika Rackley, in her prize-winning book *Women, Judging and the Judiciary*.[1] She had earlier suggested that our whole culture of judging is intrinsically male, so that the notion of a woman judge is a contradiction in terms.[2]
She wrote of:

> The importance of preserving the mythological dimension of the adjudicative process, ensuring its distance from the concerns of mere mortals. We can imagine the judge in no other way. He has to be seen as 'supra' human. We even make him dress up in his own kind of cape and mask—well wig—his own 'superhero' outfit [a man's wig, of course].

The very idea of a judge as a real human being with a life of her own will threaten this super-hero image. Just as Henry Cecil said that we should not be able to imagine a judge having a bath, we should not be able to imagine her doing the washing up.

Rackley went on to compare the woman judge with Andersen's 'little mermaid'—who traded her beautiful voice for legs so that she could join her handsome prince on dry land, and then found that he was no longer interested in her. The woman judge remains cast

---

[1] Erika Rackley, *Women, Judging and the judiciary* (Routledge, 2013), winner of the Peter Birks prize for the best academic law book published that year.
[2] Erika Rackley, 'Representations of the (Woman) Judge: Hercules, the Little Mermaid, and the Vain and Naked Emperor' (2002) 22 *Legal Studies* 602, 616.

as a mermaid. Her physical appearance threatens to upset aesthetic norms; her presence is an inescapable irritant, simultaneously confirming and disrupting the established masculinity of the bench. Like Andersen's mermaid, she is induced to deny herself and sell her voice; her dangerous siren call is silenced and in the silence difference is lost.

If there is still a grain of truth in this where women judges are concerned, how much more must this be so where visible ethnic minorities and persons with disabilities are concerned? I am determined not to be that little mermaid. I take the view that 'difference' is important in judging and that gender diversity, along with many other dimensions of diversity, is a good, indeed a necessary, thing, for several reasons.

The principal reason is democratic legitimacy—the judiciary should reflect the whole community, not just a small section of it; the public should be able to feel that the courts are their courts, that their cases are being decided and the law is being developed by people like them, not by alien beings from another planet; and this should enhance rather than undermine public confidence in the law and the legal system. The media mainly agree about this. Seventy-five per cent of the coverage of a press conference held at the beginning of the fifth year of the Supreme Court headlined not the interesting cases we had decided or the impact of legal aid changes on access to the courts, but our lack of gender diversity.[3] The recent chorus of well-nigh (almost) unanimous disapproval at the reported remarks of one of my colleagues is another illustration.

A second reason for supporting a diverse judiciary is that our laws are based on the underlying principles of justice, fairness and equality. We judges swear a very moving oath, 'to do right to all manner of people, after the laws and usages of this realm, without fear or favour, affection or ill will'. These are the underlying principles of a democratic society: a democracy which values each person equally even if the majority do not. If the people in charge of the justice system are overwhelmingly from one section of society, then the justice system does not reflect the very values it is there to uphold.

A third reason is the (otherwise potential) waste of talent: all those able young women who have been entering the legal profession in numbers equal to or greater than men for many decades now, but who somehow or other are not achieving the judicial appointments they

---

[3] Richard Cornes, '11–1 Gender Ratio Court's Achilles' heel' (18 October 2013), UKSC Blog.

deserve. Again, the same must be true of black and minority ethnic (BME) lawyers and of lawyers with disabilities.

There is a fourth reason, that different judges might actually make a difference to the judgments reached. That is much more controversial and I will come back to it.

But if judicial diversity is such a good thing, why do we not have more of it?[4] Just over a quarter of the judges in the ordinary courts in England and Wales are women. However, the percentage of women tends to be lower in the full-time, salaried posts than it is in the part-time fee-paid posts. Some 43.8 per cent of tribunal judges are women, but this includes an even higher percentage of fee-paid part-timers. The percentage of women is also lower the higher one climbs in the judiciary. In April 2015, 19.8 per cent of High Court judges were women; the two new High Court appointments announced last week have brought the percentage up to 21 per cent. Some 18.6 per cent of Court of Appeal judges were women, but there are no heads of division among them. In the Supreme Court of the United Kingdom there is still only me, despite there having been fifteen appointments since my own.[5] Only 32 per cent of the Upper Tribunal judiciary are women.

The figures do show a great improvement over the past ten years or so: in 2005 there were only ten women High Court Judges. And it is encouraging that there is a higher percentage of women in the younger age groups, suggesting that the overall percentage of women judges will increase over time. But it still seems to me extraordinary that we should be congratulating ourselves on having reached a quarter overall, and a fifth in the High Court and Court of Appeal, given the much larger proportion of women entering the profession at the relevant time.

We do not know the ethnicity of all judges, because not all judges declare it. Of the 83 per cent of courts' judges where it is known, 5.9 per cent are BME; of the 93.2 per cent of tribunal judges where it is known, 9.5 per cent are BME.[6] The overall percentage has remained steady at 7 per cent. Once again, only 3 per cent of High Court judges

---

[4] The figures as at 1 April 2015 are summarized in *Judicial Diversity Statistics 2015, Judicial Office Statistics Bulletin* (30 July 2015). The underlying tables are available on the Judicial Office website.
[5] Or thirteen, if you leave out Lord Brown and Lord Carswell, who were sworn in the day after me.
[6] So says the summary bulletin, but table 2.1 in the actual statistics gives a figure of 14 per cent.

are BME, and there are none in the Court of Appeal or Supreme Court. The percentage of BME judges in the Upper Tribunal is lower than that in the First Tier Tribunal.[7] Ethnicity is obviously a more complicated problem than gender.

Our gender figures are out of step with the rest of the world. The average across the countries in the Council of Europe is 52 per cent men and 48 per cent women. It is fair to say, however, that, across the whole of Europe, the gender balance gets worse the higher the court. But in the highest courts of the thirty-four countries in the Organisation for Economic Cooperation and Development (OECD), we are at rock bottom, with only one of the twelve Justices of the Supreme Court being female. Even the other common law countries are currently much better than us: three out of the nine in the Supreme Court of the United States; three out of the nine in the Supreme Court of Canada; three out of the seven in the High Court of Australia; two out of five in the Supreme Court of New Zealand. We have also been slow to appoint women to leadership roles, while the record in Canada and Australia is much better.

Not only that, the male Supreme Court Justices mostly fit the stereotypical pattern of boys' boarding school, Oxbridge college, and Inns of Court (what I call the quadrangle-to-quadrangle-to-quadrangle pattern!). This combination of educational establishments does turn out some of the best-educated people in the country and they must also have the brains, the energy, the determination, and the good luck to make the most of their opportunities. But it also brings advantages in other ways, in 'whom you know' as well as 'what you know', and this can smooth your path and open doors which might remain closed to others. It can also bring with it the expectation that this will happen, a sense of entitlement, which people from more modest educational backgrounds simply do not have.

So it matters that all but two Supreme Court Judges went to independent fee-paying schools (I did not). All but three went to boys' boarding schools (I only 'lived' in one). All but one were very successful barristers in private practice before going on the bench (I was not), although two did other things first. Most specialized in commercial or property law (I did not). All but two have a degree from Oxford or Cambridge (one thing I do have in common with them). All are white

---

[7] According to table 2.1, 10 per cent and 14 per cent respectively.

British (as am I). However, we do have an ethnic quota: between us, we must have knowledge of, and experience of practice in, the law of each part of the United Kingdom.[8] Traditionally this has meant two Supreme Court Judges from Scotland and one from Northern Ireland, but we are under increasing pressure also to have one from Wales.

Nevertheless, our present unrepresentative judiciary is, apparently, widely admired, not only here but in the outside world. The Russian oligarchs want to litigate here because of our judges' intelligence, industry, independence, integrity, and incorruptibility. Could this be because of who the judges are? Or could it be because we are still better paid than almost any judiciary in Europe?[9] Unlike them, we try to recruit our top judges from our top practitioners, and at every level people come into the judiciary having already achieved something in their professional lives. The rewards have to bear some relationship to the rewards of their other careers. My colleagues are increasingly beginning to voice their concern that, particularly with the recent changes to judicial pensions, the best people are no longer interested in becoming judges so that in the longer term the quality and reputation of the higher judiciary will suffer.

The status and pay of judges in countries where there are far more women judges tend to be much lower than they are here.[10] Are the status and pay lower because so many of them are women, or are so many of them women because the status and pay are lower? I incline to think that the latter is the correct explanation, for two main reasons. First, because many of the countries in which there are now so many women judges are civil law countries where there are many more judges (anyway) and that is one reason why the pay is lower; recruitment is also by examination and young women are notoriously better at examinations than young men. Second, because some of the countries are from the former Eastern Bloc where one would not expect the status of judges to be particularly high.

But all this leads some people to fear that, if we changed the system so radically, the composition of our higher judiciary will also change radically, and we might not like what we see. Would a dramatic

---

[8] Constitutional Reform Act 2005, section 27(8). Interesting that, where there are only one or two from the part of the UK in question, this would make it difficult to appoint academic lawyers.

[9] European Commission for the Efficiency of Justice (CEPEJ), *European Judicial Systems, Edition 2012* (2010 data), fig. 11.30.

[10] Ibid.

increase in the numbers of women judges lead in time to lower pay, lower status and ultimately to a less able judiciary? Are we wrong to think that improving the diversity of the judiciary will also improve the public's confidence in it?

Despite that fear, one of the biggest changes I have seen during this century is that more and more people have come to recognize that we do have a problem. Only last week, the Lord Chief Justice stated:

> I believe strongly that it is imperative to improve the diversity of the judiciary. The judiciary must be truly open to everyone of the requisite ability. I simply do not accept that this is an issue where we should be content to sit back and just wait for things to happen.[11]

One (but possibly not the principal) reason for setting up the Judicial Appointments Commission (JAC) was to increase the diversity of the Bench at all levels. The Joint Committee on Human Rights actually proposed that there should be a duty, akin to the one there then was in Northern Ireland,[12] to appoint a judiciary reflective of the community it serves.[13] But others thought that merit and diversity were competing rather than complementary values. So instead, under section 64(1) of the Constitutional Reform Act 2005, the commission has a duty to 'have regard to the need to encourage diversity in the range of persons available for selection'. But this is expressly subject to section 63(2), which provides that selection must be 'solely on merit'. So it is not enough to get the appointments' process right. We have to get the definition and assessment of merit right as well, and that is much harder.

Judicial diversity has markedly improved since the JAC came into being. More women candidates are applying and are appointed. For example, in the most recent circuit judge competition, women made up 30 per cent of the eligible pool, were 31 per cent of the applicants, and 42 per cent of the recommendations for appointment.[14] Under the old system, the Lord Chancellor's Department depended almost entirely upon the information supplied by the judges to know whose

---

[11] Speech for the Temple Women's Forum, Leeds, 19 October 2015.

[12] Justice (Northern Ireland) Act 2004, section 3, since replaced with a provision more in line with both England and Wales and Scotland.

[13] Joint Committee on Human Rights, *23rd Report of Session 2003–4, Scrutiny of Bills: Final Progress Report*, para. 1.83.

[14] Judicial Appointments Commission, *Judicial Selection and Recommendations for Appointment Statistics, October 2014 to March 2015*, June 2015, table ii.

shoulders to tap. The judges may not have set out to 'clone them-selves',[15] but, according to a former member of the Commission, 'It would be foolish to pretend that they were not occasionally influenced by unconscious stereotyping and by perceptions of ability moulded by their own personal experiences.'[16] I would merely drop the 'occasion-ally'. More important, they could only see the people who were visible to them, not equally able and suitable people whose professional lives were elsewhere.

Nowadays, appointments at all levels are based on applications (or at least on expressions of interest). The qualities thought to comprise merit have been made public. More refined assessment processes have been introduced. Nevertheless, there is a concern that these still do not identify the best candidates. Using examination papers as a sifting tool, for example, will favour those with current experience in the jurisdiction in question. Those with the potential to become excellent judges may be overlooked. And I wonder how many of us who have had to fill in the judicial referee's forms think them able to give a true picture of a candidate's merit?

A further problem is that prior judicial experience, at the same level, is usually required for any appointment.[17] The advantage to this approach is that people can be tried out, and individuals can try out the job, before either side is committed to an appointment from which the safeguards for judicial independence mean that, in reality, they cannot be sacked. The disadvantage is that you have to get on the lad-der. Not only that, Her Majesty's Courts and Tribunals Service wants people who can 'hit the ground running', rather allowing time and training to work themselves in. This puts pressure on the Commission to choose 'safe' candidates in preference to those with less experi-ence but greater potential. An important experiment, therefore, is the recent competition for deputy High Court judges, where no prior judicial experience is required and some candidates have been given intensive mentoring to help them make their applications.

The commission has also taken active steps to encourage people from under-represented groups to consider a judicial career. And the

[15] Helena Kennedy, *Eve Was Framed* (Penguin, 1991), 267.
[16] Lord Sumption, 'Home Truths about Judicial Diversity', Bar Council Law Reform Lecture 2012.
[17] The 'available pool' for circuit and High Court appointments is defined to require judicial experience, although the statutory qualifications do not.

judiciary, under the leadership of the Lord Chief Justice and Lady Justice Hallett, are now doing the same. But one major obstacle to making quicker progress is that the process of choosing the best candidates is only part of the story. On either side of the JAC there sit stages along the way which tend to disadvantage non-standard candidates.

The process begins with our education system, which, as Lord Sumption has put it, 'tends to perpetuate disadvantage'. Students from independent schools are more likely to go to Oxbridge and other top universities than are state school students with the same grades—not necessarily because the universities are discriminating but because the state school students are not applying.[18] Recruitment to law jobs, whether as barristers or as solicitors, is left to the market. The market tends to take the easy route of favouring a small number of top universities. An Oxbridge graduate with a non-law or a lower-class law degree is more likely to be recruited than a post-1992 university graduate with a first-class law degree. A recent study of twenty-six out of the UK top 50 law firms found that only 19 per cent of trainees went to universities outside the Russell Group.[19]

Then there are what Lord Sumption calls 'the patterns of working in the ancient professions'. For the Bar, this means all the reasons why many able but sensible women choose either to go into another branch of the profession or to leave the Bar after 'giving it a go' for a few years. Even in 2012, only 12.4 per cent of practising silks in England and Wales were women (risen from 9.5 per cent in 2007).[20] But there are a great many able women in the Government Legal Service, in the Crown Prosecution Service, or in commerce and industry. For solicitors, the patterns of work may be rather different, but the pressures of 'presenteeism' (coat-on-the-back-of-the-chair syndrome) may provide a clearer explanation. In the top City firms it is very hard to combine work with a normal family life. That same study found that women were 58 per cent of trainees, but only 24 per cent of partners

---

[18] Sutton Trust, 'The Missing 3000: State School Students Under-Represented at Leading Universities', 2004; Sutton Trust, 'State School Admissions to Our Leading Universities: An Update to "The Missing 3000"', March 2005; Sutton Trust, Sutton Trust Submission to Sir Martin Harris: 'Widening Access to Selective Universities', January 2010.

[19] Jon Robins, *Opening Up or Shutting Out? Social Mobility in the Legal Profession* (Byfield Consultancy, October 2015).

[20] General Council of the Bar and Bar Standards Board, *Bar Barometer: Trends in the Profile of the Bar*, June 2014, fig. 45.

(10 per cent and 4 per cent for BME). Another problem is that many solicitors' firms do not value judicial appointments in the way that the Bar traditionally has done. So they are not keen for their partners to take the part-time fee-paid appointments which are the stepping stones to full-time appointment.

Our divided legal profession is one of the principal differences between the United Kingdom and most of the rest of the common law world. There are enduring stereotypes about who gets what sort of judicial job. Only the top silks qualify for the High Court Bench. Other silks, successful senior juniors, and some solicitors, qualify for the Circuit Bench. Solicitors, and a few barristers, become district judges in the county and magistrates' courts. A much wider variety of professional lawyers, including quite a few who practise as law teachers and academics, become tribunal judges. The percentage of 'non-barristers' in each judicial post bears out these traditional assumptions: they are 1 per cent of High Court judges, 11 per cent of circuit judges, but 88 per cent of district judges in the county courts, 65 per cent of district judges in the magistrates' courts, and 84 per cent of tribunal judges (although only 59 per cent in the Upper Tribunal). Official figures do not disclose how many judges of any sort have in fact had careers as teachers, academics, public servants, or elsewhere, rather than in independent practice. This is something we must try to find out.

Of course it is possible to argue that only the top barristers become the top judges because they are the best qualified for the job. But I am simply not prepared to make that assumption, nor is the Lord Chief Justice. It is not made in other countries, such as Canada and Israel, whose higher courts are held in the greatest respect. It feels both self-seeking and implausible—self-seeking because it reserves the top jobs for the top barristers and implausible because any university teacher can list many able graduates who could have made excellent judges but who went into a different legal career. As Sir Stephen Sedley memorably put it (before becoming a judge himself), the greatest of the arts of advocacy is 'reasoning from a given conclusion'—which is the reverse of what judges should do.[21]

Finally, there is the lack of a proper judicial career structure which enables those who do have a salaried judicial appointment to make progress through the ranks. We have four separate grades of judge

---

[21] Stephen Sedley, 'Declining the Brief', in *Ashes and Sparks* (Cambridge University Press, 2011).

(High Court, circuit, district, and tribunal—tempting to think of them as the officers, the warrant officers, the non-commissioned officers (NCOs), and the privates, but that would be unfair), with direct entry, after a period of part-time service, at every level. Those hoping for promotion from one level to another have to compete with the direct-entry candidates. The Crime and Courts Act 2013 has provided some flexibility to deploy some tribunal judges in the ordinary courts,[22] but that is not a permanent solution to a more systemic problem. The principal recommendation of the Advisory Panel on Judicial Diversity, chaired by Baroness Neuberger, was:

> There should be a fundamental shift of approach from a focus on individual judicial appointments to the concept of a judicial career. A judicial career should be able to span roles in the courts and tribunals as one unified judiciary.[23]

My own solution would be to try and tackle each of these obstacles to improving the diversity of the bench: by widening recruitment to the professions, broadening the pool from which judges at all levels are in practice recruited, dispelling traditional assumptions, and creating a proper judicial career structure. Affirmative action of this sort requires concerted action from many interested parties. But it could make a considerable difference if it were done with the right amount of enthusiasm and without resorting to positive discrimination in favour of under-represented groups. I have already referred to the efforts of the Judicial Appointments Commission and of the judicial office, under the leadership of the Lord Chief Justice and Lady Justice Hallett, through appointing judicial role models, a new judicial mentoring scheme, appointing diversity and community relations judges, organizing outreach events, and preparing people for judicial selection exercises.

There is also the 'tie-breaker' clause. Section 63 of the Constitutional Reform Act 2005 has now been amended to make it clear that the duty to recommend appointments 'solely on merit' does not prevent the Judicial Appointments Commission from choosing a candidate in order to improve diversity where there are two or more candidates of equal merit.[24] The House of Lords Constitution Committee argued

---

[22] Section 21 and Schedule 14, para. 1.

[23] *Report of the Advisory Panel on Judicial Diversity*, chaired by Baroness Neuberger, February 2010, at 4, accessible at www.equality-ne.co.uk, recommendation 1, at 7.

[24] 2005 Act, section 63(4), inserted by Crime and Courts Act 2013, Schedule 13, para. 10.

that this would 'send out a strong signal that diversity in judicial appointments is important, without undermining the merit principle'.[25] Views differed about whether it would make a difference. Some thought that it might do so in the larger selection exercises for the lower ranks of the judiciary, where it could be very difficult to rank all of the candidates in strict order of merit. But for individual appointments at the higher levels, some doubted whether two candidates are ever truly equal.[26] Others argue that the assessment of comparative merit is an inherently subjective exercise—how do you rate each candidate against each desirable quality and how do you rate each quality against the others? So you might well end up with candidates who were equally well qualified but for different reasons.[27] I take the latter view, because there is so much room for variation in choosing, assessing, and then weighting the various parameters involved in merit. However, the commission's policy is only to look at the 'tie-breaker' at the final stage of any selection exercise, when an order of merit has been agreed by the selection panel.[28] In the recent exercises, seven out of 304 appointments were made in this way.[29]

One argument raised against any other kind of positive discrimination is that it would deter the best candidates from applying for judicial office.[30] The top white men would not apply if they thought that they would be discriminated against; and the top women would not apply because they do not want it to be thought that they have been appointed because of their gender rather than their merit. As for the men, if women had been put off applying for anything by the fear that they might be discriminated against, we would never have got anywhere (no progess would have yet been made). As for the women, if we think that we are good enough for the job and that there ought to be more of us, we should not be put off from applying by the fear of what ill-meaning people may say. It is our duty to our sex to step up

[25] House of Lords, Select Committee on the Constitution, *25th Report of Session 2010–2012, Judicial Appointments,* HL Paper 272, para I.101.

[26] Including Lord Sumption, JAC chair Christopher Stephens, and Baroness Neuberger.

[27] Including the then Lord Chancellor Kenneth Clarke, Lord Neuberger, Lord Justice Goldring, and Lady Justice Hallett.

[28] Judicial Appointments Commission, *Equal Merit Provision, JAC Policy,* April 2014.

[29] *Judicial Selection and Recommendations for Appointment Statistics,* 6.

[30] Lord Sumption, 'Home Truths about Judicial Diversity'.

to the plate. What also worries me about this argument is that it may well put off very able women (and other minorities) from applying for fear that they will not be welcome or will not be 'up to it' even though there is no question of discriminating in their favour.

It is vitally important that women and other minorities should not be deterred, because diverse courts are better courts, better able to draw upon a diversity of experience in reaching their decisions. This brings me back to the final reason for promoting judicial diversity: that it might actually make a difference. Erika Rackley's thesis is the argument which really matters, because it demands that something be done.[31]

I used to be sceptical about the argument that women judges were bound to make a difference, for two main reasons.[32] First, women are as different from one another as are men—in their background, experience, attitudes, and values. What may make a difference is feminism, not femaleness. Not all women are feminists but some men are. Second, we are all lawyers and judges first and have all sworn the same judicial oath. As the American judge Mary Jeanne Coyne said many years ago, 'in most cases, a wise old woman will make the same decision as her wise old man'.

There is not much serious academic work on the subject.[33] The few existing studies are mostly from the United States, but they do not tell us a great deal. For example, one tells us that white female Justices on the US Courts of Appeals from 1979 to 1981 were more liberal than their male counterparts in race and sex discrimination claims, but no different in criminal and prisoners' rights cases.[34] Other studies have told us that women judges are more favourable to claimants in discrimination cases,[35] in family law cases, and in cases raising feminist issues.[36] But these were relatively small-scale studies of the voting patterns of judges

---

[31] Rackley, *Women, Judging and the judiciary*.

[32] Brenda Hale, 'Equality and the Judiciary: Why Should We Want More Women Judges?' [2001] PL 489.

[33] The literature is reviewed in Rackley, *Women, Judging and the judiciary*, Chapter 5; and R. Hunter, 'More Than Just a Different Face? Judicial Diversity and Decision-making' (2015) *Current Legal Problems* 1.

[34] J. Gottshall, 'Carter's Judicial Appointments: The Influence of Affirmative Action and Merit Selection on Voting on the U.S. Courts of Appeals' (1983–4) 67 *Judicature* 165.

[35] S. B. Haire et al., 'The Voting Behavior of Clinton's Courts of Appeals Appointees' (2000–1) 84 *Judicature* 274.

[36] E. Martin and B. Pyle, 'Gender, Race, and Partisanship on the Michigan Supreme Court' (1999–2000) 63 *Albany Law Review* 1205.

on federal or state appellate courts. The results of large-scale quantitative studies have been more equivocal.[37] There is an interesting large study of first-instance decision making by asylum judges in the United States.[38] The researchers found a wide gap between the asylum grant rates of men and women judges—37.3 per cent for men, 53 per cent for women (and regardless of whether these people had previously been employed in helping asylum seekers or in the immigration service). It is interesting to speculate upon what the reasons might be.

There are, so far as I know, no comparable studies in the United Kingdom. So can we learn anything from the way in which the few senior female judges in this country have approached certain kinds of issue where the gender element looms large. It was a female judge who pointed out (in graphic detail) that having a child that she had negligently been made to have was an invasion of the mother's bodily integrity and personal autonomy which gave her lasting caring responsibilities, and was not just a financial burden.[39] It was a female judge in the Employment Appeal Tribunal who recognized the improper pressure put on school dinner ladies who were told that pushing on with their (justified) equal-pay claim would jeopardize the school meals service for the children who needed it, as well as the jobs of their colleagues.[40] It was the two female judges out of the eleven who considered the case of *Radmacher v Granatino* who recognized that prenuptial agreements are always designed to damage the interests of the person who is in the weaker bargaining position at a vulnerable time in their life, and might therefore require special scrutiny before it was fair to enforce them.[41]

But these are relatively rare cases. The abuse and ill treatment of women is regrettably not at all rare. It was a female judge who first recognized that women at risk of female genital mutilation belonged to a 'particular social group' for the purpose of the Refugee Convention.[42]

---

[37] Hunter, 'More Than Just a Different Face?', 8.

[38] J. Ramji-Nogales, A. I. Schoenholtz, and P. G. Schrag, 'Refugee Roulette: Disparities in Asylum Adjudication' (2008) 60 *Stanford Law Review and NYU Press*, 2009.

[39] *Parkinson v St James and Seacroft University Hospital NHS Trust* [2001] EWCA Civ 530, [2002] QB 266.

[40] *Derbyshire v St Helens Metropolitan Borough Council* [2007] UKHL 16, [2007] ICR 841.

[41] *Radmacher v Granatino* [2010] UKSC 42, [2011] 1 AC 534.

[42] Arden LJ in the minority in *Fornah v Secretary of State for the Home Department* [2005] EWCA Civ 680, [2005] 1 WLR 3773; but the House of Lords agreed with her: [2006] UKHL 46, [2007] 1 AC 412.

It was a female judge who persuaded her colleagues to recognize that domestic violence might take other forms than merely being hit.[43] Many years ago, Susan Atkins and I, in our book on *Women and the Law*,[44] pointed out that being physically hit was a form of violence which men fear, whereas women are fearful of, and can be coerced by, a much wider range of abusive behaviour.

More objective evidence for difference lies in *Feminist Judgments*, an experiment in rewriting a variety of well-known judgments from a feminist perspective and seeing what a difference that can make, not only on typically 'women's issues' but also on a much broader range of legal topics.[45] Three issues stood out to me. First, how plausible these judgments mostly were. Second, it makes a difference how the story is told. Feminist judges will take different facts from the mass of detail to tell the story in a different way, to bring out features which others discard, and to explain features which others find difficult to understand. The third issue is context. Feminist judges will set the story in a different context, a context which they understand but others may not.

So, as a result of work such as that, as well as the lived experience of being a full-time judge for nearly twenty-two years and a Law Lord/ Supreme Court Justice for nearly twelve, I have come to agree with those great women judges who think that sometimes, on occasions, this is correct.[46] One of these is Dame Sian Elias, Chief Justice of New Zealand, who points out that it is easier for those who have experienced discrimination and humiliation in their own lives to recognize it in others.

It is not that there is a different female 'voice' with which all women judges sing. It comes from the very nature of judging, especially at senior levels. Judging is not just the mechanical application of clear rules to known facts. Judges have to make choices—when law runs out, when law is not clear, when law gives them a choice. Anyone, male or female, black or white, brings their own experience

---

[43] *Yemshaw v Hounslow London Borough Council* [2011] UKSC 3, [2011] 1 WLR 433.

[44] Susan Atkins, Brenda Hale, and Brenda M. Hoggett, *Women and the Law* (Basil Blackwell, 1984).

[45] Rosemary Hunter, Clare McGlynn, and Erika Rackley, *Feminist Judgments: From Theory to Practice* (Hart, 2010).

[46] Beginning with Madam Justice Bertha Wilson, 'Will Women Judges Really Make a Difference? (1990) 28 (3) *Osgoode Hall Law Journal* 507.

and values to making those choices. These 'inarticulate premises' have been acknowledged since the phrase was first used by Justice Holmes of the US Supreme Court more than 100 years ago. Women lead women's lives—as Chief Justice Beverley McLachlin of Canada has said, we have no choice. We have as much to contribute as have the men who lead men's lives—who also have no choice. This is especially so at appellate level where judging is a collective activity and our absence may make as much of a difference as our presence can do.

Viewed in this light, diversity is an important component of the collective merit of the judiciary, not in opposition to it. This view did not cut much ice with, for example, Lord Irvine, whose evidence to the House of Lords Constitution Committee was that 'to assert that diversity is a component of merit is sleight of hand, and not a very skilful one at that'.[47] But there are other voices. Lord Bingham, undoubtedly the greatest judge of the early twenty-first century, pointed out that 'the term [merit] is not self-defining'. It 'directs attention to proven professional achievement as a necessary condition, but also enables account to be taken of wider considerations, including the virtue of gender and ethnic diversity'.[48] What a shame that Lord Bingham is no longer with us to lend his weight to the argument!

Paradoxically, however, one of the difficulties in recognizing this lies in our equality laws. These depend upon the proposition that race and sex are *not* relevant qualifications, or disqualifications, for any job save in very exceptional circumstances. So we can appoint a Justice because he comes from the north of England or because he has a different professional background, because these characteristics are not protected by the Equality Act. But, 'equal merit' apart, it is said that we cannot appoint a judge because she is a woman or comes from a minority ethnic (protected) group, however much we recognize the need for a more diverse court. Yet taking the overall diversity of the court into account would fall far short of the quotas which apply to judicial appointments in some courts.[49]

---

[47] 6 July 2011, Q28.
[48] Lord Bingham, 'The Law Lords: Who Has Served', in L. Blom-Cooper, B. Dickson, and G. Drewry (eds.), *The Judicial House of Lords 1876–2009* (Oxford University Press, 2009) p 126.
[49] See, e.g., Kate Malleson, 'The Case for Gender Quotas for Appointments to the Supreme Court' (23 May 2014), UKSC Blog.

The Home Secretary has just been chiding the police for not appointing more officers from BME backgrounds. Sir Peter Fahy, the chief constable of Greater Manchester, recognizes that he has a real operational need for a more diverse force:

> When your house is burning down you are not interested in the ethnicity of the firefighter, but when it is a long term issue of youth alienation, countering extremism or dealing with complex matters such as female genital mutilation the ethnicity of the law enforcer makes a huge difference.

He wanted to be free to make the appointments he needed to make and to change the prevailing culture, in more ways than one. How I wish that we could too!

15

Should Judges Make Law?

Lord Justice Laws

This lecture was delivered at the University of Law, London, on 5 March 2015.

The judges do make law. And it is both inevitable and desirable that they should. The real question is: what kind of law should they make?

Let me first explain what I mean by the statement that the judges make law. In very many cases the judicial act of interpreting statutes itself constitutes law making; and so, of course, does the autonomous development of the common law. I will concentrate on the interpretation of statutes. The act of interpretation often (not always: sometimes it is mechanical) makes law. This is a necessary and an unavoidable truth in a system where the law is not merely *dirigiste*, consisting in the unquestioned dictates of an unquestioned sovereign. My theme is that in the common law world the interpretation and application of the law are interwoven with its creation, because the judges mediate Parliament's legislation to the people so that, so far as possible, it conforms to civilized constitutional principles whose guardians are the courts.

Let me show how it is that the interpretation of statutes so often amounts to law making. Consider the case of *Omychund v Barker* in 1744.[1] It concerned a question whether the testimony of a witness who refused to swear a Christian oath could be received in English proceedings. Witnesses appearing before Commissioners in India would only swear in the manner of their 'Gentoo' (Hindu) religion,

[1] (1744) 26 Eng. Rep 14. I owe this reference to Poser's excellent biography *Lord Mansfield: Justice in the Age of Reason* (McGill-Queen's University Press, 2013), 96.

which was to touch the foot of a Brahmin priest with their hand. William Murray (later Lord Mansfield: at this time Solicitor General, but representing a private party in the proceedings) submitted that in the absence of precedent 'the only question is whether upon principles of reason, justice, and convenience, this witness ought to be admitted'. Then he said this:

> All occasions do not arise at once; now a particular species of Indians appears; hereafter another species of Indians may arise; a statute very seldom can take in all cases, therefore the common law, that works itself pure by rules drawn from the fountain of justice, is for this reason superior to an act of parliament.

Now compare this very different text:

> 92. It is a logical consequence of the principle that laws must be of general application that the wording of statutes is not always precise. One of the standard techniques of regulation by rules is to use general categorisations as opposed to exhaustive lists. Accordingly, many laws are inevitably couched in terms which, to a greater or lesser extent, are vague and whose interpretation and application are questions of practice ... However clearly drafted a legal provision may be, in any system of law, including criminal law, there is an inevitable element of judicial interpretation. There will always be a need for elucidation of doubtful points and for adaptation to changing circumstances ...
>
> 93. The role of adjudication vested in the courts is precisely to dissipate such interpretational doubts as remain ... The progressive development of the criminal law through judicial law-making is a well entrenched and necessary part of legal tradition in the Convention States ...

This is, of course a much more recent text; it comes from the judgment in 2014 of the Grand Chamber of the European Court of Human Rights in the case of *Del Rio Prada v Spain*.[2] It is couched in the baleful prose of European translations. But the Strasbourg court in 2014 and William Murray 270 years earlier (leave aside for the moment his claim for the superiority of the common law) are making the same point.

They describe an obvious truth: legislation typically addresses broad positions. It does not—cannot—prescribe its own application in every case; so the courts have to decide how the legislation is to be applied. The added insight of Lord Mansfield in *Omychund*'s case, and

---

[2] (2014) 58 EHRR 37.

my thesis today, was and is to recognize that this process is not merely interpretive, but evaluative. It is a creative process. It makes law.

We should regard this fact as entirely unsurprising. Consider these familiar truths.

- The common law has long held that criminal statutes must be interpreted strictly.
- The same used to be true of taxing statutes, but that, perhaps, is less clear nowadays.
- The courts lean against retrospective applications.

All of these are normative, not merely descriptive, positions. But they are part of the warp and weave of statutory construction. They, and other nostrums of statutory interpretation, are the creatures not of any rule laid down by Parliament, but of successive judges' perception of what may reasonably be called foundational principles of the constitution, about which I will have more to say. The rigour applied to criminal statutes springs from the principle that the state must prove criminal guilt strictly, according to the letter. The rigour that used to be applied to taxing statutes sprang from the principle, as it was then perceived, that private property likewise deserved strict protection from the incursions of the state. If tax law now favours the Revenue more, it is because of a shift in the principle: the good citizen should be ready to pay his tax according to the spirit, as well as the letter, of the law: so taxing statutes may be interpreted more purposively. The rule against retrospectivity springs from the principle that the citizen should know what law applies to what he does. Between them these principles exemplify more general principles of the constitution, foundational principles: freedom, fairness, reason, legal certainty. These are in the keeping of the judges.

Many other examples may no doubt be found. My point is that in the act of construing statutes, the judges very often develop, refine, and apply such constitutional principles; and in doing so, they make law. To the extent that the words of the Act do not dictate its interpretation—a statute very seldom can take in all cases—it is necessarily so. Interpretation is supposedly the servant of Parliament's will. But it is an autonomous creative process.

This autonomous creative process does not, however, arise merely from the circumstance that 'a statute very seldom can take in all cases', as William Murray put it. It is not just a matter of filling in gaps which the legislature would itself have filled, if the legislators had thought about it. The translation of words on a page into what should be done or not done is of its nature an autonomous creative process. Words on a page only come to life when they are interpreted; and more often than not there is more than one possible interpretation. Not because there are gaps; but because that is in the nature of the language, especially a language as rich as English. Consider these lines from T. S. Eliot's *Burnt Norton:*

> Words strain, Crack and sometimes break, under the burden
> Under the tension, slip, slide, perish
> Decay with imprecision, will not stay in place,
> Will not stay still.

Or this utterance by the guru of linguistics, Professor Noam Chomsky:

> Language is a process of free creation; its laws and principles are fixed, but the manner in which the principles of generation are used is free and infinitely varied. Even the interpretation and use of words involves a process of free creation.[3]

Or this rather more mysterious passage from Plato's dialogue, the *Phaedrus*, where Socrates says:

> Writing, Phaedrus, has this strange quality, and is very like painting; for the creatures of painting stand like living beings, but if one asks them a question, they preserve a solemn silence. And so it is with written words; you might think they spoke as if they had intelligence, but if you question them, wishing to know about their sayings, they always say only one and the same thing. And every word, when it is written, is bandied about, alike among those who understand and those who have no interest in it, and it knows not to whom to speak or not to speak; when ill-treated or unjustly reviled it always needs its father to help it; for it has no power to protect or help itself.[4]

Here is what these insights tell us. Time and again there will be a choice how a text is to be interpreted—how it is to be given life, how its words are to have effect in the world. And time and again the choice will not be concluded by the language of the text. When it comes to Acts of Parliament the choice will be concluded (nearly always) within the constraints of the text, but often also by the interpreter's view of what it

---

[3] Noam Chomsky, *Language and Mind*, 3rd edn (Cambridge University Press, 2006).
[4] Plato, *Phaedrus*, 275d–e (tr. H. N. Fowler, Loeb Classical Library, 1911).

should be taken to mean in light of basic principles of the common law: in light of the constitution's foundational principles. The very subject matter of the constitution is the relation between citizen and citizen, and between citizen and state; the very purpose of Acts of Parliament is to regulate what is and is not required, forbidden, or allowed, to the citizen or to the state; so time and again Acts of Parliament will touch our constitutional fundamentals; and whenever that is so, the judicial act of statutory construction—the interpretive choice—makes law, because it insists that the statute complies with the applicable constitutional principle, and such principles are themselves evolving.

I will shortly give some concrete instances of the judges making law in the act of construing statutes. But first I would suggest that in considering the question whether that is what judges do, we should have in mind this further question.

Even if the judges in some sense make law when construing statutes, is it plausible to suggest that in doing so they are merely drawing implications from the statutory language—and therefore doing no more nor less than fulfilling the will of the legislature?

It is beyond doubt that in constitutional cases, just as in others, time and again judges claim that the exercise of interpretation involves no more than the ascertainment of the intention of Parliament; and there are undoubtedly cases where the judges indeed draw inferences from the statutory language, just as they draw inferences from the language of contracts. Is that, in reality, the whole story? Is the creativity of the judges in shaping Acts of Parliament so that they conform to the constitution's fundamentals no more than an exercise in fulfilling Parliament's will?

This question calls up an old debate: is the ultra vires doctrine the foundation of judicial review? The debate has consumed the energies of academic public lawyers for twenty years and more, and has spawned a considerable literature. An effective conspectus of the controversy is to be found in a series of essays published in the year 2000 by Professor Christopher Forsyth.[5]

I cannot traverse the whole scope of that debate in this lecture. This is not the occasion on which to enter into a full discussion of the proposition that the judicial review jurisdiction depends upon an implied grant of power by the legislature—a proposition which, for what it is worth, I regard as mythological. In any case the correctness

---

[5] Christopher Forsyth (ed.), *Judicial Review and the Constitution* (Hart Publishing, 2000).

or otherwise of that proposition is not the same question as the question whether, in the creative act of interpreting statutes, the judges are doing no more than ascertaining and giving effect to the intention of Parliament.

The question I suggested earlier was whether the exercise of statutory construction, even if it involves making law by the application of constitutional principles, involves no more than the assertion of implications drawn from the statutory language—no more, therefore, than fulfilling the will of the legislature.

My thesis is that the judges' protection of constitutional principle cannot be reduced to an exercise in ascertaining Parliament's will, and the cases show as much.

Now let me turn to some concrete instances in which the courts make law in the act of construing statutes: instances in which it is not plausible to suggest that the act of interpretation does no more than give effect to the will of the legislature. I will offer four examples from the cases.

The first is the celebrated decision of the House of Lords in *Anisminic v Foreign Compensation Commission*.[6] The Commission made a determination which it had no power to make. But section 4(4) of the Foreign Compensation Act 1950 provided: 'The determination by the Commission of any application made to them under this Act shall not be called in question in any court of law.' And so the question arose: was it open to the court to correct the commission's error? It was submitted that 'determination' meant a real determination and did not include an apparent or purported determination which in the eyes of the law has no existence because it is a nullity. Here is a very familiar passage from Lord Reid's speech at 170–1:

> Statutory provisions which seek to limit the ordinary jurisdiction of the court have a long history. No case has been cited in which any other form of words limiting the jurisdiction of the court has been held to protect a nullity. If the draftsman or Parliament had intended to introduce a new kind of ouster clause so as to prevent any inquiry even as to whether the document relied on was a forgery, I would have expected to find something much more specific than the bald statement that a determination shall not be called in question in any court of law. Undoubtedly, such a provision protects every determination which is not a nullity. But I do not think that it is necessary or even reasonable to construe the word

---

[6] [1969] 2 AC 147.

'determination' as including everything which purports to be a determination, but which is in fact no determination at all. And there are no
degrees of nullity. There are a number of reasons why the law will hold a
purported decision to be a nullity. I do not see how it could be said that
such a provision protects some kinds of nullity but not others: if that
were intended it would be easy to say so …

And so section 4(4) of the 1950 Act was construed to ensure that it
does not prevent the court's supervision of subordinate bodies so as
to confine their acts and decisions within the proper limits of the
power given to them. Most certainly this was making law through the
medium of statutory interpretation. It was done, though it may not
have been so obvious in 1968 when the case was decided, to protect
the rule of law, which of course underpins all our constitutional fundamentals. And I do not think that nowadays we would find it necessary to use the metaphysical language of 'nullity'. I will come shortly,
after describing the other examples of the judges making law, to the
light which *Anisminic* throws on our question, are the judges in such
a case doing no more than fulfilling Parliament's will?

The second case is *Witham*,[7] decided by the Divisional Court in
1997. Section 130(1) of the Supreme Court Act 1981 (now the Senior
Courts Act) provided:

> The Lord Chancellor may by order under this section prescribe the fees
> to be taken in the Supreme Court.

The Lord Chancellor made a statutory instrument, purportedly
under the authority of section 130(1), increasing certain court fees
payable on the issue of civil proceedings and revoking earlier provisions which relieved litigants in person who were in receipt of income
support from the obligation to pay fees. The changes made it impossible for the applicant, who had no resources and relied on income support, to bring libel proceedings as a litigant in person. There was also
evidence of other persons on very low incomes who were prevented
from taking proceedings. In my judgment (with which Lord Justice
Rose agreed) I said:

> 7. In my judgment the 1996 Order's effect is to bar absolutely many
> persons from seeking justice from the courts. Mr Richards' elegant and
> economical argument contains an unspoken premise. It is that the com-
> mon law affords no special status whatever to the citizen's right of access

---

[7] [1998] QB 575.

to justice. He says that the statute's words are unambiguous, are amply wide enough to allow what has been done, and that there is no available *Wednesbury* complaint. That submission would be good in a context which does not touch fundamental constitutional rights. But I do not think that it can run here. Access to the courts is a constitutional right; it can only be denied by the government if it persuades Parliament to pass legislation which specifically—in effect by express provision—permits the executive to turn people away from the court door. That has not been done in this case.

The third case is *Cooper v Wandsworth Board of Works*, decided in 1863.[8] Statute forbade the erection of a building in London without giving seven days' notice to the local board of works, on pain of having the building demolished. A builder nevertheless began to erect a house in Wandsworth without having given due notice. The board of works sent men late in the evening to demolish it. 'The board did exactly what the Act said they might do in exactly the circumstances in which the Act said they might do it'.[9] But the builder's action for damages for injury to the building succeeded. The court held that the board had no power to act without first asking him what he had to say for himself. In a well-known passage, Byles J said this:

> a long course of decisions beginning with *Dr Bentley's* case, and ending with some very recent cases, establish that, although there are no positive words in a statute, requiring that the party shall be heard, yet the justice of the common law will supply the omission of the legislature.

Reminiscent, you may think, of William Murray in 1744: 'The common law, that works itself pure by rules drawn from the fountain of justice, is for this reason superior to an Act of Parliament.' Lastly, let me refer you to *R v Registrar General, ex. p. Smith*.[10] In that case the court had to consider section 51(1) of the Adoption Act 1976, by which the Registrar General owed a duty to disclose to the applicant, as an adopted person, his birth certificate. But the applicant had killed two people, one of whom he had thought was his foster mother; and if he obtained the certificate, he was very likely to use the information to find and kill his birth mother. The court upheld the registrar's refusal to disclose the certificate, reasoning that the statute was subject to an

---

[8] (1863) CB (NS) 180.

[9] Wade and Forsyth, *Administrative Law* (9th edition, Oxford University Press, 2004), 480.

[10] [1991] 2 QB 393.

implied exception based on public policy, namely that statutory rights were not given to facilitate the commission of serious crimes.

These four cases are, of course, my selection; you could readily choose others.

What should we make of them? As for *Anisminic*, I very much doubt whether anyone believes that Parliament actually intended that unlawful decisions of the Foreign Compensation Commission should be subject to what we now call judicial review for all the world as if section 4(4) of the 1950 Act did not exist. As for *Witham*, I am quite certain that there was no actual legislative intention that section 130(1) of the Supreme Court Act 1981 would not authorize the changes in court fees which the Lord Chancellor purported to make; I apprehend that the intention of the legislators, or those who thought about it, was that the Lord Chancellor should have a free hand in deciding what the court fees should be.

Cooper v Wandsworth Board of Works (cited with approval in 1964 by Lord Reid in the landmark case of *Ridge v Baldwin*[11]) was, I suppose, not really a case of statutory interpretation at all. Certainly the result in *Cooper*'s case plainly involved no inferences drawn from the statute, no complications derived from the text. It is a case where 'the common law [supplied] the omission of the legislature'. A case, in other words, where the court held that the statute was deficient when it came to the protection of basic fairness in the shape of the right to be heard. As for *R v Registrar General ex. p. Smith*, no doubt Parliament would have excluded a right of access to the birth certificate of someone as dangerous as the applicant had the legislators thought about it; but presumably they did not.

In every one of these authorities the courts were concerned with the protection of constitutional fundamentals, and in none of them were the courts in truth giving effect to a legislative intention.

I acknowledge, of course, that there are very many cases, no doubt the majority, where the words of the statute clearly dictate the result, notwithstanding the fact that as William Murray said, 'a statute very seldom can take in all cases'. Often no potential conflict with constitutional principle arises. Not every statute engages a constitutional question. Many statutes support and strengthen the principles of the constitution. And there will be cases where the words do not

---

[11] [1964] AC 40.

conclude the meaning, and the judges are left to find it, but constitutional questions do not enter into the exercise. Statutes are, of course, drafted with meticulous care to achieve a particular result—usually at least: sometimes they are drafted with the specific intention that the judges should resolve difficult questions of interpretation. Where the judges are left to find the statute's meaning but there is, so to speak, no constitutional overlay, they will straightforwardly seek to ascertain the legislation's purpose and interpret the Act accordingly.

But where an Act of Parliament touches a constitutional fundamental, then, as I have said, the judicial act of statutory construction makes law, because it insists that the statute complies with the applicable constitutional principle. And it seems to me artificial—and in the end simply untrue—that in fulfilling this duty the judges are giving effect to the will of Parliament. That is not what happens in reality, as I think the cases demonstrate. I see not the slightest point in pretending that the reality is other than it is; indeed it seems to me bizarre that the courts' duty to protect constitutional fundamentals should be covered with a fig leaf, even so apparently respectable a fig leaf as the intention of the democratically elected Parliament.

Statutory interpretation, then, is very often value-laden. It is driven by general principles of the constitution and is a means by which the judges develop, refine, and apply those very principles. The old rubric that Parliament makes the law and the judges apply it is misleading and unhelpful.

We must also recognize that the courts embark on the same exercise, the development and protection of constitutional principles, whether they are engaged in the task of statutory interpretation or the administration of self-standing issues of the common law. As for the common law, it must be plain that the development of such principles pervades our public law: Wednesbury, proportionality, legitimate expectation—all these give effect to a philosophy of the state which is rooted in reason, fairness, the presumption of liberty, legal certainty. The same philosophy characterizes our criminal law: fair trial and proportionate punishment. In the law of tort, Lord Atkin's famous question—Who then is my neighbour?—possesses so great a power because it invites a balance to be struck, a balance given concrete form by the reach of the duty to take reasonable care. Much of the law of contract also involves a balance, between freedom and fairness. These balances in our private law themselves invoke constitutional principle, in these cases between citizen and citizen, rather than citizen and state. I think that the constitutional principle is that the rights and freedoms which the law guarantees are essentially the same for every citizen; and therefore, when such rights are in conflict between one citizen and another, the law has to strike the kind of balance which the law of contract and tort prescribe.

So I suggest that in considering the question whether the judges should make law, or what law they do make or should make, the distinction between their duty to interpret statutes and their duty to develop and apply the substantive common law is nothing but a distraction, as unhelpful and misleading as the traditional view that Parliament makes the law and the judges interpret it.

But that, of course, is indeed the traditional view: Parliament makes the law and the judges interpret it. The first chapter of Lord Devlin's book *The Judge*, is headed 'The Judge as Lawmaker': it is a reprint of a lecture first published in 1976. This passage marks a striking contrast with what I have been saying:

> Judges, I have accepted, have a responsibility for the common law, but in my opinion they have none for statute law; their duty is simply to interpret and apply it and not to obstruct. I remain unconvinced that there is anything basically wrong with the rule of construction that words in a statute should be given their natural and ordinary meaning. The rule does not insist on a literal interpretation or require the construction of a statute without regard to its manifest purpose. There should be, as Lord Diplock has said:
>
>> a purposive approach to the Act as a whole to ascertain the social ends it was intended to achieve and the practical means by which it was expected to achieve them.[12]
>
>> But in the end the words must be taken to mean what they say and not what their interpreter would like them to say; the statute is the master and not the servant of the judgment.

Lord Devlin was a great judge. However, this view of statutory interpretation is impoverished. It allows no place for the judges' insistence on constitutional principle. But since 1976, when Lord Devlin was writing, the common law has begun to give express recognition to the legal category of constitutional principle, and the process has been compounded by the Human Rights Act. Once there were dangers in

---

[12] Patrick Devlin, *The Judge* (Oxford University Press, 1979). For Diplock see *R v National Insurance Commissioners* [1972] AC 914 at 1005.

judicial conservatism, timidity even: but now there are dangers in judicial activism. My views about judicial creativity in the interpretation of statutes are only credible to the extent that we recognize the dangers that may be associated with it.

The judges' express recognition of constitutional principle, and their energetic protection of it sometimes against the inroads of the legislature, confront us with an important danger. It is the risk that the judges may step too far, or be thought to step too far, onto territory that properly belongs to the elected arms of government. In considerable measure the danger has been foisted on the judges by the Human Rights Act 1998. The statutory incorporation of the ECHR, with its catalogue of rights expressed in very general terms, has amounted to an invitation—no, a requirement—that the judges decide issues which for all the world look very much like political questions for politicians to decide, and about which reasonable and informed people might readily disagree. Claims based on the right to respect for private and family life, guaranteed by ECHR Article 8, are perhaps the most notorious instance. An acute kind of case is that of the foreign criminal who has married a British citizen and has a child or children born here. He commits a serious crime; he has no settled right—perhaps no right at all—to remain here; the Secretary of State decides to remove him to his home state; he pleads Article 8. Which should prevail—the public interest in removing him or his private right to family life?

It is hardly a question of law. It is really a question of policy. In some cases, of course, the merits are so far on one side of the argument or the other that the decision is quite straightforward. But very often that will not be so. The government has made strenuous efforts—by obtaining fresh legislation from Parliament, and by making new immigration rules—to see that (broadly at least) its view of such cases prevails. But like it or not, the judges have been drawn into these controversies by the human rights jurisdiction.

Too muscular a vindication of such human rights claims seems to expose the judges to the complaint that they are making political decisions. The response that they are doing no more than their duty under the Human Rights Act is not entirely convincing: it does not answer the question, how much weight should the judges give to the public interest?

Now, I think it is very important to understand that the duty of the judges, under the Human Rights Act, to referee these passages of arms between private right and public interest is a different kind of duty from their natural and proper obligation to protect constitutional fundamentals; and there is a danger of confusion between these two quite different duties. Consider: what in truth *is* the constitutional fundamental involved in this conflict between public interest and private right? It is, surely, the very insistence by our law that both have objective value and there is a balance to be struck between them. If the public interest is denied, the freedom and security of the many are sacrificed to the interests of the few. If the private right is denied, the door is open to oppressive and capricious conduct by the state.

So the relevant constitutional fundamental in this context, in a society which is to deliver both freedom and security to its citizens, is that a balance has to be kept between these interests, public and private. The judges as guardians of constitutional principle owe a duty to see that the balance is respected. That must involve ensuring that the competing interests are properly considered by the primary decision maker. This is a duty which the common law requires of the judges, quite aside from the Human Rights Act. But it is one thing for the court to insist that the constitutional fundamental which this essential balance represents be kept and respected. It is quite another to require the court to strike the balance *itself*.

I think this distinction needs emphasis. My claim that the judges are the guardians of constitutional principle, and that in construing statutes which touch the constitution they make law by insisting on the vindication of constitutional principle, is no affront to democratic sensitivity. On the contrary: the democracy can surely thrive only in a legal milieu in which reason, fairness, freedom, and legal certainty are axioms: they are the very premises upon which democracy is constructed. But within limits imposed by these axioms it is the primary responsibility of the elected arms of the state to decide how our constitutional balances should be struck. To the extent that the courts strike it themselves, they are invitees on a territory that is not their own. Parliament can, of course, issue such invitations as it pleases.

If I am right that the judges do and must make law when construing statutes, and that they do it and must do it for the vindication of constitutional principle, there is inevitably the question, where is the proper boundary between judicial and political power? Is not the legislature also responsible for constitutional principle? In our uncodified constitution, the question offers no single answer. The legislature may of course effect constitutional innovations, as in recent years it has in enacting the European Communities Act, the devolution legislation, and the Human Rights Act. But elected government is buffeted by the rancour and asperity of party politics and the dictates of populism, so that elected governments will always struggle—sometimes they will not even try—to confine their legislative endeavours within the disciplines of constitutional principle. Democracy is our best guarantee against arbitrary and capricious government; constitutional principle is our best guarantee against democracy's own occasional aspirations to arbitrary and capricious rule. Constitutional principle is in the keeping of the judges; they are protected from overweening aspirations of their own, not by any inherent wisdom—for certain, they have no more of that than anyone else—but by the method of the common law, matured over centuries: the balance between precedent and innovation, the gradual construction of principle case by case: in short, the continuous process of self-correction. The legislature is by nature given to experiment. The common law is by nature given to conservation. Judges do, and must, make law; but they do it not by reinventing the wheel, but only by making new lamps from old.

Index